Think Positive
for Kids

Chicken Soup for the Soul: Think Positive for Kids
101 Stories about Good Decisions, Self-Esteem, and Positive Thinking
Kevin Sorbo, Amy Newmark
Published by Chicken Soup for the Soul Publishing, LLC www.chickensoup.com

The publisher gratefully acknowledges the many publishers and individuals who granted Chicken Soup for the Soul permission to reprint the cited material.

Front cover photo courtesy of iStockPhoto.com/RichVintage (© Andrew Rich).
Back cover photo is courtesy of Ania Okane. Interior illustration courtesy of iStockPhoto.com/Lazarev (© Lazarev).

Cover and Interior Design & Layout by Brian Taylor, Pneuma Books, LLC

Distributed to the booktrade by Simon & Schuster. SAN: 200-2442

Publisher's Cataloging-in-Publication Data
(Prepared by The Donohue Group)

Chicken soup for the soul : think positive for kids : 101 stories about good decisions, self-esteem, and positive thinking / [compiled by] Kevin Sorbo [and] Amy Newmark.

   p. ; cm.

   Summary: A collection of 101 personal stories about children making good decisions, doing the right thing, thinking positively, overcoming obstacles, and being grateful.
   Interest age level: 007-012.
   ISBN: 978-1-61159-927-5

   1. Children--Conduct of life--Literary collections. 2. Optimism--Literary collections. 3. Children--Conduct of life--Anecdotes. 4. Optimism--Anecdotes. 5. Children--Conduct of life. 6. Optimism. 7. Anecdotes. I. Sorbo, Kevin. II. Newmark, Amy. III. Title: Think positive for kids : 101 stories about good decisions, self-esteem, and positive thinking

PZ5 .C45 2013
810.8/02/035234   2013937414

PRINTED IN THE UNITED STATES OF AMERICA
on acid∞free paper

22 21 20 19 18 17 16 15 14 13   01 02 03 04 05 06 07 08 09 10

Think Positive
for Kids

101 Stories about
Good Decisions, Self-Esteem,
and Positive Thinking

Kevin Sorbo
Amy Newmark

Chicken Soup for the Soul Publishing, LLC
Cos Cob, CT

Chicken Soup for the Soul

www.chickensoup.com

for the Soul

Contents

Introduction for Parents and Teachers xi

Introduction for Kids.. xiii

❶
~Trying Something New~

1. Chair Challenges, *Gary Graham* 1
2. What If Nobody Laughs? *Tanya Janke* 6
3. The Spelling Bee, *Mary Elizabeth Laufer* 10
4. A New Country, A New Friend, *Diane Stark* 13
5. It's Okay to Fall, *Pamela Millwood Pettyjohn*..................... 16
6. The Color of Success, *Emily Sheera Cutler* 19
7. Sharks and Mermaids, *Jennifer Azantian* 23
8. Running with Heart, *Stacey Ritz* 27
9. How I Became a Musician, *L.A. Strucke* 31
10. On Top of the World, *David Hull* 34
11. The Art of Mistakes, *Maryanne Higley Hamilton* 38
12. The New Kid, *Debbie Acklin* 40

❷
~Doing the Right Thing~

13. Fight for What's Right, *Marius Forté*............................... 47
14. Just Do It, *Wendy Hobday Haugh* 50
15. It Just Takes One, *Shawnelle Eliasen* 53
16. Richmond Girl, *Amanda Yardley Luzzader* 57

17. Help by the Bagful, *Sioux Roslawski*..................................59
18. Tennis Anyone? *Shirley M. Oakes* 62
19. The Rescue, *Debbie Acklin*..65
20. The Sweetest Thing, *Felice Keller Becker*......................69
21. My Bad Reputation, *D'ette Corona*...............................73
22. A Puppy of Our Own, *John Berres* 76

❸

~Accepting Differences~

23. My Sister, My Hero, *Jill Burns* 83
24. Lessons from a Nursing Home, *Caitlin Brown*................86
25. Jonny and Me, *Maddy Curtis*......................................89
26. Alone, *Carol Elaine Harrison*.....................................91
27. A Sweet Lesson, *Zehra Hussain* 95
28. Father's Day, *Denise Reich*..98
29. A Different Sister, *Richard Brookton* 101
30. When Staring Hurts, *Rosalie Ferrer Kramer*.................105
31. The Hand of Friendship, *Dawn Malone*......................107

❹

~Developing Self-Esteem~

32. Embracing My Uniqueness, *Jody Fuller*......................113
33. Learning to Love My Nose, *Dallas Nicole Woodburn* 117
34. Modeling Reflection, *Michaela Brawn*.........................121
35. Learning How to Kick, *Amy Newmark* 123
36. The Middle Rock, *Deborah Roberts*...........................125
37. Be Proud, Be Strong, Be You, *Ruth Anna Mavashev*.............127
38. You Do It Your Way and I'll Do It Mine, *Jenny Mason*.........130
39. My Abilities, *Ben Jaeger*...134
40. By the Seat of My Pants, *R.K. Krochmal*....................136
41. Telling My Story, *Emily Madill*.................................139
42. The Last One Picked for Basketball, *Neal Levin*.............141

❺
~Handling Bullies~

43. Don't Pass It On, *Dani Johnson* 145
44. Bullied to a Better Life, *Mason Carter Harvey* 148
45. True to Myself, *Kristen N. Velasquez* 150
46. The Kindness Cure, *Monica A. Andermann* 153
47. The Best Way to Get Even, *Carina Lamendola* 158
48. Bullies on the Bus, *Valerie D. Benko* 160
49. The Rumor Court, *Christy Box* 163
50. Don't Fight It, Just Write It, *Neesha Hosein* 166
51. Monkey Arms, *Marya Morin* 169

❻
~Appreciating Family~

52. Already Mom, *Jeanne Blandford* 177
53. Learning from Mother Nature, *Emma Blandford* 180
54. History in the Making, *Tucker Blandford* 183
55. Easter in Ruins, *Scott Neumyer* 186
56. Three's a Crowd, *Madeline Clapps* 191
57. Me and My Hairy Legs, *Amanda Romaniello* 194
58. Bare Feet in the Waves, *Lava Mueller* 197
59. Proud to Be Your Sister, *Kathryn Malnight* 200
60. Sharing My Friend, *Kathryn Lay* 203
61. Life After Camp, *Amy January* 205
62. Taking Care of Family, *Drienie Hattingh* 208

❼
~Making Real Friends~

63. True Friendship, *Cathi LaMarche* 215
64. The Pops, *Jess Forte* 218
65. Playing Chicken, *Tracie Skarbo* 220

66. The Case of the Vanishing Sunglasses, *Courtney Conover*....223

67. My Annoying Best Friend, *Susan Sundwall* 226

68. A Great School Year, *Crescent LoMonaco* 229

69. Chosen Last, *Arlene Ledbetter* 232

70. The Nice Popular Girl, *Amy Newmark* 236

71. Those Who Mind Don't Matter, *Gloria Yaxiri Plancarte* 238

72. The Real Popular Table, *Victoria Fedden* 240

❽

~Making Good Choices~

73. Badge of Courage, *Sam Sorbo* 247

74. Guilty Nightmares, *Renee Beauregard Lute* 251

75. The Coolest Friend Ever, *Timothy Martin* 253

76. I Pledge Allegiance, *Beth Cato* 256

77. Party Invitation, *Barbara LoMonaco* 260

78. Truth or Dare, *Madeline Clapps* 262

79. The Shirt Off My Back, *Andrea Canale* 265

80. Alice and Snowball, *B.J. Lee* 268

81. Not Such a Good Idea, *Conny Manero* 270

❾

~Being Responsible~

82. A Little Effort Goes a Long Way, *Bruce Campbell* 277

83. I Can't Believe I Did That, *Pam Depoyan* 281

84. Take the Bull by the Horns, *Michael Damiano* 285

85. The Case of the Busted Lunchbox, *Joe Sottile* 288

86. Love, Loss, and a Goldfish, *L. A. E. Howard* 290

87. Cell Phone Madness, *Zulema Anahy Carlos* 296

88. The Visitor's Secret, *Teresa Bruce* 299

89. What I Learned in Gym Class, *Janeen Lewis* 303

90. Better Safe than Sorry, *Cathy C. Hall* 306

⑩
~Being Grateful~

91. Reach Out for Perspective, *Kevin Sorbo* 313
92. The Gift, *Stan Holden* 318
93. A Piece of the Puzzle, *Harriet Cooper* 320
94. Is That All? *Bill Rouhana* 323
95. The Boy Who Had Everything, *Jackson Jarvis* 325
96. Learning to Love My Messy Life, *Suzanne De Vita* 328
97. Make Your Heart Smile, *Amanda Dodson* 331
98. Like a Pendulum, *Mikaela Rose* 334
99. The Color of Gratitude, *Bailey Corona* 336
100. The Kind Police Officer, *Heather Davis* 338
101. My Final Foster Home, *Amanda Plaxico* 341

Meet Our Contributors 344
Meet Our Authors 360
Thank You 362
About A World Fit for Kids! 363
About Chicken Soup for the Soul 365

Introduction
for Parents and Teachers

By Kevin Sorbo and Amy Newmark

After the success of *Chicken Soup for the Soul: Think Positive*, a bestseller for adults, it made sense to make a version for kids. After all, why shouldn't kids have access to the same kind of inspiration about positive attitudes, gratitude, and making the best of situations?

Bringing positive messages to kids at all socioeconomic levels, in all kinds of schools, is of paramount importance in a fast-paced world filled with technology and choices, temptations and challenges for children. Now, more than ever, it's important for parents, grandparents, teachers, and other mentors to sit down with kids, get quiet, and talk. And one of the best ways to start a conversation with a child is by reading a story about another child first.

That's the goal of *Chicken Soup for the Soul: Think Positive for Kids*—to start conversations with children about core values, good examples, making good decisions, and having the courage to do the right thing. The values that children learn today will stay with them for the rest of their lives. We hope to contribute to the building blocks that create tomorrow's wonderful young adults through this book for today's children.

Chicken Soup for the Soul: Think Positive for Kids contains 101 stories about issues that are important to children. The stories can be read *to* younger children, read *by* older children, and discussed with adults. The stories are true personal anecdotes that are entertaining and also impart a lesson. We have included our own personal stories in this book, plus stories from our spouses, children, and friends. There were thousands of submissions for this book—we obviously struck a chord—so it was difficult to narrow down the field to only 101 stories, but that just means that you are getting the crème de la crème of helpful, inspiring, educational... and entertaining... stories for kids from ages seven to early teens.

These stories show children how to make good choices... even when no one is looking, how to respect the needs and feelings of others, how to develop their own self-esteem, and how to stay true to their convictions. The stories remind kids that each day holds something to be grateful for and show them that they are not alone in dealing with difficult issues.

We've addressed all the important and appropriate issues for kids, including bullying, relationships with friends and family, divorce, moving, self-esteem, disabilities, helping others, and doing the right thing even when it's difficult. We've also addressed the value of trying something new, counting your blessings, making *real* friends, and even... the benefits of putting down that cell phone.

In addition to helping your own children, grandchildren, and students, this book is going to help needy kids in Los Angeles, through our contributions of royalties and proceeds from sales of this book to *A World Fit for Kids!*, a successful mentoring program that trains teens to become heroes to the kids in their own neighborhoods by using the vehicles of school, fitness, sports, and positive role models. The program is unique because of the powerful format of "kids teaching kids"—and its success rate is astounding—working with more than 12,000 children in the Los Angeles School District, it has a 100% graduation rate in a school system that has a 54% dropout rate.

We hope you enjoy sharing these stories with your young charges as much as we enjoyed putting this collection together. Even though these stories are for kids, their lessons are universal and should prove inspirational to the adults who are sharing them and discussing them as well. We know we were inspired! Thanks for reading and sharing....

Introduction for Kids

By Kevin Sorbo and Amy Newmark

We think it is safe to say that almost every kid is insecure about something, whether it is looks, or sports ability, or schoolwork, or friends, or clothing, or just knowing what is cool. Being a kid can be tough. Your bodies are starting to change and sometimes that is embarrassing and even scary. Your schoolwork is getting harder. Your parents are giving you more responsibility and expect more grown-up behavior from you. Your friends are changing too, and sometimes you end up joining a new group of friends, or switching best friends. Boys and girls start to notice each other and that can be scary and fun and embarrassing at the same time.

The years before you become a teenager can be an awkward time but they are lots of fun and exciting too. That's why we have made you this book. Think of it as a guidebook for those years leading up to high school. You'll read stories written by older kids and adults who vividly recall their childhood years—the good and the bad times—and these people share their experiences with you so that you know that you are not alone. Millions of other boys and girls feel the same way as you do, and they are going through the same changes as you too!

We hope you will view this book as a portable support group for kids, like another friend you can turn to. You might want to encourage your parents to read it also—it will help them to remember their own childhoods and better understand what is going on in your life these days!

Enjoy the book! We loved making it for you, and we hope you will love reading it.

Chapter
1

Think Positive for Kids

for Kids

Trying Something New

Chair Challenges

What the mind can conceive and believe, and the heart desire,
you can achieve.
~Norman Vincent Peale

As a kid, I was lucky. I had loving, supportive parents and a dad who was always spouting optimism. My mom and dad both had a great sense of humor and always had a bright, cheery disposition. And something else—my father was always talking about positive thinking—and the "If you can dream it, you can do it!" type of attitude.

All through grade school I had a crush on Margaret Highsmith. Cute dimples, beautiful eyes... and she thought I was the smartest guy in the school. We were about to graduate from sixth grade and were heading off to junior high, but I decided that I wanted to play the violin. I think back now that I made that decision solely to impress Margaret Highsmith... and it worked... for a while, until she found Danny Madden's blond hair and bright white smile too irresistible to pass up.

So there I was in junior high, in orchestra, ready to play the violin. But the only trouble was everybody in orchestra wanted to play violin. And there weren't enough violins to go around. So the orchestra teacher tried to convince some of us to try the viola ... or the bass... or the cello. I picked the cello although I didn't know a thing about it.

Though I knew a little about music—my mother had put me

into piano lessons for a while when I was younger—I was clueless when it came to the cello. And the other five in the cello section had played before. Though I tried hard, I was clearly the poorest player of the six. I was "second chair, third cello"—which suited me fine, because the music was a lot easier than second cello, and a whole lot easier that the first cello parts. I settled in, struggling through the third cello parts, playing as softly as I could so that no one would realize how terrible I was.

These were nervous times for this seventh grade boy. Everything about this new school was disorienting for me. I had to ride the bus to school… the layout of the school was totally unfamiliar… my classes were all over the place and I was always getting lost and late for class.

And there were a lot of tough kids. I surrendered my lunch money once to a dude who popped a switchblade on me in the gym locker room. I started carrying my lunch in a paper bag… and avoiding the locker room.

I was on the bottom rung, a seventh grader. The eighth and ninth graders seem to feel it was their duty to make life miserable for newbies like me. Especially newbies who happened to be in the school orchestra… and who played the cello. So I kept my new interest in orchestra and classical music to myself.

Until I heard about the Christmas Concert. In Orchestra class, at the end of the week, we had on Fridays something called Chair Challenge. You could challenge the next higher-up chair to a playoff duel. The teacher selected a passage from the music and the person you were challenging would play it first—then you would play it. The teacher would determine which of you played the passage the best—and determine whether your challenge was successful or not. If you won, you switched places with the loser and moved up one chair. And at the end of November, whoever was first-chair violin, first-chair viola and first-chair cello would play the three separate solos in the big Christmas Concert in December.

Hearing this—and for reasons that still mystify me—I determined right then and there that I would be the one who played the cello solo in the Christmas concert. I only had one problem: I was second-chair, third-cello. In order for me to become first-chair, first-cello I would need to move up five positions, and do five Chair Challenges by the end of November—and win all five! And I only had six weeks to do it in.

The school allowed us to check out our instruments and take them home on weekends. I decided to take my cello home and practice my butt off until I had achieved my goal. My problem was I rode the bus. And humping a big cello case onto a crowded bus, when the only open seat was in the very back—well, it was pretty rough going. I suffered a lot of jostling, a lot of insults and snide remarks—even threats—and just tried to laugh it off the best I could.

But every single Friday and then again on Monday, for six weeks I wrestled this big cello case onto and off the bus before and after school. Then I went home and practiced. I set up out in the den, closed the door and put the music up. I rubbed resin on my bow, took hold of the cello and I worked. I played scales. I played arpeggios. I practiced Bach and Brahms and Beethoven—any music we were playing in class.

And I sounded terrible. Chilling, really—as offensive a noise as you could imagine. Picture a dying warthog being dragged across a blackboard. Looking back, I have to feel sorry for my parents who would endure this awful, screeching racket coming from the den. I seem to recall them taking many weekend trips during this period.

But on the weekends during that October and November, I played the cello for hours—until my shoulders, elbows and hands were shaking, and my fingers were so sore I could barely feel my fingertips. But I kept at it. And a funny thing happened around the second or third week. I wasn't sounding that horrible. My mother even poked her head in once with an odd look and said, "Gary… that sounds kind of… nice." And I realized—finally—I was getting good. It was a glorious feeling.

The first Chair Challenge the following Friday was a nervous affair. My hands were shaking so badly that I was sure the whole class was going to burst into laughter. But when I finished the teacher smiled and said, "Challenge successful—switch chairs." I felt a quiet thrill in my heart. First-chair, third-cello. One down and four to go. To the rest of the class this was a simple little thing, but to me it was my first step climbing Mt. Everest.

I continued my quest, humping the school cello home, practicing for hours, and each Friday, taking on the next highest chair—and winning. I was again quietly exultant—but always humble. My dad had taught me humility, from his meager childhood as a farmer's son, to working his way through college and medical school. I learned that you don't brag—you just quietly and confidently go about your business *and believe in yourself.*

I didn't dare tell anyone about my goal of winning the number one spot in the cello section. I knew they'd tell me it was impossible. The girl who was first-chair, first cello, Patricia, had been playing for years! She was an ultra-nerdy type, sweet but odd, who looked and talked like the cello was the center of the universe. Surely, to unseat Patricia would be a feat more difficult than actually climbing Mt. Everest!

But I kept practicing and winning my challenges, week after week—until it was the last Friday of November, and my last chance to accomplish my goal of the Christmas Concert cello solo. I was now second-chair, first-cello. The teacher asked if there were any Chair Challenges—and I felt every eye turn to me. I waited until the tension in the room was ripe. I had a smile on my face. Patricia turned to me and laughed. "Well…?" she said. By now she knew my plan; everyone knew it. The teacher stared at me, eyebrows raised, waiting.

My hand suddenly shot up. "Challenge!" I called out. Everyone laughed and clapped. This showdown was long in the making and the class settled in to watch as the teacher pulled out two pieces of music and arranged them in front of Patricia and me. She went first, being the challenged, and she played the passage beautifully. Only one slight bobble, and her bow screeched slightly on one attack, but it was still expertly played.

Then it was my turn. I was totally unfamiliar with this piece, but I'd been practicing, and my sight-reading had improved so much that

I was confident I could do it justice. Still, it was make or break time, and I was feeling the nerves. So rather than just jump into it… I took a moment. I don't remember whether I said a quick prayer… but I do remember dropping my head and taking a deep, deep breath before I looked up and began.

I played that passage so smoothly and steadily it was like I'd been playing it all my life. I felt like I was out of my body and it was someone else playing it. The tone of the cello had never sounded so rich and vibrant and soothing to me, and I almost felt like my soul was flying around the room, dancing to this beautiful music someone down on the floor was playing. As I drew my bow across the strings on the last note, my eyes were closed and my breath was perfectly synched… my exhale was the last note… and then silence.

The class burst into applause. I was startled as my eyes snapped open. No one had ever clapped after a Chair Challenge. Even Patricia was clapping! I was speechless, just returning to my senses… and looked around in a daze. The teacher had a small smile as he nodded. "Challenge successful, switch. And," with the slightest incline of his head, "congratulations, First-Chair, First-Cello."

It turned out that the piece he had given us to play was the actual cello solo for the Christmas Concert. And that's what I played as the cello soloist two weeks later in front of family and friends and the student body.

I learned, from my parents and my personal experiences, that you can achieve your dreams. Don't listen to anyone, not even yourself, who tell you it's impossible. Ignore the ridicule, the insults, the people who tell you can't do it, that you're not good enough, that you'll never make it. If you've got a dream—go for it. It's in your heart for a reason. You can achieve what you set out to accomplish.

Even if it's just winning the cello solo in the Christmas Concert.

~Gary Graham

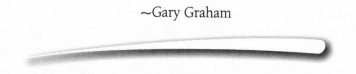

What If Nobody Laughs?

Nobody cares if you can't dance well. Just get up and dance.
~Dave Barry

My mother says I was born a performer. She still has recordings of me at three years old, singing songs and reciting poetry. I loved an audience, loved plays and recitals, and loved applause more than anything.

When I found out there was a school for the arts in my city, I begged my parents to let me audition. Their musical theatre program started in Grade 4. I was in Grade 3, so the timing was perfect. If I got accepted, I could start the next year.

My parents gathered information about the audition process and we looked at it together. It sounded easy. Kids my age only had to learn a dance routine, tell a joke or funny story, and sing the national anthem. For the high school program, the audition was much harder—memorizing a monologue, preparing a song, drama and dance exercises, improvisation. I was glad I didn't have to do all that!

"What joke are you going to tell?" my parents asked me.

I didn't know a lot of jokes. My father knew about a thousand, and gave me all sorts of ideas, but nothing seemed quite right.

"I know," I said to my parents. "I'll tell that story about the ketchup."

They asked what I was talking about.

"When I was little," I said, "I watched a scary movie with Aunt Carole. She said, 'Don't worry, nobody really got hurt. They just put ketchup on the actors to make it look like blood.' After that, I said I wanted to be an actor because I loved ketchup. When the scene was over, I would lick it all up!"

My parents exchanged glances in that way parents do when they seem to be reading each other's minds. They smiled, but they didn't laugh.

"Maybe you could tell a knock-knock joke," my father suggested. He had lots to choose from, but I was sure my story was funnier.

When my audition came around, my father took the day off work to drive me. The School for the Arts was all the way at the north end of the city and we lived at the south end, so it was a long drive. My belly was full of butterflies the whole way there, but my father kept telling jokes. He obviously wanted me to use one of his instead of telling my ketchup story, but my mind was made up.

The first part of the audition was dance. A lot of kids put on ballet slippers or fancy outfits, but I'd never taken dance lessons and I knew I wasn't very coordinated. When we started learning the routine, I couldn't keep up with everyone else. I couldn't remember the moves, but I knew I had a great singing voice. So what if I wasn't good at dancing? When I got on stage, the teachers would see how talented I was.

If I thought I was nervous in the car, that was nothing compared to sitting in the auditorium waiting for my turn to come around. There were lots of other kids auditioning. Some of their jokes were terrible, and I felt strangely glad when their performances fell flat. If other kids did poorly, wouldn't that make me look better?

But some students were hilarious. When they told their jokes everybody laughed, even the teachers. I was so jealous of those kids. They would get in for sure.

When the teachers called my name, my whole body turned to ice. I stood up, rolled my shoulders, and walked on stage feeling anxious all the way.

A teacher with curly brown hair and a pretty smile asked me to begin whenever I was ready, and I started right away with my story about Aunt Carole and acting and ketchup.

I got to the punch line about licking it all up… and nobody laughed.

Nobody laughed!

The teacher with the curly brown hair smiled, but she didn't laugh. The other kids looked bored. Farther back in the auditorium there were parents waiting. My father stood in the doorway. That was the first time I noticed him. He was smiling, but I could feel the pity in his eyes. He'd tried to tell me the story wasn't funny, but it took standing up in front of a big group of strangers for me to realize he was right.

"I'm sorry," I said to the teachers. I'd never felt so humiliated, and I just kept apologizing. "That was terrible. I can do much better, really I can."

The teacher with the curly hair and kind smile nodded before asking me to begin the vocal portion of the audition.

I'd sung "O Canada" every morning since kindergarten, but I'd never struggled like I did that day. My throat stung with tears. I meant to split the song half and half, singing in both official languages, but I was so torn up it all came out French.

When I'd finished the national anthem I apologized again and again, until one of the teachers said, "Never apologize at an audition."

That made me feel even worse, and I walked offstage and went straight to my dad. He didn't say anything. Neither did I. I'd failed at something I really wanted, and I felt awful.

We got a letter from the school that began, "We regret to inform you…"

I didn't get in. I vowed never to audition for anything ever again.

After that, I tried not to think about music and drama. I took part in school plays when there were no auditions, but by the end of Grade 8 my teachers were encouraging me to try out for the arts school again.

I didn't feel so embarrassed anymore about the joke nobody laughed at, so I went to the high school audition. I still wasn't great at dance, but I did better than before, and my monologue and drama exercises went really well.

By the time we got to music, I thought I'd be accepted for sure. The teacher who'd told me five years before never to apologize at an audition even accompanied me on piano. I felt great… until halfway through my song I forgot all the words! My mind went blank, but I didn't apologize. I just awaited instructions.

The teacher asked me to sing "O Canada" instead, and I did, French and English.

I left my audition sure I'd be rejected. After all, I'd forgotten the words to my song. Why would they want me?

A few weeks later, I got a letter from the school. It was an acceptance! My very first year, I auditioned for the school musical. This time I didn't tell an unfunny joke, I didn't forget the words to my song, and guess what? I got the lead role!

I still remember feeling queasy and embarrassed when I told a story I thought was funny and nobody laughed. I never wanted to feel that way again. But if I hadn't taken chances, I'd never have starred in two high school plays, or gone on to work in a theatre and even write my own musical. Bad feelings fade over time. The good ones shine much brighter.

~Tanya Janke

The Spelling Bee

The best way to conquer stage fright is to know what you're talking about.
~Michael Mescon

Spelling was my favorite subject in fourth grade. Every week I memorized my new words, and by Friday I was prepared to take the spelling test. I usually got all the words right. My teacher, Mrs. Casazza, wrote "100%" and "Excellent!" on the top of my paper, and when she handed it back I felt so proud.

In the desk behind me, Donna Slocum would lean forward and whisper, "What did you get?" and I'd show her my test paper. "Again?" she'd ask, with a hint of jealousy in her voice.

One day Mrs. Casazza announced to the class that we would have a spelling bee on Thursday, the day before our test. "It will be a review for those who are having a difficult time remembering their words," she said.

Oh, no, I thought. Last month when I had to stand up in front of the class and give a book report, my arms shook so badly that it was hard to read my paper. I was overly conscious of the twenty-seven pairs of eyes on me, and all I wanted was to run back to my seat. A spelling bee would be even worse. I wouldn't have a paper to read from!

After lunch on Thursday, Mrs. Casazza told us to line up by the board, and she explained the rules. "Say the word, spell it, and then say it again," she said. "Be careful not to repeat any letters."

One at a time, she pronounced a word for each student to

spell. Two boys made mistakes right away and had to sit down. With clammy hands, I waited for my turn. After the girl next to me correctly spelled her word, Mrs. Casazza called my name and said, "Your word is 'echo.'"

"Echo," I started. The sound of my own voice startled me. "E."

Then my mind went blank. I couldn't think. Everyone was looking at me, waiting for me to say the next letter. But I couldn't see the word in my head. All I could see were the other kids, and they all had their eyes on me. My face got hot. I swallowed hard. What came next? Was it K? No. It sounded like "k" but it wasn't, was it? It was "c."

"E-C-H-O," I spelled slowly. "Echo."

Oohs and aahs came from the kids beside me. "You repeated the 'E'!" Donna pointed out.

"She's right," Mrs. Casazza said. "You'll have to sit down."

I looked down at the floor and made my way back to my desk. Although I was relieved that I was no longer in the spotlight, I felt like crying because I knew how to spell the word.

Afterward, Mrs. Casazza said, "The spelling bee worked so well, and we all had so much fun, that I've decided to have a spelling bee every Thursday."

It worked so well? We all had so much fun? Every Thursday?

I didn't want another spelling bee! I was afraid that I'd mess up again. And sure enough, when the next Thursday came, I did. I started spelling my first word, and then I suddenly became conscious of everyone in the room staring at me. I stood silent a long time, unable to finish the word. The room was quiet while Mrs. Casazza waited. Finally, she sent me back to my seat.

I dreaded the spelling bee so much that I didn't want to go to school the following Thursday.

"What's wrong?" my mother asked. "Are you sick?"

I told her about the spelling bees, and how each time I messed up my first word and had to sit down.

"But you're a good speller!" she said. "You do so well on your tests!"

"I can't spell when they're all looking at me!" I said.

"Oh, so that's the problem," she said. "You've got stage fright. I heard of an easy way to get rid of that. Just imagine everyone's wearing nothing but their underwear."

I laughed. "Their underwear?"

"Try it," she said. "It will remind you that they're no different from you."

Mom seemed sure that her trick would help me, so I went to school believing it would.

During the spelling bee, my first word was "piece."

"Piece," I started. "P." The feeling that everyone was staring at me began to creep up again, but I remembered what Mom had said. I pretended my classmates were dressed only in their underwear. I must have smiled a little. My head cleared and I concentrated. Now did the word start with P-I or P-E? I knew this. We'd learned that there is a "pie" in "piece."

"I-E-C-E," I said. "Piece."

"Very good," Mrs. Casazza said.

Hooray! I did it once, so I knew I could do it again. And I did, again and again. Throughout the year, I even won a few spelling bees. That was just the beginning. My mother's trick helped me with every speech and book report I had to give. I stopped thinking that I couldn't get up in the front of the class. Of course, I could! With a little imagination, anyone can!

~Mary Elizabeth Laufer

A New Country, A New Friend

There was no language barrier when it came to kids,
and when it came to play.
~Connie Sellecca

"What are you doing today?" Mom asked.

"Nothing," I said with a shrug. "It's so boring here. I just want to go home."

"Home is a long way from here," Mom said.

"Why did Dad's job make us move to South America anyway?" I asked. "The TV shows are in Spanish and most of my toys are back home in Indiana. I miss going to school. The worst part is that I don't have any friends here. All of the kids speak Spanish."

"I know it's hard, honey. I'm lonely here too," Mom said.

"It's tough to make friends when I can't talk to anybody."

Mom hugged me. "We'll only be living here for eight more months."

At that moment, eight months sounded like forever.

A few days later, Dad said that a man at his work had a daughter my age. "Would you like to invite her over to play?"

"Does she speak English?"

"No," Dad said, "but I can teach you a few Spanish words, so the two of you can talk a little bit."

I shrugged. "It's hard to be friends with someone when you can't really talk to them."

Dad nodded. "I understand, but you wished for a friend."

"I meant a friend who speaks English."

"I know, but this might be fun anyway. I'm going to ask her dad to bring her over to our house."

The following afternoon, Maria and her dad came over. I felt funny because I didn't know how we'd play together without being able to talk to one another.

"*Hola*," I said quietly, which means "hi" in Spanish.

Maria smiled and said something I didn't understand. I looked at Dad and whispered, "This isn't going to work."

"Give it a chance," he said.

Then Maria showed me a cardboard box. She'd brought a game called *Connect Four*.

Dad smiled. "You don't need to speak the same language to play that game."

Maria and I went to my bedroom and set up the game. We took turns putting the colored disks into the board, trying to get four in a row. Suddenly, Maria smiled and pointed at the four red pieces in a row.

I grinned and said, "You won. Good game."

Although I'm sure Maria didn't understand my words, I could tell she understood my smile. I was actually having fun.

When we were done playing the game, Maria pointed at the bottles of nail polish on my dresser and held out her hands. She said something in Spanish, but I already knew what she meant.

"*Rojo*?" She asked, holding up the red bottle. She smiled and held up the pink one. "*Y rosa*?"

I pointed at each color and told her the English words for them. We each chose a color and then painted each other's fingernails and toenails.

After that, we took turns pointing at things in my room and saying the word for each item. I taught Maria to say shirt, pants, and shoes, and I learned the Spanish words for those things. We taught each other to say pen and pencil and then Maria made a face when I held up my math book.

I laughed. Long division was no fun in any language.

As we were both laughing, I realized that despite the language barrier, I'd actually made a friend.

That night at dinner, I thanked Dad for inviting Maria to our house.

"I knew you two could have fun together," he said, "even though you couldn't talk much."

"We did have fun and I even learned a little bit of Spanish," I said. "I'd like to have her over again."

"I'm sure we can work that out," Dad said.

"So can you help me work on my Spanish?"

"What for?"

I grinned. "I'll need to know a lot more words so I can e-mail Maria when we go back home."

And while I still missed my friends in Indiana, I knew the next eight months were going to be a lot more fun with Maria around.

~Diane Stark

It's Okay to Fall

Our greatest glory is not in never falling but in rising every time we fall.
~Confucius

My strict parents were picky about giving me permission to join in activities away from home, but they usually let me go with the church youth group. I was so excited when Mrs. Burks, the church youth leader who planned most of our activities, announced we were going to the skating rink. I'd never been roller-skating and really wanted to learn how to skate. It looked like so much fun!

When we got there, everyone scrambled out of the cars and rushed inside. Some of us rented our skates and soon began lacing them up. We made our way across the carpet, held onto the handrails, and stepped onto the slick floor. Then, everyone but me rolled away from the wall and started skating.

Holding onto the handrail, I pulled myself along the side as I tried moving my legs back and forth. I stiffened up and clung to the bar as I began to lose my balance. Too late! I was on the floor. After a few more failed attempts, Mrs. Burks skated over to me and stopped.

"You need to learn to fall," said Mrs. Burks.

What? I thought the idea was to go zooming around on these roller skates—not to fall down! Most of the kids in our youth group and some of the chaperones were skating around the busy rink without falling. Many of the tables between the skating rink and the refreshment area were filled with people of all ages. I didn't want them to see me try to skate, fall down, and then get back up over and over again like a circus clown.

My knuckles on both hands turned white as I gripped the bar and dug the toe stops into the floor. God, please help me skate—or at least stay on my feet, I silently prayed. The smell of freshly popped popcorn made my stomach growl. Music blaring, people laughing, and the sound of metal wheels rolling on the hard floor filled the large rink. I tried to focus again on what Mrs. Burks was saying.

"When you start to fall, relax and go on down. If you struggle to keep from falling, you'll be more likely to hurt yourself," Mrs. Burks continued.

Humph! Trying to keep my feet from rolling out from under me had already made my legs ache. My arms were sore from trying to grab the bar every time I started to fall. At least I'd learned how to use the toe stops to get back up. Sweat made long strands of hair that had escaped from my ponytail stick to my face. A cold drink certainly would help my dry throat!

I wished I could be like everyone else. The other kids in the group were flying past me. I could even feel the cooling breeze they made as they went by. Some were almost dancing to the loud music as they cut across the middle of the rink. Others shouted, "Look out!" as they skated backwards. Even when they fell, they laughed and were soon back on their feet, skating again.

Mrs. Burks reached for one of my hands. I took a deep breath, let go of the cold metal bar, and grabbed her warm hand. As we moved away from the wall, she called out, "Get your balance. Glide your foot forward at an angle and then do the same thing with the other foot—like this."

I carefully watched Mrs. Burks show me what she meant. She made it look so easy! I tried to follow her instructions in every way. But I soon landed back on the floor. My feet in the heavy skates almost tripped someone darting around me. Feelings of embarrassment hurt more than my body. I struggled to get back up on my feet, hoping to skate a little farther this time.

"That's good! You're moving your feet like you should. But remember to relax when you start to go down. Let's try again," Mrs. Burks said.

So I did. Each time I tried to skate, I stayed on my feet a little longer. Learning to relax when I began falling was harder though. But I kept trying and finally began to understand Mrs. Burks' instructions.

When I began losing my balance, I immediately crumpled to the floor. Mrs. Burks was right! It didn't hurt as much. I was able to get up faster and try again. Laughing at how silly I must have looked when I fell made it more fun. Other kids showed me how they skated and encouraged me. By the time we had to go home, I was able to skate around the rink.

Our church youth group went back there many times. I kept trying to skate the best I could. Finally I was able to go around the rink without falling. But whenever I lost my balance, I did what Mrs. Burks had taught me to do.

Later I began to see how Mrs. Burks' instructions worked for other challenges. As long as I kept trying to do my best, I could learn something even when I failed. I could get back up, try again, and trust God would be there to help me—not only with roller-skating but with everything in life.

~Pamela Millwood Pettyjohn

The Color of Success

Nothing encourages creativity like the chance to fall flat on one's face.
~James D. Finley

As I rode home from Hebrew school, I worried about my bat mitzvah. It was coming up in just one week, and I still couldn't sing my Torah portion without making at least twenty mistakes.

I have had synesthesia my entire life, a condition that mixes up the senses. For example, I see phonetic sounds in color. My name, Emily, is a light, metallic pink. Most of the time, synesthesia has been harmless and even interesting, but because Hebrew has a different alphabet than English, the letters and colors jumbled up into an ugly mess, making Hebrew difficult to read.

I could tell that my parents, the cantor, and the rabbi were worried about me. My parents came in for meetings with the rabbi on a regular basis, but that didn't help. The cantor and rabbi constantly yelled at me for making so many mistakes. We all knew that my bat mitzvah was going to be a disaster.

As my mom drove me home she asked, "How was Hebrew school?"

"Okay," I answered.

"Are you reading your Torah portion any better?" I shook my head, ashamed. "I just don't know what we're going to do about you anymore. I don't want you to mess up in front of everyone." I didn't want to mess up in front of everyone either, but I wanted to have a bat mitzvah. It was an incredibly important tradition in my culture.

The next day, I had a private tutoring session with the cantor. I still couldn't read my Torah portion smoothly.

"Do you not care about your bat mitzvah?" the cantor asked.

"I do. I am trying to get my Torah portion right. I practice every night, but nothing seems to help me learn it."

"I really don't believe that you practice every night if you still read it like this. You aren't getting anywhere."

I sighed in frustration. I had already told her about my synesthesia, but she told me that I was just making excuses.

"I'm frustrated with you," she said, exasperated. "Maybe we should tell the congregation that you won't be reading a Torah portion because you wouldn't learn it."

I didn't know what to do. There was no way I could learn my Torah portion in the few days I had left. I went home crying.

The day after that was Tuesday, and I had four days until my bat mitzvah on Saturday. My mom called the florist to make the final touches to my bat mitzvah party, and we picked out the cake. That night we had a talk.

"Emily, your bat mitzvah is supposed to be a coming of age ceremony—one that celebrates you growing up into a young woman. But not learning your Torah portion shows that you aren't very responsible, which is a sign of immaturity. I want you to have a bat mitzvah, but I want you to try harder to learn your Torah portion."

I couldn't help bursting into tears. No one could understand how hard I was trying to learn the Hebrew. I had my speech ready, and I had done my service project, but I just couldn't learn the Hebrew.

Wednesday my mom and I bought my party dress. It was so beautiful. It was red with a black belt that tied in a bow around it. I wanted to wear it, but I knew I didn't deserve to.

Thursday I broke down crying at lunch at school. I was so scared of my bat mitzvah. I knew everyone would comment about the mistakes I made and tell me I really hadn't grown up.

My best friend Christina tried to comfort me.

"It's okay! You're going to do fine. All that really matters is that you're trying your best, anyway. That's what growing up is. Being perfect has nothing to do with it."

"But it's not about being perfect! I can't even read through the first three words. I just want to be confident when I'm reading through it."

"True. I do want you to have confidence. But just remember that it's okay if you make some mistakes. I have a good feeling about this." I shook my head. Even though she tried to comfort me, I knew it would do nothing. Just then the bell rang, and I got up from lunch and went to my next class feeling dejected.

Friday night Christina called me. She said she had a present to give me.

"Meet me across the street, okay?" Christina and I lived just across the street from each other.

"Can't it wait until tomorrow? I'm trying to study Hebrew here."

"Once you get this, you won't need to study Hebrew." I laughed. She had to be joking.

"I swear."

"Um, I really need to study."

"I'm going to keep bugging you until you meet me." I took her word for that. Christina was pretty good at bugging people. It was normally for good reasons, though. I hung up the phone and ran across the street.

Christina handed me a box. It was pretty tiny. I had no idea how that could possibly help me learn my Torah portion.

"Open it," Christina said, smiling wide, practically jumping up and down.

I opened the box. It was a bracelet with many colored beads. The first three were red, blue, and green, the same colors as the first three words of my Torah portion. I looked at the other beads. They were all colors of words in my Torah portion in the same sequence. First, I felt relieved. Then, I felt guilty.

"Wouldn't that be cheating?" I asked.

"No. That's using your condition to your benefit—making

something good out of something bad. That's part of growing up, too. Learning how to make lemons into lemonade."

I nodded, slowly, not believing her at first, and then more quickly, agreeing. I hugged Christina.

"Good luck!" she exclaimed. I thanked her and went back home.

Saturday morning, I felt relieved and stress-free for the first time since I started preparing for my bat mitzvah. As I got ready for the service, I slipped on the bracelet.

I read my Torah portion perfectly, and I did a good job on my speech. I talked about the bracelet that Christina had given me and how growing up was accepting the bad things, like my synesthesia, and using them for something beneficial. I also talked about my service project. A few years ago, my grandfather had died from a heart attack, so I decided to spread awareness and raise money for the American Heart Association. This was yet another example of "turning lemons into lemonade."

At the Kiddush luncheon, everyone congratulated me and told me I did a great job. My mom was especially proud of me.

"You did a great job, Emily. You were so confident today. You've truly grown into a young woman."

That night at the party I felt great in my dress. As I climbed into my chair for the Horah, I felt a rush of excitement, relief, and happiness. The ceremony earlier had been truly special. Now it was time to celebrate.

~Emily Sheera Cutler

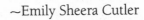

Sharks and Mermaids

Jump, and you will find out how to unfold your wings as you fall.
~Ray Bradbury

I stood on the edge of the diving board at my swimming teacher's house and peered down into the deep, dark water. All of the other kids were in the pool, or behind me, waiting for their turn, but I didn't want to jump. The shadows from the nearby fences, the trees, and an overhang obscured the water below. I squinted through the sun and tried to see the bottom. I couldn't.

"Come on, jump!" a red-haired boy yelled at me, but I didn't budge. He was the same boy who had told me about the sharks just a few minutes before. I tried not to believe him. What would a shark be doing in Mrs. Johnston's pool? But still, what if he was right? I couldn't swim faster than a shark.

My stomach started to hurt badly. Mrs. Johnston came over and put her hand on the middle of my back.

"It's all right," she said in a soothing voice. "You can do it."

In that moment, I wanted to ask her about the sharks, but what if the boy was wrong and everyone laughed at me? I eyed the water, again, wishing I was anywhere else but there.

"Jump already!" the girl behind me in line shouted, and I did. I hadn't meant to jump, not exactly, but suddenly I was falling toward the pool, the dark water coming up to meet me at an alarming pace.

Splash.

I closed my eyes, too scared to look, and just started kicking as hard and as fast as I could. Something brushed my arm, and I gasped. I could almost feel the sharks chasing after me. I could see them inside my mind. My nose and my throat hurt from the water that rushed inside. And then, bump, and my face filled with pain. I screamed underwater and kicked out, but suddenly I felt the ground. I could stand.

I opened my eyes and saw that I was in the shallow end. I was safe. I looked down through the clear water all the way down to my toes, but then a few drops of red splashed onto the surface and blocked my view. I brought my hand to my face and felt the warm drips coming from my nose. I'd hit my face on the edge of the pool. Tears welled in my eyes, and I ran to my mom. My nose wasn't broken, but she took me home anyway.

I never wanted to swim again.

Five years later, I still get stomachaches when I try to swim in the deep end, especially if there are shadows. Even though I'm ten years old and I know that there are no sharks. They need salt water and food to survive. They are way too big to fit, and how would they even get in there? I know all of this, but I'm still scared. Only now something has changed. I have a little sister. She is six years old and finally learning how to swim—and she looks up to me.

Today is her birthday, and she's having a pool party. She's standing on the diving board at our house, and she's afraid. She isn't scared of sharks, like me; I never told her about those. But she's afraid of swimming. Afraid of looking silly. Afraid of how deep the water is. She's also small for her age, and she thinks the water is too cold for her. Two years in a row she hurt herself and couldn't take lessons so now all of her friends swim better than she does.

From my place in the shallow end, I can see her shaking. I've helped her learn how to swim. I've been there, showing her how to hold her breath, and kick, and float. But now she's on the other side all by herself. I don't want to go over there, but she's alone. All the other kids at her party are eating cake and going down the slide, splashing in the Jacuzzi, and running around, but I see only her. And I remember what that feels like.

Carefully, I swim over to the deep end. I try not to close my eyes, but it's hard. I see shadows from the trees moving with the wind, and I want to run away. I want to go inside and have a Popsicle with my older friends and forget about swimming, and deep water, and sharks, but something makes me keep going. Something that was more important than my fear.

Finally, I make it. Goose bumps rise on my skin. It's colder in the deep end under the shade, but I tread water, moving my legs fast to keep me afloat, and try not to think about it. My heart is beating hard as I call out to my little sister.

"Hey Lauren, are you okay?"

She shakes her head; her blue eyes show her terror.

"It's all right," I say. "I'm here, now. Look. I'll catch you."

She shakes her head, again, "No." She's trembling so badly her teeth chatter.

"You're going to get cold if you stay up there by yourself."

She nods once, curtly.

I scrunch my forehead, thinking. There has to be a way I can help her. I think about all the stories I used to tell her. Hundreds of stories about far-off lands and magical creatures. She believed in the worlds I made for her. I look around the water, and suddenly, I have an idea.

"Lauren," I say, "do you see those shimmers on the bottom of the pool?"

She looks skeptical. "Yeah."

"Well, you know what those really are, right?"

"No, what are they?" she asks with growing interest.

"They're mermaids," I say.

She laughs, her voice shaky from the cold.

"No, really," I say. "You can't see mermaids because they're magic, but those shimmers are their reflections."

Her eyes grow wide. "Really?"

"Yup! And when you jump into deep waters, they help you. You'll feel them around you. It's like a million little bubbles all over, and they help you come up to the top."

"Are you sure?" she says while unwrapping her arms from her waist and inching forward on the diving board.

"Yes, I'm sure. Jump and you'll see. And besides, I'm here, too. I wouldn't let anything bad happen to you."

She nods her head quickly up and down. "Okay." Resolve comes over her face. "I'll do it, but if you're lying to me..."

I cut her off. "I'm not. You'll see."

After a minute, she comes all the way to the edge. After another minute, she looks right at me and jumps.

I wait, tensely, and a few seconds later, she breaks through the surface with her cheeks blown out like a puffer fish because she doesn't know how to hold her breath inside yet.

"Jenny! Jenny! I felt them. I felt them." My sister pumps her arms and legs rapidly. Glee covers her face. "You were right!"

I swim over to her and spin her around. "You did it! Good job."

"I want to go, again," she says.

"You should," I answer.

"Will the mermaids always help me?"

I beam. "Yes, always."

I watch her pull herself out and then jump in again and again. And I forget my own fears along with hers. The sharks are gone forever.

~Jennifer Azantian

Running with Heart

Without passion you don't have energy, without energy you have nothing.
~Donald Trump

My name was missing from the list. I looked again, hoping that it might somehow appear. All my friends had made the cheerleading squad. But somehow my name was not there. I fought back tears, wanting to be strong, and I forced a smile and congratulated those who made the squad. But the moment I saw my dad's car pull up to the curb of the school, I hopped inside, closed the door and began to cry.

I was devastated. How could I have not made the cheerleading squad when all of my friends did? I felt lost, betrayed... an outcast among my own friends. I was embarrassed, too.

My friends spent their afternoons practicing cheers and gymnastics after school; they bought matching cheer charm necklaces and wore their uniforms to school every Friday before the game. I still sat with them at lunch, still laughed at their jokes, but it felt different now. I felt as if I didn't belong. Knowing that next year would bring a new round of try-outs I began practicing routines on my own, with my mom watching in support. I took gymnastics lessons and asked for training from one of the local college cheerleaders. I had a year to build up my skills and I was determined to see my name on the list after the next try-outs.

During that year, although I was practicing cheerleading on my own, my dad suggested that I get involved in a school activity or sport—just to try it out for a year. He suggested running track, as anyone could join the team. There were no try-outs, just a sign-up. I had always been the fastest kid to run the mile in gym class every year, so I figured I might as well sign up for one season of track; I could participate in it until I made the cheerleading squad the next year.

On the track team, I quickly learned that out of 100 students, no one wanted to run the long-distance events—and so I volunteered. I had no idea what I was getting myself into. In the first race I took last place. My lungs were burning and my face was flushed. I had never worked so hard at anything in my life, yet I was the slowest one on the track. Race after race, I continued to place last and I continued to feel my lungs burning from the effort. I wanted to quit, and I felt like a failure. But my dad reminded me that once you commit to something, you should always follow through. And so I finished the track season, continuing to come in last every race.

The next year came and I was thrilled to make the football cheerleading squad. But when spring came around and track season started up again, I felt myself drawn to running. Although track was not a popular activity, like cheerleading was at our school, I signed up again to run the long-distance races. I had no idea why, because I hadn't experienced success. Looking back, I can only guess that I wanted to challenge myself, to see if I could personally improve my running times. I wasn't running track to be cool or to prove anything to anyone else—I was running simply for me.

The races were still brutally hard and although I didn't place last that year, I wasn't winning. At the end of the season, I told my parents I never wanted to run again and I was just going to focus on cheerleading.

The funny thing was, the next year I received a letter from the new cross-country coach, asking me to consider joining the team. Our school didn't have enough runners to make a full cross-country team and the coach was hoping to fill the spaces. For some reason, I carried that letter with me all summer as I contemplated whether or not to join the team. If I ran cross-country, I couldn't cheer because they were both during the fall season. I hadn't had any success at running and it wasn't regarded as "cool" at our school, so I'm not sure what drew me to the sport, other than the fact that it was different.

When I called the coach and told him I would give cross-country a try, I never realized that one simple decision would change the direction of my life. All of this time I had wanted to be a cheerleader because it was cool, but something deep down inside of me wanted to run, even though it wasn't popular and it made me a target for being different among my classmates. There was something exciting to me about being unique.

Within one year I became the fastest female cross-country runner on our school's team. A few years later, when I was a senior in high school, I won the conference meet in cross-country and in several track races and I placed 3rd in the Ohio State meet. Not only that, but I was offered an athletic scholarship for college.

Classmates may have laughed at me for choosing running over cheerleading, but I didn't care. Running made me happy. It made me different and it made me proud of who I was. I didn't have a reason for choosing running over cheerleading, other than that I simply followed my heart; I listened to my intuition — that little voice inside me. And because of one simple decision, the decision to be myself — to run — the course of my life was changed. I ran cross-country and track at a Division I NCAA university and became an All-American Cross Country runner. I met talented runners from around the world and I traveled the country from coast to coast for races of various distances. I wouldn't trade those experiences for the world. And more than a decade after high school graduation, I was inducted into the school's Athletic Hall of Fame.

I knew when I chose to be a runner that I would be perceived as different. I knew that being a runner wasn't a cool sport; but I chose it because it felt right. I chose to be a runner because I liked the challenge. Running pushed me to work harder than I ever knew I could. And when I chose to be a runner, I chose to be true to myself. And that is a decision I'm glad I made. We all make that choice every day—we can be who we were born to be or we can simply follow the crowd. For me, I'm happiest to simply be... me.

~Stacey Ritz

How I Became
a Musician

Music is your own experience, your thoughts, your wisdom.
If you don't live it, it won't come out of your horn.
~Charlie Parker

M y mother stood before me as I practiced my clarinet. I had been playing for a while, trying to get a clear sound from the reed.

"I'm sorry," she said. "You're going to have to choose between clarinet and piano. I can only afford to pay for one instrument."

My heart sank. I loved my shiny new rented black clarinet. I practiced every day, and music came easily to me, but playing it was an entirely different story. No matter how hard I tried, I couldn't seem to get a great sound out of it.

As for the piano; I had been playing it since the age of six. My father gave me my first piano lesson before he died. The clarinet was great but I loved the piano. It was the instrument my father had played so well. Every time I played a song on his black upright piano, I felt closer to him. I gave back the clarinet and chose piano lessons.

That decision affected my entire childhood. I watched from the audience as all my musical friends at school played in the band at holiday and spring concerts. They had started in fourth grade and every year they played better and better. I felt left out of all the fun.

Nobody at school even knew I was musical at all. Every day I would go home and play the piano by myself. By the time I was in seventh grade, I was writing my own songs, but no one heard them. I played them when my mom and stepfather were at work.

One day I took a break from piano practice to watch an afternoon talk show. They were making a huge deal out of a young boy who could play the piano by ear. He would listen to music and then play it without sheet music.

"Not fair," I yelled at the TV. "I can do that! How come I'm not on TV?" Nobody heard me.

I was sitting in class one day when a friend mentioned that the music teacher was looking for a bell player for the school band. I thought about it for a week. Should I dare to volunteer?

It took all the strength I had to get the courage to approach the school music teacher. To my surprise, he asked me to stop by the music room after school. He showed me a glockenspiel and asked me if I could read music. The glockenspiel was not a difficult instrument to learn to play, so he said I could learn on the school instrument. My mom wouldn't have to pay for a rental instrument or lessons. Now I could play in the school band! It was like a dream come true to be performing in the concerts at school.

Sometimes, during breaks at band rehearsals students would get up and practice on the band room piano. I longed to play it, but I was too shy to get up and play.

One day after band practice, I summoned all my courage and wandered over to the piano in the corner of the room. No one was around, so I started to play a popular song I knew. It was something I had figured out by ear. After a few minutes I looked up and realized the band director was listening. "Keep playing," he said. My heart was racing. I was so embarrassed yet I wanted to play more than anything in the world. I wanted people to hear me. So I kept playing.

"Would you be interested in joining a little trio I have?" He smiled in an encouraging way. "We have a bass player and a drummer. We could use you on the piano." I was in complete shock.

"Sure." He had no idea how excited I was. Secretly, I was terrified.

I was not one of the popular kids and I could see myself messing up and everyone making fun of me. I was so scared, I almost didn't show up at the first practice. Then I thought of my father. When he was alive, he played the piano in front of everyone. He wasn't afraid. I was his daughter. I had to do this, for him and for me.

The first day of practice was a pleasant surprise. My band mates were great musicians. They were also really nice. They complimented me on my playing. It was so much fun! I made new friends who thought I had talent. People heard me play piano in the music room and one of the most popular girls in my grade asked me to play a piano duet with her. When I had volunteered to play the bells a year before, I never dreamed it would lead to this.

At my eighth grade graduation, I played the piano duet, and performed with our band trio in front of the whole school. My mom and stepfather were in the audience cheering me on. And I know my father was there too, listening from heaven.

~L.A. Strucke

On Top of the World

With innovation and technology, seems we have forgotten to cherish the true
beauty the world has to offer.
~A.C. Van Cherub

This past summer I joined my family for their annual Adirondack vacation. Every July my sister and her family rent a cottage on a lake, the same place my family has stayed since I was a little kid. They always take my parents along. And every few years I join them too.

There are plenty of activities to keep everyone busy: swimming, fishing, canoeing and sand castle building on the beach.

Every evening at dusk, everyone gathers on the beach for a bonfire and s'mores and, at least once during the week, a pair of melted flip-flops when someone gets their chilly feet too close to the fire.

Anyway, by the third day of the vacation, I had noticed that my ten-year-old niece had spent most of her time watching cable TV, playing pinball at the arcade and browsing through the gift shops in town. Not exactly the wilderness experience I remembered from my youth.

So that night at the bonfire I told my niece I thought this was the year she and I should hike to the top of the mountain across the lake. The mountain is called Rocky Point because the peak is bare and rock-covered. It is considered one of the smaller mountains in the Adirondacks. Since nothing was planned for the following morning, we could hike it the next day.

"Well," replied my niece. "Tomorrow there are some shows I want to watch on the Disney Channel, so I'm going to be pretty busy."

"When your mother and I used to come here when we were your age, the cottage didn't have a television," I informed her.

My niece looked incredulous for a moment, and then asked: "So you had to watch all your TV shows on your laptop?"

I closed my eyes for a moment and rubbed my temples.

"We didn't have laptops either. We just didn't watch TV," I said. "We were too busy swimming and canoeing and hiking up mountains."

"Sounds more like punishment than a vacation." My niece shrugged her shoulders. "Besides, I don't think I can walk that far."

"Your mother and I hiked it every year when we were kids," I said. "It only takes a half-hour of steady walking to get to the top."

"Fine, I'll go," my niece grumbled. I knew she was agreeing just to shut me up, but I would take anything I could get. "If you and Mom could do it, then I can too, I guess."

The next morning was a perfect day for a hike, with sunshine, clear skies, and the temperature in the low seventies. I got up early and made some sandwiches and filled a couple of water bottles, which I tucked into my backpack along with the bug spray and the camera.

My niece came shuffling downstairs and announced in a very unenthusiastic, robot-like voice. "I'm ready to go hiking, Uncle David." Then she turned to her mother and asked: "Can I take my $10 spending money?"

"Why are you bringing your money hiking?" her mother asked.

"In case I see something I want to buy at the gift shop on top of the mountain," she replied.

"There are no shops," I said

"What's at the top?" my niece asked.

"Rocks mostly," I answered, "and an incredible view of the lake. You can even see this cottage from up there."

There was a moment of silence. "That's it?" she said. "You mean there's not even a restaurant or an ice cream shop?"

I shook my head. "It's a mountain, not a mall. It'll still be a fun trip," I insisted.

My niece sighed dramatically and rolled her eyes, but we climbed into my car and drove to the trailhead about ten minutes away.

"I'm still not sure this is a good idea," my niece said as she stood at the edge of the gravel parking lot and looked down the shaded trail that led into the woods. "But if you and Mom could do it, I can too, I guess."

For the moment she was determined to start our journey.

About 200 yards into the forest, the trail began to climb a steep slope. I pointed out birch bark trees and a natural spring that bubbled out of the ground and a flowering plant called trillium, which I explained was an endangered species. My niece didn't share my enthusiasm.

She was thirsty.

She was tired.

She was sweaty.

She was bored.

I handed her the water bottle as she sat on a fallen log and took a break. "You know, I think we're almost to the top," I told her.

"You already said that three times," she replied. "And we're not there yet."

She grumbled another complaint as we continued on. She might not have been happy, but at least I was proud that she had the determination not to quit before we reached the top.

A while later we did make it to the top. First, my niece looked up, noticing we were no longer under the trees. "Where are we?" she asked.

She stopped, looked around and saw where we were.

Her jaw dropped, her eyes opened wide and she shouted: "Oh my gosh, I don't believe it. We're on top of the world. It's awesome!" It had taken us almost an hour to make the climb, but it was worth it.

A refreshing breeze brushed the mountaintop, not a cloud was in the sky and miles and miles of trees and lakes spread out below us.

We sat on a large boulder and took in the view, while eating our peanut butter and jelly sandwiches and pointing out islands and roads and, of course, the cottage where we were staying.

"This is the best, Uncle David. Can we come up here another day before we go back home? It's so cool."

No stores, no restaurants, not even an ice cream shop, but she had learned it was cool to climb to the top of a mountain.

And if I had given in to her complaining we never would have attempted it at all; which is a good reminder that sometimes a little determination is all you need to get to the top of the world.

~David Hull

The Art of Mistakes

Never say, "Oops." Always say, "Ah, interesting."
~Author Unknown

"Mrs. Hamilton, I need a new piece of paper. I don't like my drawing! I drew the house too small," moaned the new student standing at my desk. He showed me his art work, which reflected twenty minutes of diligent effort and advanced artistic skill for a fifth grader.

"You have so much detail completed already. Let's see if we can think of a way to fix it," I empathized. "Mistakes are often a great opportunity to enhance your art work."

Students I'd had the previous year, some since kindergarten, knew two of the guiding principles in my art room were creative exploration and self-expression. New students were often insecure and easily frustrated, which sometimes led to torn-up papers or smashed clay.

"Let me tell you about a mistake I made while creating wall murals in someone's home," I began. "One was a painting in a little girl's bathroom. After spending the morning planning and sketching, I painted a dog. I made him over four feet tall so that it looked like he was holding the bar for her towel."

Gesturing with a paintbrush in the air for emphasis I went on, "While I was putting the finishing touch on the black dog collar, the paint dripped on part of the wall where I was not supposed to paint."

Nearby students exchanged smiles and stopped what they were doing to listen.

"It was a wall! I couldn't throw it away and start over," I said dramatically to stress the extent of my crisis. "I had to figure out a way to fix it."

I paused a few moments to give him time to consider what he would have done, then continued: "So I studied the painting for a while until I thought of a way to cover the spot: I added a red heart-shaped dog tag over it, and included the little girl's initials."

"Did the little girl like the painting?"

"The next day my client called to tell me her daughter loved the painting, and she was thrilled when she spotted her initials on the dog tag," I replied, accentuating the solution to the problem.

"So when you make a mistake, make something good out of it!" chanted the other kids, who had heard me say this before!

Since retiring from teaching art in the public schools five years ago, I've maintained a friendship with some of my students and their families. I recently overheard two of my past students, now in college, reminiscing about their experiences in my classes. They both chanted, "When you make a mistake, make something good out of it!"

~Maryanne Higley Hamilton

The New Kid

The best way to find out if you can trust somebody is to trust them.
~Ernest Hemingway

I was a happy child and I loved school. I couldn't wait to get there every day to be with my friends. Most of us had gone to the same school since first grade and many of us lived in the same neighborhood. It was an old school with a lot of character. I still remember the smell of the cleaner that was used on the floors. I remember how huge the playground seemed and the good times we had there. It was great.

One year, the city decided that our school was too old and they rezoned the school districts. As a result, many of the students from our old school were sent to other schools, depending upon which neighborhood we lived in. I cannot remember the name of my new school, but I will always remember how that year began.

The new school was located in a neighborhood that was nicer than mine. Our homes were small and old. Our streets were narrow and some of them had not been paved for many years. Our new school was in a fancy neighborhood with large brick homes and the kids wore more expensive clothes and shoes than at my old school. I felt very self-conscious.

I was miserable at school every day. I hated going. I felt like everyone was secretly talking about me and making fun of me. I became very shy and only talked when I had to. That was normally when the teacher asked me a question. I even hid behind the bushes on the playground so that I wouldn't have to play with the other children in my class. I was sure they were mean and they didn't like me.

One day we had to bring homemade miniature floats to school. They were the kind of floats that you see in parades. Each child's float represented a different state. When I walked into class, a group of children were gathered around my float and they were laughing and talking. I knew they were making fun of my float because I had to make it out of a Kleenex box, Q-Tips and tissue paper. Some of the other floats were fancy and well made. Mine looked so cheap and puny beside them. I was devastated and hurt.

Many of my old friends, from my old school, were also at the new school. I slowly began to notice that they were not having the same problems adjusting to the new school that I was having. They acted the same way as they always had. They dressed in the same clothes, but unlike me, they had developed new friendships. I asked them if they liked the new school and they all did. They could not understand why I felt the way I did about it. It seemed like I was the one who felt like an outsider.

Then one day, the girl who sat next to me in class leaned over and said, "Your float is so pretty! Everyone is talking about how clever you are and that obviously your parents didn't make it for you. I just wanted you to know." She gave me a big smile and I smiled back. The person in front of her turned around and agreed that the float was very pretty. I had been wrong.

If I was wrong about the float, what else was I wrong about? That day, I sat with those girls at the lunch table. Much to my amazement they were eager to talk to me. They asked me many questions about my family, my old school, and the things that I liked to do. Lunch was over quickly. I went home that day feeling happier.

It was much easier to go to school the next morning. I had made two new friends. They invited me to join them on the playground, and through them, I began to make other friends. I was invited to birthday parties. I was an accepted part of the class and I was no longer self-conscious or shy. I was my old self again. I was a happy child.

I realized that my only obstacle to being happy had been my own imagination. My classmates were not mean. They just didn't know me and, like me, they were not sure how to make friends. My float opened the door for my first real conversation with them.

I have always been grateful to those two girls who showed me such kindness and included me in their circle of friends. It made me a stronger person and I have never again felt like an outcast. Being the new kid can be very hard. I never forgot that and always tried to be the person who welcomed new kids and showed them the ropes. I made a lot of great friends that way!

~Debbie Acklin

Chapter
2

Think Positive for Kids

for Kids

Doing the Right Thing

13

Fight for What's Right

To know what is right and not do it is the worst cowardice.
~Confucius

One sunny afternoon, when I was about fifteen, I was walking home from my school in Vienna. I attended the international school there because although my mother didn't speak much English, she loved America and everything the United States of America represented. She had lived through World War II and she was grateful to the United States for what it had done to fight communism and Hitler.

I didn't particularly enjoy school, so it was with a happy heart that I set out on the beautiful Viennese roads. As I came to a crosswalk, I noticed a crowd of people standing around looking at something I couldn't see. At first, I thought it was just some street artists, of which there were many in Vienna, performing their acts to a crowd, but as I approached to satisfy my curiosity, I realized it was a very serious fight between three older teens and a younger teen. To my amazement, no one in the crowd did anything to prevent this uneven match.

I stood for a moment, assessing the situation. I didn't personally know anyone in the fight, nor did I recognize any of the people, mainly kids, who were watching. After about a minute, I sprinted through the crowd to stop the brawl, yelling at the aggressors.

At first, they ignored me and kept beating up the scrawnier kid. So I grabbed one of them—we were pretty evenly matched—pulled him away, and slugged him as hard as I could. As he went down, one of the others turned on me. I was amazed that at this point none of the bystanders had come to my aid. I grappled with the second thug and punched him also. But this served only as a distraction, which allowed the third bully to continue his vicious attack on their original defenseless young victim, pummeling the boy relentlessly. The first bully got up to confront me again, and I took a few hits, but I wouldn't give up the fight.

Finally, after what seemed like a very long time, one young guy came to my aid. And again after a short while, a second, then a third and a fourth joined in to confront the attackers and break up the fight. Eventually, once we outnumbered the thugs, they gave up and ran off like the cowards that they were.

I had a few bruises and my shirt was torn, but other than that, I was okay. The young teen victim did not fare so well. He was bloodied all over and needed help. While aiding him, I could hear the police sirens getting closer. Someone had called them. I looked up at the crowd and I will never forget the expressions on their faces. Some of them were indignant or some seemed ashamed, disgusted, or angry, but many of them simply stared, like sheep, unwilling to do anything. It seemed like they just didn't care.

Because this incident happened off school property, I didn't get in trouble at my school, which frowned on fighting. But I told my mother about it, and she said she was proud of me. I had learned an important lesson, she said: The masses are indifferent in most cases, not only to others' affairs, but even to their own. That crowd's behavior sadly explains the rise of Stalin and Hitler, with whose atrocities we were intimately acquainted in Vienna, and in fact, throughout Europe. Those brutal totalitarians found easy prey in their own people because they knew this little secret—that while many people will get upset, they are cowards and will do nothing to stop aggression. I had been raised to be aware of this and I was not going to let myself act like a sheep too.

So, when confronted by brutality and bullying, I took a stand, even when others wouldn't, and I became stronger for it. And while I was alone at first when I tried to defend that boy from the bullies, eventually other people in the crowd joined me to fight off the bullies. You are not as alone as you might think when you fight for what's right.

~Marius Forté

14

Just Do It

No one is useless in this world who lightens the burdens of another.
~Charles Dickens

As a preteen, I was pretty lazy when it came to "doing" for my family. I worked hard at school, did tons of homework, practiced for piano lessons, and sometimes babysat my younger sister. Still, I found myself regularly resisting the urge to help out at home with even the simplest things.

If my mother or father asked me to do something, I would do it: not a problem. But the fact that I always needed to be asked or told to do things—things I could plainly see needed doing—undoubtedly bugged my parents. What Mom and Dad didn't realize, though, was that by age ten my resistance to chipping in even bugged me!

For a long time, I wasn't bothered enough to actually do anything about it. But my guilty conscience—knowing I could and should do more for my folks, and not just when asked—led me to feel pretty bad about myself.

Every Wednesday afternoon, for example, my mother drove me to another town for a piano lesson. During my half-hour lesson, she'd rush to the nearby grocery store and buy a week's worth of groceries. Given the fact that my mom had just driven me twelve miles there, twelve miles back, paid for my lesson, and bought me a candy bar, you'd think I'd be grateful and gracious enough to help her bring the groceries into the house without being asked. But I wasn't.

I knew I should help her. But with homework weighing heavily on my mind—and with "me" still the center of my universe—I generally just brought in an armload and left the rest for Mom as I ran to my room, shut the door, and started studying.

Don't get me wrong: being conscientious about school is a good thing, and I know my parents appreciated my hard work and good grades. But the thing is, even holed up in my room, I still felt guilty about not helping my mother more. Sure, I had work to do—but she'd worked all day, too! And after hauling in those bags, and putting the food away, Mom still had to whip up a tasty dinner for the five of us. Small wonder I felt guilty.

A similar situation occurred on summer weekends as my family headed north to our rustic lakeside cabin. Each of us kids was expected to pack our own basket of clothes and toys, carry it to the car and, later, bring it inside the camp. But besides our individual baskets, that station wagon was always jam-packed with coolers, camp gear, and bags of food. Once again—if asked—I'd help carry in everything else. But if left to my own devices, I was much more apt to dump my basket inside, then head outdoors to explore the woods. Exploring trumped helping every time.

Exploring is a good thing, sure, and it turned me into a lifelong naturalist. But my "not helping" was gradually becoming a bigger and bigger problem for me because in my heart and my head I knew I was skirting responsibility—not to mention, it obviously made my parents cranky to have to continually ask for my help.

Deep down I wanted to change my ways. But I also realized that once I did change, there'd be no going back. Once I took on more responsibilities, my parents would start expecting more of me. At age ten, I sensed that this one small change would mark the start of something far bigger: my personal transition from a cared-for, semi-spoiled child to a more mature, responsible, caring and giving young person.

I'll never forget the Wednesday I made a conscious decision to jump in and see what happened. Returning home from my lesson, I disappeared into my room, as usual. But once inside, I felt that deep and burning shame. Dumping my schoolbooks and music on the bed, I abruptly opened my door and headed back to the garage to help my mother.

I'm sure Mom thanked me that day, but her thanks are not what I remember. What I remember most is the incredible sense of peace and satisfaction I felt after helping her. Working hard at school always made me feel good. But what surprised me that day was how happy I felt just helping my mom—all on my own.

At the time, I imagine Mom wondered: "Is this a one-time deal or will Wendy help me again next week?"

Unknown to her, I'd already vowed to pitch in every single Wednesday—and from that day on, I did. It was such a small action. Yet what a nice little difference it made in my mom's life! And what a huge difference it made in mine. The selfishness and guilt I'd struggled with for so long suddenly vanished, replaced by a warm glow of pride.

As for those summer treks to the lake, ditto! Instead of just carrying my own stuff, I began returning to the car for more loads—even when my father was in a really grouchy "long week at work" mood. The first time I did it, Dad probably wondered the same thing as Mom: "Is this a one-time deal?"

But over time, I showed my sincerity by continuing to help out with the loading and unloading. The neat thing was, the more I helped out, the better I felt about myself and my place within my family. As Mom and Dad realized they could count on me more, our trips became far less stressful, too. In short, it was a win-win situation for everyone.

Sometimes the little things we put off doing the longest turn out to be the simplest things to accomplish. Helping out more—and offering to help rather than waiting to be asked—made my parents and me a lot happier. And feeling happy trumps feeling guilty any day.

~Wendy Hobday Haugh

It Just Takes One

Fortune befriends the bold.
~Emily Dickinson

"Do I have to go, Mom?" My son looked down at the party invitation that came in the mail. It lay on the table, between us.

He picked it up and read it again.

"It's a week from Friday. I think we're busy that night." He smiled a big smile. A hopeful smile. A wishful, wanting smile.

"I don't think we're busy that night, Logan. And I'm not going to make you go. But I do want you to give it some thought. Andrew doesn't have many friends."

Not any. That we knew of.

Logan sighed. "Okay, Mom," he said. "I'll think about it." He stood, pushed his chair under the table, gave me a quick hug, and disappeared to the living room to build Legos.

Logan was just ten years old, and he was a thoughtful, kind boy. But Andrew pushed his buttons. Logan was sensitive, and Andrew was loose with words. Logan was calm and quiet. Andrew was active. He often did or said things that Logan found to be inappropriate. Sometimes when he shared these things with me, Logan blushed a deep, rich scarlet.

And though he would never be unkind, Logan enjoyed Andrew's company about as much as he enjoyed a sunburn. Or a rash. Or a case of itchy, irritating poison oak.

An overnight birthday party would be a big, hard stretch.

Logan and Andrew had been on the same Little League team. They were in the same grade, but Logan was homeschooled and Andrew went to public school. Twice a week, all summer, they donned maroon and black T-shirts and came together to play ball. They often played warm-up catch together, since Logan wasn't familiar with most of the kids and no one else would play with Andrew.

It was evident that Andrew struggled to have friends. He was that puzzle piece that just didn't fit into the picture on the box.

One afternoon, Andrew's mom sat next to me at the ballgame. We kicked our sandals off and sat, on the grass, on my old, flannel quilt. Andrew's mom looked at me through round, dark sunglasses. "We're so grateful that Logan plays catch with Andrew. Last year he had to warm up with the coach."

I smiled, though I hurt for Andrew. I ached for what it must be like for him in gym class when the children chose teams. Or on the bus. Did anyone sit with him? "It's nice for Logan, too. He doesn't know many of the players." But in my heart, I knew that it was a half-truth. It was harder for Logan to get to know the other players with Andrew stuck to his side like Velcro.

I let Logan's decision about the party rest for about a week. Then one afternoon, while we drove to the orthodontist, I asked him about it.

"Have you given any thought to Andrew's party?" I asked. "We should get back with his mom, one way or the other."

Logan looked at me and took a deep breath. "I think that I need to go. It would be so sad for Andrew. For no one to go to his birthday party."

"I think that's very kind, Logan. You're thinking of someone else, and that's an important thing. We'll stop after your appointment to pick out a gift."

Logan looked at me as if I'd just asked him to eat a double portion of broccoli.

Without cheese.

He had the same look a week later when we pulled in front of

Andrew's house. It was attractive and welcoming, though I could tell from Logan's tight shoulders that the curb appeal brought him little comfort.

Logan lumbered to the door, backpack over his shoulder and sleeping bag tucked under one arm. I toted his pillow and followed behind.

We were about halfway up the sidewalk when the front door flew open and the long barrel of a popgun poked out.

"Better get in here fast or I'll shoot your kneecaps off," came the boyish voice from behind the door.

"Now Andrew," said his mother. "That is not welcoming."

Then the door opened fully and there she stood. A grateful mama lovingly welcoming the one and only guest at her son's party.

Logan gave me a smile and a hug. I held him extra tight.

I prayed for Logan through the night. That he would be strong. That he would be patient. And that he would be blessed and would even have some fun.

And when I picked him up early the next morning, I knew that he had done just fine.

"Give me the skinny," I said as we pulled out from Andrew's driveway.

"Andrew did some things that I didn't enjoy," he said. "But he also is great with Legos and he likes to draw. He was so happy to show me his sketchbook." Logan's face warmed to a gentle smile. "He's okay, when he's not trying so hard. I'm glad that I went. I think it meant a lot to him."

Logan and Andrew continued to play catch at baseball, and they hung out sometimes outside of Little League, too. While they were never best friends, in a lot of ways, they helped each other grow. When Andrew's family eventually moved away we were sad to see them go.

And a few years later, my own son found himself alone. Sort of like Andrew. Without a friend. The piece that didn't fit.

In the ninth grade, Logan transitioned to public school. We'd just moved to a different community. A small community that wasn't used to newcomers. And Logan struggled. His quiet, gentle nature made it hard for him to blend. One older boy targeted him and made Logan's school days tough. The others were not unkind, they just weren't used to pulling someone in.

Logan's most dreaded time of the day was lunch. He ate his sack lunch alone.

"It feels so terrible, Mom," he said. "Everyone busy around me. And no one even seeing that I'm there."

Logan's face had matured to adolescence, but his kind eyes were the same. The hurt in those eyes went straight to my own heart.

And day after day, no one reached out.

Until Brian.

Brian was an upperclassman. He was handsome and well liked. He was also confident. Confident and kind.

One afternoon, Logan came home, eager to share. "Mom, a guy named Brian sat with me during lunch. He didn't make it weird. He just came over. Sat down. Asked how I was doing. It was nice. To not eat alone."

Brian was also wise. If he had invited Logan to his table, his senior table, Logan would've felt self-conscious. But Brian met him where he was, ate with him every day, until he made a few more friends. He extended a warm hand of companionship and friendship.

Just as Logan had with Andrew years before.

My son learned that all it takes is compassion, courage, and confidence to stretch into someone else's life.

And sometimes, others are willing to stretch into ours.

"One person can make the biggest difference," he'd tell you. "Sometimes it just takes one."

~Shawnelle Eliasen

Richmond Girl

Honesty is the best policy — when there is money in it.
~Mark Twain

I was twelve when I got my first regular babysitting job. It didn't pay much, just two dollars an hour, but I was thrilled to be earning my own money. The job was fun, even if it was tiring at times.

I was so excited to receive my first paycheck. I was expecting $18, a veritable fortune for a kid who only saw money on her birthday. I waited as Mrs. Little wrote the check and handed it to me. I smiled and said, "Thank you." Then, without looking at the check, I gathered my things and left. I was barely out the door when I excitedly pulled the check out to examine it. Eighteen dollars, just like I expected. I had such plans for the money! But, there was something else I noticed about the check. Mrs. Little had been in a hurry when she wrote the check and in her rush, she had made the number one in the eighteen look like a seven. The text was written correctly, but if you just looked at the numbers, it looked like $78.

The next day, I walked to the bank. I lived in Richmond, Utah, a small town with just the one bank. I didn't have an account at the bank, but they would cash the check for me. I handed the check to the teller and waited while she processed the transaction. She handed back an envelope, containing my money and a receipt. I took a couple steps to leave, and as I did, I peeked in the envelope. I knew instantly a mistake had been made. The teller thought the check was for $78 and that is what she had given me!

Earning $18 was a fortune; $78 was like hitting the lottery! I could think of many ways to spend this money. The exit door was right in front of me, beckoning me to escape with my riches. I could easily leave without anyone trying to stop me. But, I knew it wasn't right either. Two elderly ladies were just entering the building as I went back to the teller. "Excuse me," I said timidly. "I think you've given me the wrong amount. The check was for eighteen dollars."

The teller pulled my check out of her drawer and exclaimed, "Oh, my goodness! You are right!" She quickly began to correct the transaction when I heard cheerful voices behind me.

"That's a Richmond girl, for you!" gushed one of the grandmotherly ladies, smiling.

"So honest," said the other one, "A true Richmond girl!"

I didn't know what it meant to be a "Richmond girl." But their comments lasted much longer than $78 would have and meant substantially more. Doing the right thing felt good. Even years later, I still feel a swelling of pride to think of how my actions represented more than just myself. After all, I was a Richmond girl.

~Amanda Yardley Luzzader

17

Help by the Bagful

Sometimes when we are generous in small, barely detectable ways it can change someone else's life forever.
~Margaret Cho

Almost immediately, when I walked into my third grade classroom, I spotted the bag in the corner by my desk. It was thick cream-colored plastic, making it impossible for anyone to tell what was inside. I picked it up and asked, "Who does this belong to?'

No answer. Opening it up, I rooted around and saw a blue and red shirt, some shorts, and what looked like some tennis shoes. Unaware of whose bag it was, I asked again, but nobody volunteered. I scanned the faces of my students. They all looked clueless until I got to Timothy. Looking up, he glanced at me and shook his head a little—side to side—just enough to make me stop digging into the bag. I sensed he was responsible for the bag of stuff. I also sensed that if I made him stand out from the rest of the class or if I exposed what was in the bag, I would embarrass him.

Later in the day I took him aside. "Timothy, are those your clothes? Are you going to a sleepover after school? What's going on?" Timothy scuffed his tennis shoes and told me the clothes were for his friend—one of the other boys in our class—a kid he saw every day. He was concerned that his buddy wore the same two outfits and the same pair of shoes every week. He told me he'd noticed that the clothes didn't always fit, and since they had been worn by two older brothers before being passed down to his friend, they were kind of ragged. Also, the shoes were sometimes smelly.

I was curious, because most kids in third grade are just worried about themselves. They don't often reach out to others like this. Later, when I asked Timothy why he had done it, he looked me in the eyes and said, "He's my friend. I just wanted to be nice."

I asked him if his mom knew about it. There was no way I wanted one of my students giving away his clothes without his parents' permission, but Timothy reassured me.

"First," he said, "I asked my mom if it was okay and she said, 'If somebody needs something and you've got it, you can give it to them.' So I went into my closet and drawers. I picked out things that were getting too small for me, things I thought he would like. I picked out that blue and red shirt, with a polo guy on the front, especially for him."

Pulling it out of the bag and examining it, I said, "It's a colorful and sharp-looking shirt, Timothy. I'm sure he'll love it."

"It still kind of fits me but soon, I'll be too tall to wear it anymore, and my friend is shorter than me."

I looked at the expression of pride on Timothy's face, touched his shoulder and said, "Instead of shoving the shirts and pants to the back of your closet, you decided to give them away to someone who could wear them?"

"Yeah, and my mom taught me how to do laundry last year, so I washed the clothes and put the stuff in a bag."

I asked Timothy when he was going to give them to his classmate. He said, "I already did. I handed him the plastic bag this morning and said, "I have some clothes for you."

Timothy looked around to make sure no one was close enough to overhear us. "He said he'd take 'em. So together, we decided that the safest place for them would be in a corner by your desk until the end of the day."

That afternoon, I walked out with the car riders and talked to his mom. Leaning into her car window, I told her, "You have such a kindhearted son. You should be really proud of what he did."

Timothy just shook his head and smiled. From the expression on his face, it looked like he didn't think he had done anything special. All he had done was help his friend. But when I saw his friend wearing his "new" clothes in the weeks that followed, I knew both boys had learned a life lesson: little gestures from the heart mean so much.

~Sioux Roslawski

18

Chicken Soup for the Soul

Tennis Anyone?

Character is doing the right thing when nobody's looking. There are too many people who think that the only thing that's right is to get by, and the only thing that's wrong is to get caught.
~J.C. Watts

One summer when I was about ten years old, my brother and I received a wonderful gift—tennis rackets and balls. We had never had the opportunity to play tennis, so this was exciting. However, there was one problem—the small town we lived in did not have a tennis court.

One Saturday morning my brother said, "Hey, I've got an idea. Let's take our tennis rackets and balls to the school and hit the balls against the school building."

"Great idea! Let's go," I agreed, not realizing what a lesson we would learn before the experience was over.

When we got to the school ground, no one was around, so we began hitting our balls against the side of the two-story brick building.

"I'll hit it the first time," my brother suggested, "then you hit it the next time. We'll hit it back and forth to each other."

So we began taking turns hitting the ball, getting more confident with each stroke. Actually, we became pretty good at returning the ball and we were hitting the ball higher and faster each time.

Suddenly, the unthinkable happened—the ball got out of control and went crashing through one of the upstairs windows.

We looked around and no one was in sight — except — there was an old man sitting on a porch halfway down the block.

Quietly, I asked, "Now what should we do? Our ball is inside the school."

"Well," my brother responded, "no one will know whose ball it is. And no one saw us, except that old man down there. And he probably can't see this far."

"He probably doesn't know who we are anyway," I added.

"Let's go home," my brother suggested.

"Okay," I agreed. "Should we tell Mom and Dad?"

"I don't know," my brother answered.

As we picked up the rest of our balls and headed for home, the decision as to whether we should tell what had happened was carefully weighed out. But that decision was made for us the moment we walked into the house.

Our mother was always in tune with her children. "What happened?' she asked as soon as she saw us.

"Well," my brother slowly began. "We had a great time hitting the tennis balls against the school."

Then I interrupted, "until we hit it too hard and too high and it went right through the school window."

"Oh, my goodness!" my mother exclaimed. After a short pause, she continued, "You will have to tell your father as soon as he gets home."

And so we did. As soon as he walked in the house, we both hurried to him and poured out our story.

His response was typical. "Well, today is Saturday and tomorrow is Sunday, but first thing Monday, I will call the school janitor and see what we need to do. You will probably have to pay for the window."

We had two agonizing days to wait until our dad got home from work on Monday.

He looked very somber and we were sure that the news was bad. We were sure that every penny we had saved would have to go to fix the window.

Then my dad smiled. "Well, I talked to the school janitor and he was surprised to hear from me. He had been sitting on his porch watching while you two were playing tennis on Saturday. He saw the whole thing and was surprised when I called to tell him what had happened. He said many windows had been broken, but we were the first ones to call and admit that we were responsible. He said the school budget allows for window repair, so we will not have to pay for the window, but he was glad we called."

He could see our relief as he continued. "I am proud of you kids for having the courage to tell us what happened."

I'm not sure at that moment whether we were happier to be able to save our money, or to hear our dad say he was proud of us. But either way, we discovered that there is always someone who sees what we do and we might as well confess our mistakes and be willing to take the consequences.

~Shirley M. Oakes

The Rescue

We must reach out our hand in friendship and dignity both to those who would befriend us and those who would be our enemy.
~Arthur Ashe

t was a cold fall day. The wind gusted under a cloudy gray sky. My children, who were seldom deterred by the weather, were outside playing. Suddenly there was a commotion on the front porch. I opened the door to find my young daughter shivering as she held her damp jacket against her.

Cheeks red from the weather, she stood on the porch and looked up at me. In her eyes I could see both defiance and tears. I pulled her inside and asked what had happened. "What are you doing with your jacket off?" She just looked down and said nothing. Her jacket moved slightly. I pushed aside the folds of the jacket to find a pitiful wet kitten. The kitten shivered and mewed in protest.

"They were throwing the kitten into the swimming pool," she sobbed. "I begged them to stop, but they just kept doing it." She hugged the bundled kitten close. I waited patiently for her to continue. "I grabbed it and ran." Once again, defiance dominated her small face. My daughter had championed this kitten and she did not care about the consequences.

I hugged her and took the kitten from her. Ordering her to immediately change into dry clothes, I found a soft hand towel and set about drying off the unhappy kitten. The kitten wiggled with my efforts to dry him, but soon a fluffy little yellow creature began to emerge. The kitten looked to be about half grown.

Her clothes changed, my daughter hugged the kitten close as I warmed up some milk for him to drink. She placed him lovingly on the floor so he could lap it up.

"Momma, it was awful," she said. "Why would they do that?"

She explained that a couple of neighborhood boys kept tossing the kitten into one of those small children's pools that had filled with rainwater from the night before. One of boys was the owner of the kitten.

"I don't know," I said soothingly, "but I'm proud that you had the courage to put a stop to it."

"I'm not in trouble?" she asked in a surprised voice. "I just ran off with the kitten," she said, as if she did not believe that she was not in trouble.

"No sweetie," I said, tears now in my eyes for my brave little hero. "I am very proud of you." I held her close and tenderly, just as she had held the kitten.

Now warm and full of milk, the kitten began to meow again. "I think he's confused and a little scared," I told my daughter. She picked him up and cuddled him in her lap, stroking him softly until he fell asleep.

"We need to call his family," I said. "They need to know what happened and where their cat is."

My daughter's eyes widened. "No! They'll hurt him again."

I was uncertain about what to do. I knew I needed to make the call, but I also knew that the boy was likely to mistreat the kitten again. I began to pray about it as I got up to make us some lunch.

In his usual fashion, our son burst through the door. Slow and easy were terms that he was unfamiliar with. He stopped when he saw his sister sitting with the kitten in her lap. "Are you in trouble for stealing that kitten?" he asked her.

"She didn't steal the kitten," I said. "She rescued it. I'm going to call the family in a few minutes and let them know what happened."

He shrugged his shoulders and headed for his room. I headed

for the telephone. I spoke with the mom and told her what had happened. She was disappointed in her son, but not surprised. This son was born after her other children were in high school. Shortly after his birth, her husband had died from a heart attack. She was left on her own to raise her son and provide for her children. Life was difficult for them. She had hoped he would consider the kitten a nice companion.

"Well, he's young," I said. "Sometimes children don't realize how harmful it is to play roughly with animals." She agreed to walk over to get the kitten after supper.

Coming home from work, my husband was surprised to see our children, on the floor, giggling and playing with the little ball of fur. He looked over at me with a question on his face. "No, I did not bring home a kitten. It's not ours."

"She rescued it," my son said, pointing at his sister. "It was awesome." We explained to my husband what had occurred that day. While we ate, we discussed the fate of the kitten, trying to reassure my daughter that everything would be okay. We said the boys had just gotten carried away and did not see how much they were harming the kitten, although we were not entirely sure that was true.

After we had eaten and were settled in our favorite seats, watching TV, we heard the knock at the door. My daughter, once again, had a panicked look on her face.

"Don't worry," I said. "It will work out. Just wait and see." I prayed very hard that I was right about that.

My husband answered the door and asked the mom to come in. Behind her, his head hanging low, was her son. He shuffled behind her as my husband led them into the den and offered them seats. My daughter was on the other side of the room, protectively holding the kitten.

The mother explained how she had spoken with her son and thought he now understood that what he had done was dangerous and that the kitten could have died. Then she spoke to her son. "Is there something you would like to say?"

For the first time, he looked up and we could see that his eyes were red as if he had been crying. He looked directly at our daughter. "I'm sorry," he said. "I just thought it was funny. I didn't think about the kitten getting hurt." He looked at the kitten and then hung his head again.

Again, his mother spoke. "We have agreed that maybe a kitten was not a good choice for him."

The boy looked up, his face more animated. "I'm going to get a dog!"

"Yes," his mother said. She looked at us. "We are going to the animal shelter to pick out a dog. We want a full grown dog, not a puppy. I want a dog my son can roll around and play with."

"The kitten is going to my sister," she continued. "She doesn't have young children, so he will have a good home." She reached for the kitten. Satisfied, my daughter laid him in her arms.

The boy got his dog and it was just what he needed. He was lively and fun and followed him everywhere he went. All of the neighborhood children loved him, including my little hero.

~Debbie Acklin

The Sweetest Thing

No legacy is so rich as honesty.
~William Shakespeare

had been following my mom and her shopping cart around our small-town grocery store for what felt like forever, at least six aisles and the bakery department. At ten years old, I was obsessed with candy and got permission to head up front to the checkout aisle. Once there, I ran my fingers over the rows and rows of goodies trying to settle on a favorite and dreaming of what it would be like to devour the entire rack full. I smelled large shiny brown wrappers and shook palm-sized purple boxes. I loved almost all of the treats, but chocolate was always my first choice. Skittles and Starbursts were okay, too, especially the yellows and reds.

As I was pondering all things sweet, I noticed a man a few feet away pushing buttons on the ATM machine. Most people I knew didn't use that magic cash machine. My parents still preferred to drive to the bank to get money. This man, though, looked younger than my parents. He was dressed in a suit, had dark hair, and seemed to be late for something, anxiously waiting for his cash to appear. The machine made a grinding noise, and he immediately grabbed a stack of bills and headed out. Bored with the candy, I wandered over to the ATM, where I started pushing the buttons as if looking for some secret combination. Eventually, I peered into the bottom of the machine and saw it: a beautiful, crisp $20 bill. Though I wanted to believe my magic had made the cash appear, I knew the man in the suit must have left it behind.

I held the money in my hand, staring at the number "20" and feeling richer than I ever had. The bill was so smooth, without a crease on it, so perfect that I wondered if maybe it had been printed inside that machine. I thought about slipping the money into my pocket. No one would know, but it didn't feel right. I knew it wasn't mine. I hadn't earned it. I saw how hard my dad worked to make money. I watched him come home from work exhausted each evening. Sadly, this $20 didn't belong to me. I needed to find its owner, but first I had to find my mom.

I started running through the market frantically, when I finally found my mom wandering the produce aisle. "Mom!" I panted wildly.

She whirled around, clearly concerned. "What's wrong?" she asked.

"There was this guy using the money machine, and he left $20 in it. We have to find him and give it back!"

She paused a moment, then pushed her full cart to the side and took my hand. "He might be gone already," she said kindly, trying to lessen the potential disappointment that always followed when I had my mind set on something that didn't or couldn't happen, like receiving a perfect score on a test or that coveted solo in choir.

"But we'll look for him," she said reassuringly.

"I think he was walking to his car," I said.

We scurried out the automatic doors, only to see several men in the parking lot. "That's him," I cried, as I pointed my finger toward the man in the suit. "I think…" He was stepping into his car.

"Are you sure?" my mom asked, looking at me nervously.

"Pretty sure," I replied.

"Excuse me, sir," my mom asked as she approached the young man. "Were you just at the cash machine?"

"Yes," he said tentatively, wondering what was coming next.

"Well, my daughter found money in there and thinks it may belong it you." She pointed to me and he smiled.

"Let me check," he said, as he pulled out his brown leather wallet and multiple bills. "Twenty, forty, sixty, eighty... I think I got it all."

"Okay," my mom said, as she turned away.

"Mom, that's him," I insisted in a whisper.

"Oh wait," he said with surprise. "You're right! I'm missing a $20 bill."

"Here you go," I said, beaming with pride. "Twenty dollars," I proclaimed, as if I was a detective who had solved a major mystery.

"Thank you so much," he said in an official tone. "That was so nice of you," he said, bending down and shaking my hand as he would an adult. My heart swelled. I felt important. I felt special. "Thank you," he repeated.

"You're welcome," I said.

"You must be so proud," the man said, turning to my mother.

"I am," she smiled.

"Can I get your address?" he asked. "I want to send your daughter a thank you card. What's your name, honey?" he said, turning back to me.

"Felice," I answered. My mom gave him my dad's work address, and we said goodbye.

When my mom and I returned to the store, my mind was racing. Twenty dollars. What could I have done with that $20? I bet I could have bought a puppy or every single candy bar in town! But now none of that would happen. I knew I had done the right thing. My parents had always taught me to be a good citizen, but usually that just meant holding open doors or being polite to adults. I had never had to give up money before, especially not twenty whole dollars.

A few weeks later, my dad came home from work with a big brown box in his hands. "Felice!" he called, "I got a package for you!" I jumped up from the recliner I was sharing with my little sister and ran toward the front door. "Here" he said, as he put the box on the floor so I could get a good look at it. "Let's open it up." Within the box was a note and a smaller shoebox. I ripped it open to find dozens of packages of candy, Applets & Cottlets, a Pacific Northwest powered-sugar treat.

"Oh my gosh!" I screamed as my dad handed me the card. "Dear Felice, Thank you very much for returning my $20. You are a great girl, and I appreciate your honesty. I hope you enjoy this candy. Best Wishes, Tom." Tom included his business card. Turns out he was vice-president for the candy company, which sounded like the coolest job ever. I had done the right thing and now I had been gifted with candy. And though it wasn't chocolate, I loved it, sharing with my family and eating one bar every night until it was gone. It tasted sweet, sugary, and also satisfying, each bite reminding me that what I had done mattered. That I made someone happy. That my honesty, although it wouldn't always be rewarded with candy, would make a difference to someone. And that was the sweetest part of all.

~Felice Keller Becker

My Bad Reputation

A lie may take care of the present, but it has no future.
~Author Unknown

Every day after school my parents made me sit and write… "I will not tell a lie! I will not tell a lie!" I repeated the sentence over and over until my hand felt as if it might fall off.

It was the middle of third grade and I am not sure what had gotten into me. I lied for no reason at all and about the dumbest things. I lied that I had eaten all my dinner, when in fact I buried it in the bottom of the trashcan. I lied that I had made my bed, when clearly by entering my room it was obvious I had not. I lied that I had brushed my teeth; with a quick check it was obvious the toothbrush wasn't even wet. My lies were not hurting anyone, but for some reason I felt the need to say things that were not so.

My parents tried everything to understand why I felt the need to make up stuff. I was grounded; I was watched closely so that I did what I was supposed to do, I was talked to and lectured while they tried to get to the bottom of where my poor behavior was coming from.

Was I looking for attention? As the middle child, maybe I wanted attention I wasn't getting. I soon realized the new attention I was getting was horrible. I was labeled a liar and my parents did not trust me. I promised to stop telling lies.

A few days later my sisters and I were invited to spend the

weekend with my aunt. We all loved the times we were invited to Aunt Kim's house. She did not have children of her own so she spoiled us with her time. Not much of a cook, she gave us the perfect food for a third grader—hot dogs and macaroni and cheese. She took us roller-skating at a park with a long path and she was an amazing artist so arts and crafts were a big part of our afternoons. She had cool pencils, erasers and other supplies that any young girl would love to get her hands on.

The day finally arrived for the fun to begin. As my parents dropped us off and visited a few minutes they made it a point to tell my aunt to keep an eye on me and to not let me fall back into my world of silly lies. I was embarrassed and angry but when they pulled out of the driveway I forgot all about their lecture.

Then it happened… sometime that day someone took one of Aunt Kim's good art erasers and rubbed it across the entire top of the TV. The eraser ruined the shiny finish on the TV's casing. When Aunt Kim discovered the destruction all three of us were called into the TV room and asked to confess. Nobody did! Boy was she mad. I had never seen that side of her. She told us how disappointed she was and that someone would have to take responsibility. Again, nobody said a word. The next thing I knew she was on the phone with my parents and they were on their way to pick me up.

It had to be me! I was the liar. No amount of protesting could convince any of them that I had not committed the crime. I was taken home and sent to my room for the rest of the day. I begged and pleaded my case, but no one listened. Why would they? I had been telling lies for the past few weeks so of course it had to be me.

I stayed in my room the rest of that day thinking of all the things my sisters were getting to do without me. I was labeled a liar and now I sat alone with nothing to do. My parents finally let me out for dinner. And then there was a knock at the front door! Aunt Kim was standing there. I could not believe it. I was sure she and my sisters were already watching a movie from her big collection. Why had she come? It turns out my younger sister finally felt guilty! She confessed that she was the one who rubbed the eraser on the TV. Aunt Kim had come to get me. I was invited back!

Funny, I don't even remember being mad at my sister. I learned a valuable lesson about lying. No matter how big or small your lies, once you are labeled a liar earning trust takes a lot of work and time. I promised myself right then and there to never lie again.

~D'ette Corona

A Puppy of Our Own

My goal in life is to be as good a person as my dog already thinks I am.
~Author Unknown

We lived on a quiet street with very little traffic so my mom let my brothers and me play out in the front yard a lot. One day we were outside playing when I saw something move under a bush at our neighbor's house. It looked weird so we went over to check it out.

It was a puppy! I sat down in the grass and clapped my hands and it came running over to me and jumped in my lap. I was so happy. I had been begging my parents for a puppy for a long time and here it was. My brothers were going crazy.

I carefully carried the puppy to my house and went inside to look for my mom. "Mom, Mom, guess what I found under the bush next door?" My mom came into the room, looked at me, looked at the puppy and then back at me. "Mom, I think it's lost; it doesn't have a collar or any tags. And Mom, it sure looks hungry."

Mom got a bowl and filled it with water. Then she got some food from the refrigerator and put it in another bowl and put both bowls on the floor. I put the puppy down. She ran right over to the bowls and started eating and drinking. I was right… she was hungry. After she ate she curled up into a ball and went to sleep. My brothers and I just sat on the floor and watched her sleep.

My mom said that we needed to try and find the owner of the puppy. I didn't want to do that. I wanted to keep the puppy for my own. But Mom said that the owner was probably worried about the puppy and sad that she was gone. She asked me how I would feel if I had lost my puppy. Would I want the person who found it to try and find me? Or just keep the puppy? She was right. We needed to try and find the owner.

We made "Found Puppy" signs and put our phone number on them. We hung the signs up around the neighborhood. My mom put an ad in the newspaper about finding a lost puppy. Every time the phone would ring I would get scared. Almost a week went by and no one had called about the puppy. I was so happy.

Then one day that dreaded phone call came. I could hear my mom asking lots of questions: What does your puppy look like? What does your puppy like to eat? And then I heard her giving our address to the person on the phone and saying we would wait outside for him. I felt sick. I loved this puppy so much and now I might lose her.

The man drove up in his car. There were two kids in the car with him. They all got out of the car and started walking up the front walk to our house. The puppy went wild! It ran to the man and his kids and was jumping all over them. The kids were screaming and laughing and jumping too. The man got down on his knees and the puppy jumped into his arm. There was no doubt that this was their puppy. And the puppy was really happy to see them even though we had been so nice to her.

My mom and brothers and I were sitting on the front porch and the man walked up to us. He was so happy. He thanked us for finding the puppy and for taking such good care of her. He told us that she had gotten out of the yard about a week ago and had run away. Puppies do that. He and his kids had looked all over for her. They had never given up hope of finding her but, since a week had gone by, they weren't sure they would ever see her again. The man wanted to give my mom some money as a reward but my mom said no. She was just glad that we were able to do the right thing and return the puppy to her family. They drove away.

I watched them go and I cried. So did my brothers. We were so sad. We only had the puppy for one week but we loved her so much. My mom was very sad too but she told us to think of how happy the other kids were now that they had their puppy back. And then she told us something that my brothers and I had wanted to hear for a very long time. She and my dad were going to get us a puppy! Our very own puppy! She told us that she was proud of us for taking care of the puppy for the week we had her. And she was proud of us for understanding that giving the puppy back was the right thing to do. My brothers and I started yelling and screaming.

We got our own puppy the very next week. We named her Princess and she ruled our house. My brothers and I took good care of her and we didn't ever have to worry about having to give her up. She was OUR puppy. Keeping that other family's puppy would have never felt right to us. Princess was like our reward. We got her because we did something that was hard to do but it was the right thing to do.

~John Berres

Chapter
3

Think Positive
for Kids

Accepting Differences

My Sister, My Hero

You cannot do a kindness too soon,
for you never know how soon it will be too late.
~Ralph Waldo Emerson

The first full choir rehearsal of the school year took place in the school auditorium. Each grade had been practicing the songs separately, but this was the first time all the grades joined together to sing. My sister was a year older than I was and I watched as her grade filed in and took their places next to us on the stage.

Off to my right and in back of me I could hear giggling. As I turned my head around to see what was going on, I saw older boys and girls pointing down at a girl a few rows below them. I'd never seen this girl before but a couple of kids away from this girl stood my sister. She turned and glared at the group that was now openly making fun of this girl, saying things like "diaper" and "pee your pants" at her.

The teachers were too busy discussing the order of the songs to notice the commotion. Finally, the rehearsal started. After each song, the teachers would discuss any problems and while they did that, the little group of bullies were pointing, laughing, and talking just loud enough so that the girl, whoever she was, could hear what they were saying. One of the girls in my class whispered in my ear, "Did you know she's wearing diapers?"

At home that evening, I asked my sister about the girl I'd seen.

She said that her name was Theresa and that she was a very nice girl.

"Why were those kids being mean to her?" I asked.

"Because they're jerks, that's why," she snapped, turning and stomping out the door.

The scene was the same at each choir rehearsal but as time went on more kids joined in teasing poor Theresa.

The day before the program, I was walking home from school when I heard voices behind me. The closer they got, the more I realized they were talking about me.

"There's little idiot's sister—you know, the one who loves pee-pee pants. Does your sister pee her pants too?"

I walked a little faster and then I felt a pebble hit me in the back. "Knock it off, you jerk!" I stuttered in the bravest voice I could find. By this time I was almost running.

"I'll bet you pee your panties too, don't you?"

Just then, one of the neighbors came out of her house and I took off running for mine. When I got home I ran down to my sister's room and knocked on her door.

Jannelle opened her door and I pushed my way into her room, screaming at her. "Why do you have to stick up for that girl, Janelle? Now I'm being bullied because of you. Why do you have to be her friend? I don't see anyone else being nice to her."

Janelle yelled back, "Because she's a wonderful person and she's dying!"

I will remember those words for as long as I live. Theresa wet her pants because she had an illness, an illness that was killing her. My sister was the only one nice enough to be her friend and stick up for her.

The choir program was great and since there were parents in the audience it was the one time that no one tortured Theresa. When the program ended, I watched as she introduced my sister to her parents. Theresa's mother had tears in her eyes as she hugged my sister. Smiling, Janelle turned around and gave Theresa a big hug. I noticed a lot of looks coming from some of the bullies but this time instead of being embarrassed I felt proud that Janelle was my sister. A few months later, Theresa passed away.

On that night, so very long ago, my sister became my hero. Throughout the years I watched her, always making friends with everyone. It didn't matter if they were fat, thin, brilliant, not so brilliant, shy, or loud, she never left anyone feeling isolated or alone. We never talked about Theresa or the night I was mad at her for being Theresa's friend. All I know is because of that night, something inside me changed and I never looked at anyone in the same way again.

~Jill Burns

24

Lessons from a Nursing Home

Wrinkles should merely indicate where smiles have been.
~Mark Twain

One chilly autumn day when I was ten my mom took my siblings and me to visit our great aunt in a local nursing home. As we entered the building, the smell of watery soup, mashed potatoes, and cleaning solution filled our nostrils. My siblings and I looked warily around the room, a large common area with a braided rug, wilting potted plants, and an old coffeemaker. Elderly residents napped in wheelchairs around the perimeter, and the only noise came from an old television. We started as an old man to our left started muttering in his sleep. An ancient woman wrapped in a yellow quilt clutched a plastic baby in her arms, singing a lullaby as if it were a real infant. Another woman stared into space with beady black eyes, nibbling on her bony fingers with toothless gums.

We gingerly made our way across the room and found our aunt asleep in an overstuffed armchair. My mom decided not to wake her, and my siblings and I breathed a silent sigh of relief. Now we could get out of this creepy room and away from all the strange old people! But then a voice sounded from our right.

"Sweetie, you have such pretty hair," said a little old lady to my six-year-old sister. "You remind me of my granddaughter."

"Oh, look at the kids!" exclaimed a woman with long white hair. "Aren't they sweet?"

One by one, the elderly people noticed us, rolled their wheelchairs closer, and greeted us cheerfully. Surprised, but not as frightened as before, we introduced ourselves and answered the many questions asked by the eager seniors. They wanted to know all about us: our names, ages, grades, and hobbies. We met Ethel, a frail woman who loved talking about her three grandchildren. Mary, a crusty but good-natured soul, made sure we all had a chair to sit in. Rose still remembered all the recipes she used to cook, and told us what it was like to be a teenager more than half a century ago. My siblings and I left the nursing home feeling like we had just made a dozen new friends.

We visited the nursing home several times after that, sometimes bringing homemade cookies or muffins, sometimes just dropping in to say "hi." Many of the seniors loved to talk and were thrilled to have so many listeners. My younger sister befriended the lady with the doll, whose name was Caroline. She was a sweet old lady who loved children and had a huge doll collection from when she was young.

We also made a surprising discovery—the old ladies loved playing beach ball! The nursing home staff taught us to stand five feet away from an old woman's wheelchair and toss an inflated beach ball right at her. To our surprise, all the ladies in the home loved to bat the ball away with their hands, feet, and even heads! They could spend hours playing catch with us—we wore ourselves out from throwing the ball long before they tired of playing!

All these events helped me realize that underneath all those wrinkles, crooked backs and missing teeth, these ladies were just ordinary, friendly people. Although they looked different from me, on the inside we were very much the same. Despite my first impression, they weren't crazy or scary or strange—in fact, they had the same feelings, worries, and hopes as normal people. Just like me, they liked to laugh, talk, and make crafts. And, like me, they wanted to be loved, and to know that somebody cared about them.

The nursing home taught me that appearances are often only

skin deep, and that with an open mind and a caring heart, you can discover the beautiful person inside.

~Caitlin Brown

25

Jonny and Me

The only disability in life is a bad attitude.
~Scott Hamilton

My family sometimes talks about Before Jonny and After Jonny. But I've never known life without my special brother.

Not that we're not all special—at least that's what my parents say. We have twelve kids in our family altogether. Jonny's Number Eight. I'm Number Nine. We were born one year and two weeks apart and we were like twins when we were little.

That's because Jonny has Down syndrome. My mom calls it A Little Extra. An extra chromosome on the 21st pair. That makes him different, but aren't we all a little different? And isn't Jonny more like me than not?

Still, the differences are enough to make Jonny stand out in a crowd. And over the years I've seen a lot of different reactions from people in all sorts of situations. But while I've heard of kids giving kids with disabilities a rough time, I've never seen that in the places where we've lived. In fact, Jonny seems to bring out the best in people he meets. When he walks down the halls of our high school, he's greeted with tons of high-fives and "Hey, Jonny's!"

For a while in middle school I even worried that Jonny was more popular than me. When I told my dad he said that Jonny had a long road ahead of him—that he needed all the confidence he could get in these early years. That someday those people high-fiving and

Hey-Jonnying him would be the people who gave him and other people with disabilities jobs. And that soon middle school would be over, that what I was feeling was pretty normal for a girl with an older brother in the same school, and that eventually—like my parents always say "This too shall pass." I used to hate it when they said that, but as I'm getting older I see they've got a point.

It did pass—the weird feelings I had about Jonny's popularity. Now I'm happy for him. And happy we live in a town where he can have a lot of friends. I'm proud of our high school, where five years ago a senior girl with Down syndrome was voted Homecoming Queen. I thought that was unusual until I Googled "Down syndrome" + "Homecoming Queen" and found it happens all over.

While my mom and dad have had to work hard to help Jonny reach his potential, they've worked pretty hard to help me reach mine too. Jonny and I share a love of Broadway musicals and someday hope to work onstage.

God has given me the gift of music and I love to sing. Seeing his plan for Jonny unfold has helped me see that God has a plan for me as well. Jonny's Down syndrome and our love of music and acting are things that He built into us from the day we were born.

My parents say having a baby is like getting a gift from God, then unwrapping it slowly to see what's inside.

Jonny's little extra was obvious the minute he was born—his almond-shaped eyes, for instance. Unwrapping my package may have taken a little longer, but one thing Jonny's taught our family: Each of us really has a little extra. But what's most important is the ways in which we are the same.

~Maddy Curtis

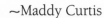

Alone

Be yourself; everyone else is already taken.
~Oscar Wilde

"How was school today?" I asked my youngest daughter as she walked in the door.

The sad look on her face and in her eyes gave me the answer before she spoke these words: "Why doesn't anyone want to be my friend?"

After two years in our small town we had begun to know a few people. Yet even though Amee had already spent those years with the same group of students no one from her class chose to get to know her and become her friend. Amee walked to and from school alone. She played alone at recess and ate alone at lunch since no one in her class wanted her around. No one picked her to be on their team in gym class or for class projects. There were no after-school homework groups or fun times, no birthday party invitations, no sleepovers with the girls, no one to whisper secrets and dreams to. Her classmates simply excluded her.

She just wanted to be accepted, to belong to a group, to have some friends. In her loneliness she begged me to talk to the teacher. "Mom, help them understand why I need help. Tell them I just want to be friends. I try my best."

Thinking Amee had a great idea I talked to the teacher but her reply made us sad.

"No, we don't need to tell the students anything about her

disabilities. You know how mean children can be. This will only single her out."

Then, some of the girls began yelling at her to quit staring at them. They didn't realize the staring indicated that Amee was having an absence spell seizure and not simply staring to be rude. Some of her classmates tried to push her aside so they could spend time with her teacher assistant. Occasionally some of the girls said mean things that hurt her feelings and once they even pushed her. Each day my daughter came home sad. She became so frustrated she did not want to go to school anymore. She begged me to talk to the teacher again. I did but the teacher refused to change her mind. No matter how sad and hurt Amee felt, she continued to treat her classmates kindly, even the ones who tormented her, hoping they would become her friends.

Finally school finished for the summer. The holiday meant visits to her older sisters, which she looked forward to. Summer holidays meant time with grandma and grandpa whom she loved very much. This summer meant being a junior attendant at her oldest sister's wedding. This summer meant time away from those who chose to exclude her, tease her and hurt her.

As summer drew to a close and the start of school drew closer Amee began to beg, "Mom, please talk to the new teacher. Maybe she'll let you talk to the kids. They'll all be the same. I don't know why they don't like me. Tell them why I sometimes stare. Tell them why I need help. If you help them understand maybe they'll be my friends this year."

It hurt to see her so fearful about the new school year. This year's teacher agreed to let me talk to both grade six classrooms during health class. I planned my presentation. I checked with Amee to see what she thought. She smiled, hoping this year would bring friendships and fun. She remained convinced that a talk to the class would change everything.

On the day of the presentation, Amee's lopsided ponytail bounced as she rushed to school with a smile on her face. Later that morning I gave my talk to the students. "Put the hand you use all the time on your desk." Once every student had one hand on the desk I continued. "Now put that hand in your lap or behind your back. You can't use it for the rest of the class no matter what you have to do."

They had fun trying to print and then write their names. I assigned the second task and stood back to watch the students problem-solve their way through tying shoelaces. Some students began working in pairs to have two hands available for the job. Some attempted it on their own and frustration soon showed on their faces and in their actions. Finally one boy put up his hand and said, "I can't do this with one hand. I need help."

The rest of his classmates nodded in agreement.

I began to simply explain brain injury, cerebral palsy and epilepsy to the class. I personalized all the information by sharing Amee's story. Cerebral palsy affected her right side especially her hand and arm. The hand and arm would not work the way their hands worked but her leg functioned well enough to allow her to run races with Special Olympics. I explained the small absence spell seizures that mimicked staring and how medication did not always work as well as it should. Brain damage due to the stroke she suffered at birth caused both these conditions, as well as learning disabilities, which meant she needed more time and lots of repetition and help to learn simple lessons.

I ended with an object lesson especially for the girls in the class. I asked them to put their hair in a ponytail with only one hand and then change their earrings. The girls looked at me and then at the very crooked ponytail Amee had accomplished on her own. One girl shouted, "So that's why her ponytail is always messy."

Another girl said, "That's not fair. She's had lots of practice. We've never tried that."

I smiled as I watched awareness show in the faces of her classmates. Maybe this new understanding would make a difference in attitudes and actions. Maybe Amee's idea would work.

Changes began to take place. Some of her classmates asked her to be in their group for class projects. Some included her at recess and noon hours. They quit yelling about her staring and began to acknowledge her need for a teacher assistant. They excitedly cheered for her when she ran her races with Special Olympics and helped celebrate her abilities.

Total change takes time. Amee still walked home alone after school. No birthday invitations or sleepover invitations arrived. But knowledge provided more understanding. Meanness and exclusion decreased during the school day. Amee started to feel like she belonged and enjoyed going to school. She remained convinced that friendships would follow.

~Carol Elaine Harrison

A Sweet Lesson

*Our most difficult task as a friend is to offer understanding
when we don't understand.*
~Robert Brault

Many people have vivid memories from their kindergarten years. From finger painting to nap time, it was non-stop fun. What I remember most from kindergarten was meeting Christopher, who was diagnosed with diabetes at the age of four.

Christopher came to our school in the middle of the year, right after Christmas break. He was the only new kid who transferred in the middle of the year but he wasn't shy at all. He stood in front of the class and introduced himself with full confidence. Right away, I felt as if I found my other half. I immediately ran to Mrs. Rose and asked if Christopher could sit next to me.

Weeks passed and I realized Christopher was in fact exactly like me. We both were funny and liked sports, food, playdough, as well as causing trouble. Our parents even got a chance to meet and put us on the same soccer team! Every day I'd tell my classmates hilarious stories about how much fun we would have, but they didn't find it as amusing. My classmates stayed away from Christopher because he had to get pricked every time after he ate sweets like cookies. He also wore a metal medical alert bracelet and had a lot of bandages.

The day before spring break all sorts of candies and desserts were being passed out. Mrs. Rose invited all our parents too. I stuffed my face with every sugary sweet I could find. I made sure to grab a couple for Christopher too but he didn't touch them. He just looked at the floor.

"Why aren't you eating, Christopher?" I asked.

He replied sternly, "I can't."

I kept bugging him and then he got mad and said, "I told you I can't eat it! Stop it!" He then stormed out of the room and along followed his mother. I sat there stunned and puzzled.

I went home that night with a million questions. My mom sat me down and told me that Christopher had diabetes and that was the reason why he couldn't eat as much sugar as everyone else. She also told me that the reason he had to get his finger pricked was to make sure that his blood sugar wasn't too high, because if it was he could be in serious danger. Plus my mother explained that he wore the metal alert bracelet because it had all his medical information engraved in it, in case he had an emergency. I felt so bad for Christopher and couldn't imagine what he had to go through on a daily basis.

During spring break I thought about various ways to make Christopher feel completely welcomed once we all returned to school. When we got back, I asked Mrs. Rose if I could share with the class about Christopher's medical condition and she agreed. As I told them about his diabetes, I could see from their faces that they were getting it. I also proposed that every snack or sweet that we brought to class had to be appropriate for Christopher to eat. Surprisingly, all of them agreed.

Months went by and Christopher was happier than ever. He had even more friends now and he didn't feel so left out during snack time because everyone was eating the same treat. There was even a time where everyone wanted to get tested, just to see how it felt. Mrs. Rose made everyone get parental permission and then we as a class felt the same small pinch Christopher felt daily. All my classmates were delighted to see their sugar level and laughed when Christopher told us it was fun to suck the blood that comes out. As we all sat there laughing I realized that this was exactly what Christopher wanted—friends who could accept him and love him for who he was.

Seeing Christopher's wide smile spread across his face was the greatest "thank you" I could ever receive. I learned about living life to the fullest from Christopher, who enjoyed every day despite his serious medical condition. At such a young age I couldn't have asked for a better eye-opening experience.

~Zehra Hussain

Father's Day

*A father may turn his back on his child, brothers and sisters may become
inveterate enemies, husbands may desert their wives, wives their husbands.
But a mother's love endures through all.*
~Washington Irving

There were loops and curves and long squiggly spirals; rings and letters and bow ties. The pile of uncooked pasta made a faint clicking sound as I sifted through it, searching for the very best pieces for my art project. I carefully dabbed glue onto each bit and attached it to the empty frozen-orange juice can I had brought from home. I tried to ensure that every last inch of the can was covered; ziti and macaroni protruded at jagged angles. When our masterpieces were finished they would be pen and pencil holders, and they would serve as Father's Day gifts. Our teacher, Ms. Z., told us to leave our cans on sheets of newspaper at the back of the classroom. The projects would be spray painted gold after school and left out to dry overnight.

We put our glue bottles away and settled down at our desks to make Father's Day cards. I picked up a crayon and stared at the piece of paper before me on the desk. On either side of me, my classmates were drawing pictures of their fathers: stick figures with scruffy hair and ties; smiling faces with and without beards; men holding baseball gloves or footballs. I chose, instead, to draw a spring scene. Smiley faces, rainbows, butterflies and a bright sun danced across my card. I folded it in half and wrote my message on the interior:

"To Mommy... Love Denise"

There wasn't anything else I could write. I'd never met my father. I didn't know his name or what he looked like. He had actively and consciously chosen to be completely absent from my life, although I would not be aware of that detail for years to come. When I was in the first grade, all I knew was that he didn't exist for me. I was honestly fine with that, because I didn't miss someone I didn't know. I wasn't thinking about the things I didn't have; I was enjoying what was there. I had a mother and aunts and baby cousins; I had an uncle and a grandmother and a sweet German Shepherd dog named Cindy who liked to play catch. A few of my classmates lived with their grandparents; others had huge extended families. Some of my friends had siblings and others were only children, like me. One of my friends from dance school had a parent in the military who wasn't home very often. I knew that there were all kinds of families out there and that mine was just one more possible permutation.

For me, addressing my Father's Day card to my mother was simple logic: it was supposed to be a present for a parent, and my Mum certainly was one. Ms. Z didn't get it, unfortunately. She was somewhat unsettled, and she questioned me about it. It was the first time I'd ever encountered a teacher who didn't understand that I really meant it when I told her that I didn't have a father, but it would not be the last. As I progressed through my school career, I would meet other teachers who were perplexed that my family configuration did not mesh with their expectations. They would ask why my blue emergency card—which listed family contact information—wasn't completely filled out; why my Father's Day cards were addressed to my mother; and why I didn't talk about my father at all. Some of my classmates' parents would sneer at my mother behind her back. I was occasionally upset that people felt the need to judge me, but for the most part, I took it in stride. I knew that if anyone had a problem with my family, it was their issue, not mine.

At that moment, though, in first grade, my concern was with my art project. Part of me fretted that Ms. Z. would throw it away. What if she decided that if I didn't make a Father's Day gift, I couldn't make anything at all? I needn't have worried. When I returned to school the next morning my work was still on the newspaper, right where I had left it. It had been spray-painted gold along with all the other cans; it was sticky and tacky and it still reeked of fumes.

I gave the presents to my mother as soon as I brought them home. Mum loved my card and gift, and she kept the pencil holder in her office. Whenever I visited her at work that summer I smiled to see it, shimmery and sparkling, on her dark desk.

~Denise Reich

A Different Sister

I choose not to place "DIS" in my ability.
~Robert M. Hensel

I was standing in the park on the other side of our street watching the old Henderson place. My best friend Sam and his little brother TJ were with me.

"They're monsters, Richard," Sam said. "Someone told us at bowling. There are two sisters and they're monsters."

Sam was talking about the new family that had moved into the house. We'd seen the parents. They looked ordinary, but we had never seen the two girls. And there had never been any monsters living on our street before, so we wanted to find out all about them.

"How big are they?" TJ stretched his hands up high over his head. He knew about T. Rex and other dinosaurs.

"As big as full grown bears," Sam said with a nod to me. "And they hate little boys."

TJ moved behind his brother, but kept his eyes on the house.

That's when the garage door opened. We expected to see someone drive out but two girls walked out instead. They were pushing bicycles.

The girl in front was very pretty. She had curly blond hair and pink clothes. She was about as old as me.

"She looks all right," I said. "She's not a monster."

"Look at the other one!" TJ's voice was more squeaky than usual, as he pointed at the second girl coming down the driveway. She was bigger than the first one, and she had a crooked face. She swayed from side to side as she walked.

The girls pushed their bikes across the road toward us. That's when I noticed the big girl's tongue seemed to be blocking her mouth.

TJ became very brave. He jumped out from behind Sam and pointed and laughed at them. "Monsters! Monsters!" he yelled.

The two girls took no notice. The pretty girl was helping the other girl put on her helmet. TJ bent down, picked up a stick and threw it at them. The stick didn't even go close.

"TJ!" Sam and I both shouted at him at the same time, and he stepped back and looked very guilty.

I wanted to find out what the pretty girl's name was. She looked nice. And she didn't seem to be frightened of the other girl.

"Come on, Sam. Let's go and talk to them," I said.

TJ wanted to go home. He was almost crying and kept dragging on Sam's hand, so I went by myself.

"Hi, my name's Richard," I said.

"I'm Holly. This is my big sister Claire." Holly finished tightening both helmets while I looked closely at Claire. Her eyes were bulgy and she stared at the ground beside me.

"Hi," I said to her.

She didn't answer. She just stood and stared.

"Can she talk?" I asked Holly.

"I can talk!" Claire shouted. "And I can ride a bike. Can you ride a bike?"

"Yes, I can," I said. "I didn't mean to be rude. Don't be angry."

"She's not angry." Holly looked straight at me and smiled. "That's how she talks."

Holly had the best smile in the world. It was like it was a special smile just for me. And I couldn't help smiling back.

Then Claire got on her bike and nearly ran me down as she started off along the track.

"Sorry," Holly said, as she rode after Claire.

By this time Sam and TJ were almost out of sight. I ran home to get my bike so I could ride with the girls. When I got back to the park they were still going slowly around the track. I rode next to Holly with Claire riding ahead.

"What happened to her?" I said.

"What do you mean?" Holly said.

"Why does she look so strange and talk so loud?"

"Nothing happened to her," Holly said. "She's always been like that."

"Don't you mind going out with her, when kids point and laugh?"

"They soon stop when they get to know her," Holly said. "She says some funny things you know."

After a while the girls propped up their bikes and sat down to have the cookies and drinks they'd brought with them. I sat next to Holly and looked at Claire. She hadn't said anything funny since I'd been with them. In fact she hadn't said anything at all. She sure looked strange, but not scary-strange like she did at first.

"Do you eat cookies?" Claire shouted at me. She was holding out a cookie for me. I took it and she smiled for the first time. It was a lopsided smile and her tongue got in the way, but that was all right.

The next day I rode with them to the library. Claire waited outside to mind the bikes while Holly and I went in to find some books.

We'd only been in the library a few minutes, but when we came out the police were there. One of them was trying to talk to Claire, and the other one was talking to a woman next to her car. The side window of the car had been smashed and glass was on the ground.

"Did you see anything?" the policeman said to Claire.

"Yes," she shouted back at him.

The policeman waited a while and then said, "Well? What did you see?"

"Two men."

"Which way did they go?" the policeman asked.

"Nowhere," Claire shouted.

"They must have gone somewhere." The policeman seemed to be getting impatient with Claire.

"No. They're over there." Claire pointed at two men watching from behind a blue truck. They saw her point and they scrambled to get in the truck. But the police were too quick. They had their guns out and the men gave up.

The police found the woman's bag in the truck and lots of other things as well.

The woman came over to speak to Claire.

"Thank you," she said. "You're a very clever young lady."

"I know," shouted Claire. "They said I was stupid. They didn't care if I saw them smash your window."

"Well, here's a $20 reward for being such a good witness." The woman held out the bill to Claire. But she wouldn't take it.

"I don't have money," she shouted. "Holly has money."

"Thank you," Holly said as she accepted the bill. "I'll buy her something nice."

On the way home, Holly had to ride in front because Claire didn't know the way.

As I rode beside Claire I realized I had become used to her already. There wasn't anything scary about her at all. She might look unusual, but she was really a very nice person—just different.

~Richard Brookton

When Staring Hurts

Be curious, not judgmental.
~Walt Whitman

Once upon a time, whenever I was out with my children—Iris, Marc and Danny—strangers stared at them and told me how attractive they were. But that was before my Marc and Danny became wheelchair bound due to muscular dystrophy. Then, going anywhere with the boys led to a different kind of staring.

It's sad that even in these times, when people are supposed to know better, my boys still get stared at. A quick glance would be one thing, but the veiled look, the pointing, or the unabashed, open-mouthed gawking is difficult to bear.

Watching us enter a restaurant is quite a sight and we get lots of stares. We charge in with our electric wheelchairs, we make adjustments to the table, we cut the boys' food, and they wear splints on their wrists so they can hold their forks. The boys like to go out to eat so we decided to do something about the staring. Here's what we do—we stare back.

However, just getting into a restaurant can be a problem. One time Marc wanted to go to the new Big Boy restaurant for his birthday. The eateries were being furiously advertised on television with the big Elias Brother's chubby Big Boy, in the red and white checkered outfit, going around and around on a thirty-foot pole beckoning to one and all. Watching that commercial caused Marc to think that he was being personally invited. So I wasn't surprised when he said that he wanted to go there for his birthday.

First I called the Big Boy to make sure our group of seven, including grandma and our aide could be seated there. I explained the situation to the manager but he said, "We don't take reservations."

I was dumbfounded so I explained, "Well I just didn't want to cause a sensation, and I thought you could put us in that quiet corner in the back where you have the super big booth. There will be seven people, two in wheelchairs."

"I told you lady…"

Mister, this is a special situation." He hung up.

I put the phone down and called the corporate offices of Elias Brothers who owned the Big Boy franchise. As an advocate for the disabled, one must be prepared to ask for help. Mr. Elias listened to me without interrupting. When I paused for a breath he said, "Mrs. Kramer, you just call me anytime you want to go to any Big Boy, and a table will be reserved for you and your party whether is it seven people or twenty-five."

We went, as quietly as possible, to the Big Boy near our home. The manager greeted us at the door bowing and walking backwards, like a maitre d' in a fancy restaurant. Every eye in the place was on us, but our son was very happy. He said with a grin, "Let's do our thing, Mom."

"Okay Marc, who seems like the prime culprit to you?"

"I see a kid in a red hat. Even his mom is staring; they're being very rude. And that busboy is standing stone cold still just looking and looking."

We stared away and it worked, as always. Sometimes everyone laughs—the starers and the starees. It breaks the ice and shows people around us that we are just a regular family with a few problems.

~Rosalie Ferrer Kramer

The Hand of Friendship

Labels are for filing. Labels are for clothing. Labels are not for people.
~Martina Navratilova

The third graders tumbled into the classroom for our after-school Bible study program, screeching metal chairs on the linoleum floor as they found places to sit. Chatter filled the room and the kids couldn't help fiddling with the plastic caddies of supplies in the middle of the table—scissors, glue bottles, markers—for our project that day.

"What are we making, Mrs. Malone?" asked a girl with a green polka dot bow on the top of her head.

"Handprint butterflies," I said, showing them my sample, a paper butterfly made from the outlines of my hands traced on cardstock and glued together at the bottom of each palm. It fluttered at the end of a piece of yarn. Some of the kids grasped at it as I fluttered it over their heads.

I passed out two pieces of cardstock for each of the kids. "As soon as you choose a marker to outline your hands, you can begin," I said. Most were swirling a marker tip around their hands before I finished the sentence.

As the handprints morphed from blank canvasses into rainbow-winged creatures, I noticed one boy who hadn't started yet. He tapped the table with the tip of his marker and held his left hand firmly in his lap.

"Why aren't you working, Michael?" I asked.

He shrugged.

"I'd like everyone to at least try to do the project. Do you want me to help you trace your hand?"

"Mine won't look like everyone else's," he said.

"No two people can make their butterflies exactly the same. That's what makes each one special."

He shook his head. "No. That's not what I mean."

Puzzled, I struggled to understand. Michael looked down, clearly upset. Why would a simple coloring project be so troublesome? Never before had he refused to do a craft. Across the table, his best friend Andy's expression was just as grim as Michael's.

I knelt down so Michael and I were eye to eye. "What's bothering you, Michael?"

He sighed and laid his left hand, the one he'd been hiding on his lap, on the table. "My hand is different."

I looked at his hand. For the first time in the four years I'd known him as a classmate of my daughter since kindergarten, I saw his missing fingers. There were only four fingers. Two of his four fingers were partial, pink nubs. He tapped them with the marker in his other hand. "My butterfly wings will look funny."

At first, I didn't know what to say. Here was a boy who was always smiling, surrounded by friends at school and out on the playground, a polite boy who talked easily to adults and who towered over others his age. Not once had I noticed his hand. How could I explain to an eight-year-old that the shape of his hand was not important to the people who mattered to him? At a loss for words, I looked to Andy for his reaction to Michael's words. Then I noticed Andy's picture.

Andy's hand was splayed across the page as he finished tracing his second handprint. Only he had three fingers folded under his palm, creating the same outline Michael would have displayed had he traced his own hand, with its shorter fingers.

The gesture almost brought tears to my eyes. It was a perfect example of what I wanted to tell Michael but didn't know how to put it into words.

"Look at Andy's butterfly," I said to Michael.

Michael looked sharply at Andy. "Why are you doing that?"

"Because we're the same. We're friends," he said without hesitation.

Michael and Andy exchanged looks. Andy made a goofy face at his friend and then picked up an orange marker to color the wings.

I patted Michael's left hand. "Your friends don't care what your hand looks like. I didn't even know about it until you showed me just now. I've known you only as someone who smiles a lot and makes his friends laugh. That is what's important to Andy, too, and your other friends."

Michael nodded. His mouth hinted at a smile. He wiggled his hand from underneath mine and flattened it on the paper. With the black marker, he finished tracing both hands by the time I got up from the floor.

As I walked between the tables, helping those who had finished coloring their handprints to glue them together, one of the adult assistants in the room pulled me aside.

"Whatever was bothering Michael before seems to be forgotten now," she whispered. "What was the problem?"

"He was worried that his project would look different."

"Whatever you said to him worked."

"It wasn't me," I said. "Andy made him feel better."

True friends have that power.

~Dawn Malone

Chapter
4

Think Positive
for Kids

Developing Self-Esteem

Embracing My Uniqueness

*The one thing I've learned is that stuttering in public
is never as bad as I fear it will be.*
~John Stossel

My grandfather stuttered, as did my uncle. My brother stuttered, too. And, at forty-one years old, I still stutter.

I'm fine with it now but that wasn't always the case.

It wasn't too terribly difficult the first couple of years of school. In fact, I don't recall being made fun of at all, although there was a great deal of curiosity about my abnormal speech.

In the second grade, one of my classmates asked me why I talked funny. With a straight face, I told her that I had a piece of meat lodged in my throat, which caused my words to get stuck. She believed me.

Several years later, she asked me if I still had that meat stuck in my throat.

To this day, stuttering can be difficult, in more ways than one, to explain.

Less than one percent of the world's population stutters; however, there was only one stuttering kid in first grade at Jeter Primary in Opelika, Alabama, and that stuttering kid was me.

Kids love recess, naps, and show and tell, and I was no different. Recess and naps came easy, and in spite of my speech disorder, I still took part in show and tell just like all the other kids. I just did a whole lot more showing than I did telling.

At the time, I didn't like being different. I felt that I stood out for all the wrong reasons.

It's never easy being a kid, but it's especially tough when you're different. Just imagine the pain, shame, and embarrassment of not even being able to say your own name. I would often give fake names when meeting new people, because it was easier. It was not uncommon for me to be Jason or Mike, Chris or Kevin or just whatever sounds I was confident I could say at that particular moment.

Most little boys are shy when talking to girls, but I was downright terrified. I can probably count the number of times on one hand that I talked to a girl in elementary school. Years later, many of those same girls told me they thought my stuttering was cute. I wish I'd known that then.

As I got older, some kids started getting meaner and the teasing started. Unfortunately, I let it bother me. I shouldn't have, but I did. I put more stock in what they had to say rather than being thankful for the overwhelming majority of kids who treated me with kindness, respect and compassion. In hindsight, I know that it was a reflection of them and not me. Again, I wish I'd known that then.

I had sessions with Ms. Watson, my speech therapist, biweekly. Although challenging, my time with her was special. While in therapy, there was no pain, shame, or embarrassment. I could simply be myself and work on my speech at the same time.

Class was a different story altogether. It was a constant struggle.

It was not uncommon for me to know the answers to questions, but it was quite common for me to remain silent out of fear of being ridiculed.

Reading aloud in class was pure torture. The buildup and anticipation of being called upon created more stress and anxiety than I am able to put into words, which often resulted in tension headaches.

When it was my time to read, I would lower my head, focus, and stop breathing. I would instinctively hit my thigh with my fist over and over to literally beat the words out of me, whereas other times,

I would hit the underside of my desktop. This technique helped me get my words out but there was also a shadow side to it. When talking to my friends, I would often beat their arms until I finished saying what I had to say.

Could anything be worse than that? Yes, it could.

Giving an oral presentation in front of the class was the ultimate challenge, which usually resulted in ultimate shame. There was nowhere to hide. All eyes were fixed upon me as the secondary effects of stuttering stole the show. My eyes closed and my face contorted as I struggled to get out each word. There was no desk to pound and beating my leg in front the whole class was incredibly awkward.

Kids were mean and I let that bother me. There were very few days this future soldier didn't find himself crying by the end of the day. I didn't like who I was and didn't want to be me. The pain, shame, and embarrassment were too much for me to bear, or so I thought.

The funny thing, though, was that it wasn't the stuttering that caused any of the negative feelings I had, and it wasn't the bullies, either. It was my reaction to both the stuttering and the bullying.

I let it bother me, but it didn't have to be like that.

Sometime in the eighth grade, my attitude changed. I don't recall exactly when, where, how, or why, but I turned what I'd always perceived as a negative into a positive.

I wasn't a star athlete and I wasn't a genius. I wasn't in the band and I certainly couldn't sing, but everyone still knew me, because I stood out, and that was a good thing. I was different and I finally embraced that difference and ran with it.

Instead of waiting in fear for the teacher to call my name, I raised my hand when I knew the answer to a question. I always volunteered to read and even used oral presentations as an opportunity to show-case my comedic talents.

I was in control and would not allow the anxiety or insecurity to control my feelings, attitude, or behavior.

In subsequent years, I'd go on to speak in front of the entire student body on multiple occasions.

Being in control eased most of the tension; inevitably, there were fewer headaches, secondary effects, and, to a degree, stuttering.

I surrounded myself with good kids and didn't overly concern myself with the occasional wisecrack. At this point, I knew it was a reflection of them and had no bearing on my character whatsoever. Besides, my own wisecracks were much better than anything they could dish out.

Self-acceptance is crucial to happiness and success in and out of the classroom. It doesn't mean we can't strive to improve upon our so-called flaws, but it doesn't mean we shouldn't love ourselves and embrace our uniqueness either.

Individuality should be celebrated, not suppressed, and certainly not mocked.

I went from a stuttering kid who seldom spoke a word to a stuttering man who now speaks for a living. Self-acceptance continues to be essential in the success I've experienced as a speaker, comedian, writer, and soldier.

My lone regret is that it didn't happen sooner.

It's never easy being a kid. It's especially tough when you're different, but it doesn't have to be.

The time to embrace your uniqueness is now.

~Jody Fuller

Learning to Love My Nose

Beauty is not in the face; beauty is a light in the heart.
~Kahlil Gibran

t was a sixth-grade Friday afternoon like any other. I was riding the bus home from school, sitting next to my friend Krystal, both of us joyous that it was finally the weekend. At the bus stop before mine, a few boys I didn't know very well pushed down the aisle past us.

"Bye, Big Nose!" one of them called, waving to us. He and his friends laughed and scrambled off the bus.

Big Nose? Was he talking to us? I glanced over at Krystal. Her nose was a tiny ski slope, delicate and dainty. There was no way anyone would call her Big Nose.

My cheeks flushed. That must mean they were referring to me. I knew I didn't have a cute button nose like Krystal, but I had never thought of my nose as particularly big, either.

"Those guys are mean," Krystal said. "You have a great nose."

She was trying to make me feel better, but her words only confirmed my fears: those boys had been addressing me. I had a huge honking nose, and all this time I hadn't even known it. I fought the instinct to cover my nose with my hands. When my stop came, I ran off the bus and into the safety of my mom's car.

"What's wrong, sweetheart?" Mom asked as I slumped in the front seat, trying not to cry.

"My nose is ugly. I hate it."

"What? That's nonsense. You have a beautiful, strong nose. Your nose is perfect."

I stared gloomily out the window, my sunny Friday mood completely gone. I didn't want my nose to be strong. I wanted a delicate, dainty nose like the other girls at school.

As soon as we got home, I raced upstairs and shut myself in the bathroom. Usually, I looked at myself straight on, and my nose didn't seem very big from the front. It was fairly thin and not too long. But then I opened the mirrored medicine cabinet, tilting it at the right angle so I could see myself in profile.

Oh, no! I did have a big nose!

I felt like I'd been punched in the gut.

Even worse, there was a slight bump in my nose at the bridge, in the exact place my sunglasses perched. I experimented, putting the sunglasses on and peering at my profile through the dark lenses. Did the sunglasses hide the bump, or draw attention to it? I decided they made the bump—and my nose—seem a little bit smaller. If only I could wear sunglasses all the time!

I spent much of the afternoon staring into the bathroom mirror, studying my big-nosed profile like I had stared at my bloody, badly-scraped knee a few years before on the blacktop basketball courts: it disgusted me, but I couldn't seem to look away. I tried pressing down on my nose, momentarily flattening it, but as soon as I took my hand away it regained its normal shape with the awful bump.

Finally, on the verge of tears, I closed the medicine cabinet and looked at my face straight on in the mirror. All this time, the world had known I had a huge nose and I had been oblivious. I imagined that everyone at school secretly referred to me as Big Nose behind my back. I wanted to crawl under my bedcovers and hide in my room forever.

A couple days later, we were over at my grandfather's house for dinner. My grandmother Auden had passed away when I was in kindergarten and Gramps never remarried. My family joined him for dinner at least once a week, and I always looked forward to these visits. Gramps told the best stories about growing up in a small Ohio farm town, playing football in college, traveling the world. My favorite stories were about Auden, who Gramps described as the most beautiful lady he'd ever met. One day, I dreamed, I would meet someone who felt that way about me. Maybe then I would feel beautiful, too.

Gramps always left the front door unlocked for us, but he wasn't in the kitchen or the living room when we arrived. "He's probably upstairs," my dad said. "Go tell him we're here."

I climbed upstairs and found him in his bedroom, staring at a framed photograph in his hands. He looked up when I came in.

"Dally!" he said. "How are you, my girl?" He smiled, but his eyes looked sad. I walked over and sat down on the bed next to him.

"Is that Auden?" I asked, looking at the photograph. It was a black-and-white photo of a glamorous young woman with short-cropped blond hair and wide, pretty eyes. She was smiling at the camera like she knew a wonderful secret. I could tell why Gramps fell in love with her.

"Yep, that's your grandmother. I was missing her a lot today and wanted to look at her. This photo was taken the year we met."

"She's so beautiful," I said.

"The most beautiful woman in the world," Gramps said. "Inside and out." He looked over at me and smiled. "Next to you, of course."

"Thanks, Gramps." But I knew he was just being nice. In my head, I heard the echoing laughter of those boys on the bus: Bye, Big Nose! Remembering it made my cheeks flush with embarrassment.

"You look just like her, you know," Gramps said. "The older you get, the more and more you resemble her."

"I do?" This was news to me.

"Yep. You have the same nose. You got your profile from Auden, that's for sure."

I traced my fingertip down my nose, over the bump that had made me feel so self-conscious. I looked again at the photograph of my grandmother as a young woman.

And then, I saw it. At the bridge of her nose, a tiny bump.

She really did have the same nose as me! And she was smiling like she couldn't be happier.

That was the day I began to love my nose. When I look in the mirror, I don't see a huge honking nose anymore. Now I see a link to my heritage. I look at my nose and imagine the long line of strong, loving women who came before me. And I think of my grandma Auden, who in some small way is kept alive through my own nose with its beautiful bump.

~Dallas Nicole Woodburn

Modeling Reflection

Young people need models, not critics.
~John Wooden

had been standing in line for over an hour when my number was finally called: "547, you're up!" I walked in front of the seamless and stood on the X. The photographer took my card and information sheet before quickly snapping a few shots of me and sending me on my way. As I walked out of the studio to where my mother stood waiting, the girls signing in were taking numbers in the 800s.

"Well that took a while!" my mother exclaimed before seeing the expression on my face. "What's wrong?"

"They barely looked at me, and there were over 800 girls trying out."

A few days later, I was contacted by my agent at Wilhelmina Models, who informed me that I had booked the H&M shoot. I hadn't seen it coming at all, and I was thrilled that out of over 800 people, I had been one of the few selected.

Castings are often unpredictable in their nature. Sometimes a model is specially requested and is only among a few others being considered for the job. Other times, a model can arrive at a casting to find that she is up against a huge number of other people. In my experience there were many times that the odds seemed in my favor, yet I still faced a disappointment, but there were also many times when the odds were against me, and I prevailed. Modeling can seem a game of chance because you really never know the outcome of any casting. All you can do is try your hardest and be your most confident self.

It is not always the most beautiful girl in the room who gets the job, but really it's the one who stands out from the crowd. Maybe it's her smile; maybe it's her personality, her confidence, or just the way she walked into the room. Modeling has taught me a great deal about patience and about being true to myself. It is easy to feel inferior in this industry or in anything that is this competitive, but I have learned that as long as I remain positive and try my best, things tend to work out well.

This last year, I was reminded of this when I began the college application process. I set my goals high, and I knew that, but it is still never easy to hear someone say, "Don't set your heart on Brown. They'll never accept you," especially when it's coming from your college advisor. I did not let this stop me however. I knew Brown was the school for me, so I ignored this negativity and got to work on my application.

When my college advisor told me that despite my qualifications, I didn't have much of a chance of getting into my first choice, I did not fear rejection. I saw a challenge. I spent a great deal of time writing and rewriting my essays and supplements. I needed to perfectly express who I was because, as I had learned in the past, being yourself and showing how hard you are willing to work for something you truly want is very impressive and can often help you to stand out from all the rest.

I knew the odds were not in my favor with a school that has an acceptance rate of only nine percent, but I wasn't going to give up just because of that. I put my all into my application and my interview and then I settled down to wait for the news.

I am now proud to say that I will be attending Brown University in the fall. A lot of people and things have shaped who I am today and helped me pave the way to this next part of my life, but I know that a lot of what kept my head up during this stressful and competitive time was what I learned from working with Wilhelmina Models.

~Michaela Brawn

Learning How to Kick

A positive attitude can really make dreams come true — it did for me.
~David Bailey

I went to a private school through third grade. It was far away from my house and most of the kids who went there lived in other towns. Then my parents moved me to the public school that was close to our home. I was happy to finally be in school with kids who lived nearby, since it would be much easier to go to their houses and have them over to mine.

It was a little difficult making the transition to a new school in fourth grade, since all the other kids had been together since kindergarten. Luckily, my two best friends from the private school moved to the public school when I did, so we had each other right from the beginning of the school year. It wasn't too hard making new friends either, and the schoolwork was okay, even though it was different from my old school.

The one thing that was difficult, however, was recess. At my new school, the whole class played kickball together every single day. We had never played it at my old school, so I had no idea what to do.

Every day the best kids would act as captains and pick their teams. I was terrible at kickball and would always be one of the last kids picked. Since I was very good at academic subjects like math and writing I found it difficult to be one of the worst kids at anything! But this situation continued all year. I started to dread recess, but I showed up for kickball every day anyway. There wasn't any option, since that was what the whole class played at recess.

The summer between fourth and fifth grade, I decided that I needed to do something about kickball. I couldn't go another year with recess hanging over me like a cloud every day. I confessed my problem to one of my best friends, Carlta, who was a great athlete. It turned out that I had been kicking the ball all wrong, using the front of my sneaker and trying to hit the ball with my toes. My kick had no power that way. Carlta showed me how to kick that red rubber ball with the front of my ankle, right where my leg and my foot met. That transformed my kick. I practiced all summer and I developed a strong kick that went far.

When school resumed, everyone was surprised at how much better I played and I started being one of the first girls picked each day at recess. It hurt a lot to kick the ball with my ankle because the rubber ball really stung my skin. But it was worth it! I kicked the ball far, we scored a lot of runs, and I was finally a valuable member of my team. I loved recess from then on.

Unfortunately, kickball didn't continue in the middle school where we went for sixth grade, so I only had one year of being really good at recess! But I learned a valuable lesson—I could solve a problem by asking for advice and practicing what I was taught. And I am still grateful to my friend Carlta for teaching me how to kick properly.

~Amy Newmark

36

The Middle Rock

Wanting to be someone else is a waste of the person you are.
~Marilyn Monroe

One day we went to pick up our grandson at his school in northern Virginia. It was a beautiful spring day so we decided to go to the local gardens where we had taken many walks before with our grandchildren. Normally, our grandchildren were very enthusiastic about going to the gardens, especially Mark, who was quite a nature lover and loved being out in the woods among the plants and the trees.

It truly was a gorgeous spring day, with many flowers blooming, birds singing and the waters from the brook below rushing fast over the many rocks that lined its path. Despite all of this, we noticed how sad Mark was. Kicking pebbles along the tree-lined path, he mumbled, "There is nothing special about me."

"Why do you say that?" I asked.

"Well, I am smaller than my older brother who is fussed over for being the biggest and I am bigger than my younger brother who is fussed over because he is the baby. There is nothing special about me."

"Ah, I see your dilemma." Although, I knew how much he was loved I knew how easy it was to praise the oldest son for accomplishing new things for the first time. I also knew that his parents were busy helping the youngest, for he was the littlest. By Mark's statement

I knew he felt that he, the middle son, was not getting the same attention.

We walked a little farther into the woods when Mark stopped and asked if we could throw rocks into the brook to see which one would go the farthest.

"Okay," I said.

Mark enthusiastically said, "I am going to throw the biggest rock, because I know it will go the farthest." Mark picked up the largest rock he could and threw it. Although it made a very big splash, it didn't go very far. Mark thought for a minute and said, "Since the big rock didn't go very far, I am going to throw a little rock instead." He picked up a little pebble and threw it but it didn't go very far because it was too little. Mark was puzzled.

Thinking quickly, I said, "Why don't you pick up a rock that is in between the two other sized rocks and see what happens." As a family we had always spent a lot of time out in nature and I thought this was a very good opportunity to use nature as a teacher.

Mark reached over and picked up a medium sized rock and threw it.

Mark said, "Look, Ika, the middle sized rock went the farthest!"

I stopped for a moment and smiled at Mark. "You see, Mark, you are like the middle rock. In this situation the little rock was too light, the big rock was too heavy but the middle rock was just right.

"So, I am special?"

"Yes, Mark, everyone and everything is special and has a special purpose, especially you."

Mark smiled and picked up another medium size rock to throw again.

~Deborah Roberts

37

Be Proud, Be Strong, Be You

When you have decided what you believe, what you feel must be done, have the courage to stand alone and be counted.
~Eleanor Roosevelt

At my school, I was the foreign girl. I was also short, I didn't dress fashionably, I had a problem saying my R's and I was Russian. I was usually teased about my hair or my clothes or my height. I did feel bad but I had lots of friends who cared about me. I was called midget, shortie, and the worse name of all—Russian spy. But people thought of me well too, well at least the girls. Over the years, I was also the smart one, the one who could give good advice, the one who could share and the one who would never give up on you.

One day, when school ended, I was walking to the buses with my best friend Macy and her friends. One of them was having serious girl trouble. I was about to give some advice when suddenly a kid stepped in front of me and said, "No one cares what you say, Ruthy." The other guys laughed.

"Back off!"

"Russians are so violent and dumb," he said. All the guys laughed and started talking about movies, games, books and all these other things that made Russians look cruel. I turned away. Macy ran up to me.

"Ruthy, don't listen to them; they are just stupid and jealous," she said. Wow, who would be jealous of me? I got teased every day. Macy went on to say, "Ruthy, do you know why I became friends with you?"

"What does that have to do with this problem?" I asked while trying to fight back my tears. I actually never knew why she wanted to hang out with me. We had started talking and then we started hanging out and we became friends.

Macy said, "Because you aren't like anyone else I know. It's cool that you are Russian. You teach me words in Russian and you are also caring, helpful and the greatest friend I have ever had."

"Really?"

"Absolutely," she nodded with a smile.

We walked a little more and talked about schoolwork. But, I still didn't feel totally okay. I was still sad inside even though I was relieved to hear why she was my friend.

Later that day, I was digging through my backpack when I found a rectangular piece of pink paper. It had my name on it. Then I remembered. My science teacher, Miss Ostapuk, had taught us about self-esteem. She had told us to keep these pieces of paper because we might need them one day.

The paper was a questionnaire that we had filled out. We had to answer questions about what we liked about ourselves. I remembered having a hard time doing the assignment because we had to brag about ourselves and I never really did that. But then I had decided to answer the questions by writing down what other people had said about me.

"What is your best feature?" I had put my eyes because I remembered my older sister commenting on my eyes. "What is your proudest achievement?" I put playing the piano for old people. At the very bottom of the paper there was a comment. It said, "Never let people bring you down because of who you are. You are special." I realized that maybe I was teased not only because I was different but also because I could do things that other kids couldn't do, like speak two languages and play the piano for an audience.

The saying on that paper is my guide now. I live by it. I learn by it. I achieve because of it. I think of my qualities and strengths, not weaknesses. My unique traits and thoughts make me who I am. I still feel sad sometimes and I still get teased but it doesn't affect me the way it did before. So if you are different, like I am, be proud, be strong and most importantly, be yourself.

~Ruth Anna Mavashev

You Do It Your Way and I'll Do It Mine

If you hear a voice within you say "you cannot paint,"
then by all means paint, and that voice will be silenced.
~Vincent van Gogh

The hardest part about being the youngest kid in the family is not that you're shorter than everyone else. It's not that you can't keep up, or that you're the first one hurt when the roughhousing starts. It's not that you're the last to get a serving of whatever snack just came out of the oven.

All that stuff is pretty annoying. But it's nowhere near as bad being told, "No, do it this way." I used to hear that all the time.

If I asked to help Grandma when she was baking her famous crispy golden cornbread, she'd slide the big mixing bowl to where I could reach it and then tell me to mix up the ingredients. I'd grab that big wooden spoon and stir the batter, but Grandma would stop me and say, "No, do it this way or you'll spill it." She showed me how she wanted it stirred, and I did my best to imitate her on the second try.

If I asked Dad how I could help when he was working in the garage, he'd hand me a wrench and show me which bolt to loosen or to tighten. I could get about two cranks in before he'd stop me and say, "No, do it this way or you'll strip the bolt." I watched and did my best not to blunt the corners.

When my older sister Missy and I dressed up our dolls for a

fancy dinner party, I was put in charge of doing the dolls' hair. Three wraps into a lovely braid, my sister would reach for the doll and say, "No, do it this way." She would twist the hair and pin it just right, and I'd try hard to do it that way on the next doll.

I couldn't even color in a coloring book without the teacher pausing by my desk to say, "No, do it this way." Color in the lines, she advised. Stroke the crayon back and forth carefully so it fills in the shapes thoroughly.

I knew they were all trying to teach me how to do something faster or better, or without making a mess. But I didn't like feeling wrong all the time. I was so frustrated. I wanted to tell everyone, "Stop telling me what to do."

One weekend, my family got together to help Grandma and Grandpa with spring cleaning and gardening. My cousin Brian, the oldest of all the grandchildren, got to work mowing the lawn. His sister Jaime and my sister Missy got to plant all the pretty flowers in the garden. The adults took up shovels and started cutting a route for a stone-paved walkway that would go around the garden.

I asked what I could do to help. Grandpa led me to the big juniper bush at the front of the lawn. The bush had once been trimmed to look like a big green square with blue berry bells. Now, long frizzy branches grew out in all directions. The bush looked like a big green porcupine. Grandpa used a pair of long-handled gardening shears to chomp off the green bristles.

Clip! Clip! Clip! Grandpa flattened out one side of the juniper in three quick cuts. He gave me the shears and told me to trim the other side. He waited to watch, but I didn't do anything. I worried that as soon as I tried, I would do it the wrong way.

"I can do it by myself, Grandpa," I said.

Grandpa tipped his hat with a wink and said he would come back to check on me. When he was gone, and when no one was looking, I lifted the big heavy shears and clipped at the jagged bristles sticking out of the bush.

I missed.

I clipped again. This time a big wad of green bits crunched

between the blades. But they didn't clip away. Instead, they jammed the blades together. I pulled and tugged and finally freed the shears. I couldn't do it! I couldn't trim the juniper the right way. I wanted to cry.

I leaned the big shears against the fence and ran into the house. I took a pair of regular scissors from the junk drawer in the kitchen and ran back out to the bush.

Snip. Snip. Snip.

Little bits and bristles fell to the ground.

Snip. Snip. Snip.

I took a step back to inspect my work. The porcupine pincushion looked flat and neat on my side.

Grandpa strolled back to the juniper. He watched me with the scissors and said, "That way will take all day."

He picked up the big shears and I knew he was about to tell me: "No, do it this way." But he stopped. He shouldered the big shears and looked at the side he had trimmed, then back at mine. After a minute, he lifted his cap, scratched his head, and laughed. "Your side looks better than mine."

I gawked. "You mean my way isn't wrong?"

"No ma'am. Your way works just fine." Grandpa leveled the big shears at the juniper bush and said, "I'll bet we can get this bush trimmed together in no time. You do it your way, and I'll do it mine."

I was so happy my way wasn't wrong. Grandpa cut the really big and bristly branches and then I trimmed up all the pokey, prickly bits. We squared off all four sides in no time. The top of the juniper was too high for me to reach, so I showed Grandpa my little-scissor trimming techniques. For the most part, he did exactly what I showed him, but a few times he snipped in weird ways. I didn't correct him though. His way might have been a little different, but it got the job done.

As I grew up I still learned from other people when they showed me new methods, but I realized the point is not always to imitate or copy cat. It is okay to do things just a little bit differently. Grandma's cornbread was always so crispy golden good because she did it in her own, unique way. Missy's dolls always had such beautiful hairstyles, and Dad never stripped a bolt, because their ways were different from anybody else's. Being different is fine, which is why I figure out my own way of doing things.

~Jenny Mason

39

My Abilities

Always be a first-rate version of yourself,
instead of a second-rate version of somebody else.
~Judy Garland

once had a blind friend in elementary school named Easton. I remember one day when I asked him, "Easton, if they came up with a way to cure blindness, would you want to get your blindness cured?" To my surprise, he said no. He said that this blindness was a way of life for him. It was what he was used to. It was what he had known all his life. I was confused. I mean, if I were blind, I surely would want to see. Then, when I was in middle school, I was diagnosed with a nonverbal learning disability and Asperger's syndrome. It was because of these that my social, organizational, and handwriting skills (among other things) were less than up to par.

Several years after I was diagnosed, I started thinking about that day when I had asked Easton if he wanted to have his blindness cured. It was then that I was able to see what he meant. I realized that I was thankful for my disabilities, and that I wouldn't want them to be cured. Like Easton, my disabilities have become a way of life for me. Sure they inhibit my social skills, so I tend to be the kid who sits there quietly and reads while everyone else talks with their friends. And sure my social mannerisms can be awkward at times. But I do have a few very close friends who mean the world to me. And you know what? Sometimes it's nice to be alone. I can't really explain it; it just is.

Sure I tend to be somewhat uncoordinated and not very good at sports. But I'm pretty good at acting. I've been in several school productions: I've been Daddy Warbucks in *Annie*, Ike Skidmore in *Oklahoma!*, Francis in *The Tempest*, Charles in *My Fair Lady*, and even Grandpa in *You Can't Take It With You*, and I have also gotten inducted into the International Thespian Society. Acting is something for which I have a passion.

Sure my handwriting tends to be sloppy sometimes, and sometimes it hurts to write, but because of that I get to type my notes—except in math, where someone takes notes for me. Sure my disabilities have inhibited my math skills, but they have also helped me to become pretty good at English. Statistics say that most kids with the disabilities similar to what I have struggle in math but are pretty good in English.

I don't expect you to understand why I am thankful for my learning disabilities instead of wishing they could be taken away. It wasn't until years after I was diagnosed with my disabilities that I could fully understand Easton's reasons for accepting his blindness. I don't think you can understand it unless you've experienced it. When it comes down to it, my learning disabilities are just my way of life. They are a part of me. It is the way God made me, and I cannot wait to see how He uses these disabilities in the future. Sure my disabilities have taken things away from me, but they have given me so much more. That is why I am thankful for my learning disabilities.

~Ben Jaeger

40

By the Seat of My Pants

Humor is merely tragedy standing on its head with its pants torn.
~Irvin S. Cobb

"Let's go, Rob," Mom screamed up the stairs. "We're going to be late."

"We don't have time for this," my older brother, Lee, yelled.

I rolled my eyes. I could picture Lee standing at the bottom of the stairs, tapping his foot and looking at his watch. He was never late.

"I'll be right down," I yelled. But that probably wasn't true. I couldn't find my basketball shorts.

Someone stomped up the stairs. My door opened and Lee stepped inside. He looked around with disgust at the mess I call a room. "What's the problem?" he asked.

"I can't find my shorts."

"We don't have time to look for them," he said. "Just borrow my extra ones."

"They'll be too big." But he was already getting them from his room.

I shrugged. It's not like it mattered. Coach wasn't going to let me play no matter how much I practiced at home. Lee was the star player and I was the bench warmer. That's just how it was. I put on the shorts and hurried downstairs.

The rest of the team was already on the court doing warm-ups when we got there. Coach was tapping his foot and looking at his watch. He looked like an older version of Lee.

"It's Rob's fault," Lee said as he hurried to join the others on the court. Coach glared at me as I took my seat on the bench.

The first half of the game went like it usually did. Lee scored basket after basket and racked up point after point. We were beating the pants off the other team.

The second half started and that's when things started to go wrong. Sam, one of our best players, missed an easy basket. Lee had the ball stolen from him. The other team was starting to catch up.

Then Lee tripped and fell hard. He didn't jump back up. The players and coaches gathered around. When the group parted, Coach helped Lee to the bench. He wasn't putting any weight on his right foot.

"Are you okay?" I asked him.

"Yeah," Lee answered. "Just twisted my ankle."

Coach looked around, searching the crowd. He sighed. "Okay, Rob," he said. "You're the only other player we have. Take Lee's place."

My heart raced. I couldn't take Lee's place. The only reason I was on the team was the Parks and Recreation Department said Coach had to let anyone join. I'd never played in a real game before.

"Go on, Rob," Coach pointed. "Get out there."

I swallowed hard and stepped onto the court. "Please don't let me mess up," I thought. I followed as my team ran from one side of the court to the other.

The other team scored a few more baskets. The score was tied and there were only a few more minutes left in the game. The other team had the ball and their best player was running toward me. He lost control of it right in front of me.

"Get it, Rob!" Lee screamed from the bench.

I grabbed it. I looked for someone to pass it to. No one was close enough.

"Try for the basket!" Lee yelled.

I ran down the court, concentrating on my dribble. I didn't want to mess up. This was my chance to show Coach I really had been practicing. The other team tried to block me. I weaved one way and then the other, not really sure what I was doing. Avoiding blocks wasn't something I could practice by myself.

Suddenly, I was under the basket. If I could make the shot, we'd win the game. I closed my eyes and imagined I was practicing in my driveway. No crowd, no other team… just me and the hoop. I jumped and released the ball.

"Please make it," I said. "Please make it."

Swish! The crowd cheered. I'd done it. I'd won the game. Then I heard the laughter. Just a few chuckles at first but soon everyone was laughing. I looked around. What was so funny?

They were all looking at me. I looked down. My borrowed shorts were around my ankles. My face turned red as I scrambled to pull them up. My team gathered around me, blocking out the laughing crowd, as they congratulated me. Even Lee limped onto the court.

"Good job, little bro," he said. "You won the game. That's all that matters."

He was right, I did win the game. But more important, I proved I could do it. If I wanted something bad enough, all I had to do was practice. I just wish I could have done it with my pants on.

~R.K. Krochmal

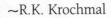

41

Telling My Story

A true friend knows your weaknesses but shows you your strengths; feels your fears but fortifies your faith; sees your anxieties but frees your spirit; recognizes your disabilities but emphasizes your possibilities.
~William Arthur Ward

O h no, here it comes... the familiar feeling I dread. It always starts with my cheeks warming up as they turn red. Next, the palms of my hands begin to sweat. It all seems to happen in slow motion. All I hear is the loud thud of my heart beating in my ears. All I really want to do is run and hide.

I sit at Alison's dinner table, her beautiful dinner table, at her perfect house with her picture perfect family. I am careful to practice my manners: yes please, no thank you, oh wow that looks delicious—that kind of thing. It isn't hard to do. Alison's mom is a great cook and the dinner and conversation go well until her mom starts asking about me.

Where was I born? What do I like to do for fun? What does my mom do? And then the next question, the one I dread: What does your dad do? It gets me every time. My dad passed away when I was six months old and at my house it's just my mom, my older brother Eric, and me.

It shouldn't be that big of a deal, yet for some reason, anytime I meet new people I dread having to tell the story. Mostly because there is an immediate uncomfortable feeling in the air because whoever asked the question is so sorry and wants to know what happened and the whole thing just feels yucky. I never knew my dad, so to me, it's the way it has always been. The embarrassment is more from the reaction of others and feeling different because I don't have a dad.

So, there I am at dinner at my new friend Alison's house, and all eyes are on me as I muster up the courage to tell my story. Everyone listens closely and then something different happens. Instead of acting apologetic for ever asking me the question, they tell me something I didn't know about them.

Alison had a little sister who was born premature and she passed away at a week old. They talk about how that affected them and how they are happy to have known her for a short time. I am not sure if they sense my shame and embarrassment or whether maybe they too can relate to questions being asked about why they don't have more kids. Either way, I am pretty happy that they asked the question because it helps me learn something really important. My dad passing away is not something I need to feel ashamed about. It is a part of my story that makes me who I am.

~Emily Madill

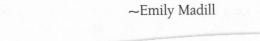

42

The Last One Picked for Basketball

Wisdom is always an overmatch for strength.
~Phil Jackson

The last one picked for basketball
Is never on the court.
He's way too weak and clumsy
And he's certainly too short.

His arms are full of notebooks
And his head's too full of knowledge.
But the last one picked for basketball
Might be the first picked for college.

~Neal Levin

Chapter 5

Think Positive *for* Kids

Handling Bullies

43

Don't Pass It On

Be kind whenever possible. It is always possible.
~Tenzin Gyatso, 14th Dalai Lama

Have you ever seen that little kid alone on the playground? The bell rings and everyone bolts out of the classroom—except this little girl. She slowly walks out of the room, looks around to see where the other kids are, and then goes off to play by herself. That was me.

I did everything I could to avoid the other kids on the playground. I loved playing tetherball and twirling on the monkey bars, but if a lot of kids were there, I would avoid those places.

Why? Well, my parents were a little "different." They didn't work. They did a lot of drugs, and there was always a lot of yelling and violence in my house. I held in a lot of pain and anger. I worried what people would think of me if they knew my parents were doing illegal drugs. So I kept to myself.

But that provoked some of the other kids to bully me. There were three girls in my grade who were bigger and taller than me. They would come and find me when I was playing alone, and they'd push me and say terrible, mean things to me. They would call me a monkey, because my arms and legs were kind of long and I had dark hair, dark eyes and darker skin than they had. They would even make fun of my clothes.

You see, my parents were poor. My sisters and I didn't have the kind of clothes the other kids had. We had hand-me-downs from the neighbors because our parents spent money on drugs instead of on clothes for us.

Those girls did everything they could to provoke me, and I would just scream, "Leave me alone! I'm going to tell the teacher!" which caused them to make fun of me even more.

I can remember so many days after school being chased home. They would say, "You're so stupid! You're so ugly! You dress funny! Those pants are gross; I would NEVER wear anything like that! Why are you even here?" I spent a lot of my younger years terrified of those girls.

One time, the last bell rang and I packed up my stuff slowly, waiting for everybody else to leave. I hoped they would forget about me, but as soon as I stepped off school property, there they were. I started running as fast as I could. My heart was beating so fast and I was gasping for air. I dove behind a bush in somebody's yard to hide from them.

When they found me, they sneered and laughed at me as I shivered in absolute fear. Fortunately, a woman opened the door and said, "Get out of here, kids!" The girls went running in one direction and I ran home as fast as I could.

I remember believing people hated me, because there was no love in our house, only abuse. I felt like I would never fit in and nobody would ever love me. After I was bullied by these girls (and many others), I took in everything they said about me—I believed I was ugly, stupid and weak.

But the sad part is, I began to bully my two little sisters. I did the very same thing to my sisters those girls had done to me. I called them nasty names and we even had fistfights. I caused them to believe things about themselves that just weren't right. I hurt their minds, their hearts and their bodies because of what was done to me.

I didn't know what to do with the pain, rejection, anger and confusion I felt, so I did what most people do—I hurt others.

If there is one thing I could change, I would change that. My sisters didn't deserve for me to pick on them. My sisters didn't deserve to take the wrath for what somebody else did to me. That was a mistake I never should have made!

You see, when we get hurt, we try to hold it all in. We don't want to tell our parents or friends about it, but that's the worst thing you can do. It's important to talk to somebody you trust.

I'm not that kid anymore, the one those kids and my family made fun of or called horrible names. Today I have a good life, a loving husband, wonderful kids and great friends! And when I look back, I just wish somebody had told me what I'm going to say to you.

First, forgive them. They don't know what they're doing to you. When people are hurting, they hurt others. We have to do the right thing, the nobler thing. We have to choose to forgive.

Second, seek help from an adult. I'm sure there were people I could have talked to, but I didn't know that, so I didn't get help from the school principal or a teacher. It's important to talk to someone, even if you don't think they will listen or believe you. It's okay to ask for help. That's what adults are around for—to help and guide us!

If you ask for help once, and nothing happens, keep asking. If you persist, correction will come and justice will be done. Don't hide out like I did. When you hide, the hurt gets worse. I didn't begin to heal until I started to get help.

And last, don't take your pain out on your brothers and sisters, or other kids. Be sure you speak what is good, noble, encouraging and uplifting. Speak to others the way you wish they would speak to you. Tell them they are beautiful, wonderful and talented. You will reap what you sow. What you say to others will be said to you.

Can you imagine if we all learned how to forgive? If we all learned how to encourage others, lift people up and make people feel good about themselves? We could make the world a completely different place!

~Dani Johnson

Bullied to a Better Life

It's wonderful when you can bring sparkle into people's lives without fading away from your own true color. Keep the hue in you.

~Dodinsky

was in third grade and my parents said I was a cute kid with a great personality who loved to laugh. The problem was that I was overweight, and that year the bullying began. A couple of kids at school started picking on me. Before school, after school, at recess, on the bus. "Fatty, Tubbo, Jelly Roll" were names I was called every day. They would throw stuff at me too. I was so scared I wouldn't ride the bus and my mom had to take me to school. Even when I got to school I would scream and cry, begging my mom not to leave me there.

I didn't tell my mom and dad why I didn't want to go to school anymore, so instead I would fake being sick all the time. I just wanted to stay at home where I was safe. My parents talked to my teacher, my principal, and a school counselor. They finally found out I was being bullied and I got to switch to a new class with an awesome teacher, Mrs. Willhoite. There were not any bullies in her class and she would let me bring my lunch to her room and eat with her so I didn't have to go to recess and be around those mean kids from my old class.

The bullies were still picking on me in fourth, fifth, and sixth grades. I would see them in the halls. They'd be there at recesses. But I had finally been truthful and asked for help. My mom and dad worked with the school to make sure I was in good classes and protected as much as possible. Would the bullying have been so bad if I had asked for help in the very beginning? I don't know, but I do know that once my parents found out they got me help. And once I got help, I didn't have to deal with the bullies by myself.

By sixth grade, even though I was hardly being bullied, I started to get sick for real. I weighed 206 pounds by the time I was eleven. I had solved the bullying problem, but now I had to take care of my health. I started drinking water instead of soda, eating fruits and veggies instead of chips and candy. I even put down my Xbox controller and went outside. I got active and started getting healthier. I lost some weight and felt great. I lost some more it was awesome! The harder I worked, the more I lost. The better I felt, the harder I worked. By the time I got to seventh grade I lost 85 pounds! My friends hardly recognized me. The bullies didn't even think I was the same kid and left me alone. I was back to being what my parents had described when I was in third grade—a cute kid with a great personality who loved to laugh.

I started a project called Strive for 85, since 85 is the magic number of pounds that I lost. I shared my story with 85 important people, including Michelle Obama. I inspired 85 other kids. I hosted or attended 85 events that raised awareness. I've been on TV, in magazines, even got to fly to Washington, D.C.... twice. I've spent the last year traveling around to schools and telling them bullying is never okay. I was overweight but I didn't deserve to get picked on.

Here's what the bullies say to me now: "Can I have your autograph?"

If you are being bullied, get help. You don't have to deal with this alone. You have to believe in yourself and not let mean kids decide who you will be and what you can do. If you are being the bully, stop! Come run with me instead or go ride a bike, climb a building, hit a punching bag. Do anything other than try to make a kid, like me, feel bad about himself. You never know... the person you're picking on could turn out to be the president one day.

~Mason Carter Harvey

True to Myself

*Our wounds are often the openings into
the best and most beautiful part of us.*
~David Richo

When I was six years old, I developed a type of cancer called leukemia. It made me very ill and I spent most of my days at the Chicago Children's Hospital.

After I had two years of treatment, the cancer went into remission for almost five years. I was no longer showing signs or symptoms of the disease. But just when I thought my future looked good, my cancer came back. I had just turned eleven years old and was starting middle school. This time it hit me even harder and I had to fight to survive.

School was the last thing on my mind but I still had to complete my course work one way or another. Most of my schoolwork was done at home but when I was feeling up to it, I went to school. I couldn't walk very well, so I had to use crutches. The medicine I had to take made me weak.

I also wore a baseball hat to school because the medicine I took made all of my hair fall out. Losing hair was not fun, especially being a girl. I was teased and even told I was in the wrong bathroom by someone who thought I looked like a boy.

The teachers and other staff members did their very best to try and help students understand my cancer. But some of the kids still chose to tease or pick on me. Dealing with cancer and school was very difficult.

Middle school was even harder to deal with because in middle school you have to switch classrooms for every subject. Since I couldn't walk well, my teachers let me leave class a few minutes before the bell rang. This gave me enough time to get to and from my next class without all the other kids rushing through the hallways.

On one particular day when I felt super weak and too tired to make it to my next class, I rested for a minute up against a wall while leaning on my crutches. Suddenly the bell rang, the classroom doors swung open, and the hallways filled up with students trying to get to their next class.

I took a deep breath and started to crutch my way through the crowd. I didn't make it very far. I remember my hat being lifted off my head and a boy shouting, "Go get it," while other kids giggled. Another kid kicked my crutch from behind me and I lost my balance. I tumbled forward and fell flat on my face. My backpack landed on top of me still strapped to my back. I lay there trying to find enough energy to get up.

The final bell rang and the doors closed. All of the students had vanished into their classrooms except for me. Still lying on the floor, I felt humiliated, in pain, and most of all, defeated. At that very moment I hated everything about what was happening to me — my health, my weakness, my existence. I never wanted to go back to school again.

Before my cancer I thought kids' jobs were to play, have fun, and be silly. Little did I know there was more responsibility to being a child and that sometimes life wouldn't work out the way I wanted.

The next morning I had to make a choice. I could stay home and feel sorry for myself or I could go to school and accomplish what I had set out to do. All night long I kept thinking that if I went to school it would be just another day of humiliation, not to mention a lot of stress.

I closed my eyes and thought a while. I thought about the children I had met at the hospital who were also sick. I even thought about the kids I went to school with who had other types of problems. Unlike some of their illnesses or disabilities, mine were not permanent. I had a chance of recovering.

Right then and there I opened my eyes, sat up, and decided tomorrow was a new day and no matter how the day played out, I was going to make it, crutches and all—one step at a time.

That night I picked out my favorite T-shirt to wear, grabbed my lucky ball cap and gave myself a pep talk. I was not going to let the bullying behavior of others take me down. I told myself that my looks were just temporary, that my hair would grow back, and that one day I was going to walk again just like I used to.

To my surprise, the next school day went smoother than usual. I had regained a little bit of confidence, enough to keep trying my best and to not let others' behaviors or words bother me. I even made a new friend that month. Her name was Kristen like mine.

Eventually I got healthier and my cancer went away. Later, I became the fastest runner in my class! I even played flag football with the boys.

I didn't choose my cancer or disabilities, but I conquered them. The only thing I regretted was not telling someone about the bullying behavior. But I stayed true to myself and that is what matters.

~Kristen N. Velasquez

The Kindness Cure

If you can, help others; if you cannot do that, at least do not harm them.
~Randy Rind

"Hey!" the voice called from behind me. "Are you a girl or a duck?" I ignored the comment even though I knew it was directed at me.

I ran to my class, causing my slight limp to become even more apparent. I didn't care. I just wanted to get away from the group of mean girls behind me. It was my first day at a new school and I was still trying to learn how to find my class. I wasn't prepared to handle this type of treatment also.

Already, I could see that things would be different here. At my old school, I had a group of friends to protect me. If those friends had been there, I just knew they'd be yelling back, "Hey! Leave her alone!" I could actually see Maryann and Elisa waving their fists at the name-callers and howling their warning, "Or else!"

Yet starting today, in this new school, I was on my own. I took my place in the first row of desks, grateful for alphabetic seating. My last name came at the beginning of the alphabet and the mean girl Betsy's last name came at the end of the alphabet. That put a full five rows between us.

By the time lunch hour arrived, I was feeling better about my situation. Betsy and her group had been quiet during class and polite when speaking to the teacher. Surely, they had calmed down and wouldn't be repeating their behavior. Or so I thought. The minute I walked into the hallway, I felt a hand at my back. It was Betsy.

"I don't like being ignored," she said. "I asked you a question before and I expect you to answer it."

"Yeah," chimed her chorus of friends, "answer it."

I looked at her, "What question?"

"Are you a girl or a duck?"

"I'm a girl."

"Then why do you walk like a duck?"

I felt my face redden. "I don't walk like a duck," I insisted.

"Yes you do," Betsy smirked. "Quack, quack."

"Quack, quack, quack," sang her chorus. Then they all broke into fits of laughter and went off to take their seats for lunch. I, however, went to the far end of the cafeteria and ate my lunch alone and in silence. Was this how I would spend the rest of my school days?

As the weeks went on, though, I made friends with two girls named Fran and Lisa who sat near me in class. They didn't seem too thrilled with Betsy either and whenever she made one of her snarky remarks they would wave it off and tell me to ignore her. Eventually, I also gained skill in avoiding Betsy and her group of crazy quackers. I didn't linger in the hallway before and after class and I went directly home at dismissal time.

Still, I hated that I didn't walk like everyone else. I didn't like not being able to run as fast or as straight as the other kids and I didn't like getting picked last for teams in gym class. Mostly, though, I really hated it when people like Betsy made dumb remarks about how I walked. Yet I learned to live with it until one day the game changed.

"Class," our teacher addressed us one morning, "you've been in the same seats for a full semester and you've become friendly with the students around you. Now it's time to change seats and make some new friends."

The class let out a collective moan, yet our teacher would not be dissuaded. As she assigned the new seating, Fran, Lisa, and I looked at each other while we waited for our names to be called. We didn't want to be separated. And we especially didn't want to sit anywhere near Betsy.

Fran and Lisa's names were called first. Though they weren't sitting right next to each other, they were sitting close. Then my name was called. I took my seat. Then Betsy's name was called. She took her seat — directly behind me.

I knew this wasn't going to be good and I soon discovered I was right. For Betsy, her new seat assignment was like hitting the bully jackpot. I could practically hear her rubbing her hands together in delight. She was as close to her target as she could get and she didn't waste any time getting to work. The torment started within minutes. Betsy leaned into my back: "Quack, quack." When I ignored her, she kicked my seat. When that didn't work, she poked me. This went on daily until one morning I simply refused to go to school.

My mother sat me down after I told her the details of my harsh treatment. "Look," she said, "there will always be mean people in this world. That will never change. But you can change the way you handle them. Did you ever hear of the saying 'Kill 'em with kindness'?"

I shook my head, no.

"It's simple. Just give Betsy a compliment from time to time. If she drops her pen, pick it up and hand it to her. Things like that. Just be so nice to her that it takes the fun out of teasing you."

I was doubtful, but I was also desperate. Even though Mom's "kill 'em with kindness" idea didn't seem logical to me, I was still willing to give it a try. After I took my seat that morning, I turned toward Betsy. Her hair was a mess. She was wearing a pair of old jeans and the same worn pink and purple shirt she wore every Monday morning. How could I possibly compliment her?

"Betsy," I squeaked, "did I ever tell you how much I like that shirt? Those colors are my favorites."

She looked back at me blank-eyed, "Uh, thanks."

Maybe my mother was on to something because Betsy only quacked once and poked me twice that morning. My new tack seemed to be working and I kept at it. Instead of rushing out of class on Friday afternoons, I began to wish her a good weekend. On Monday mornings, I'd ask her if she'd done anything special on Saturday and Sunday. She usually would only answer with a mumble, but I did notice she was being less mean to me and some Fridays she would even wish me a good weekend first. It almost seemed as though Betsy was starting to like me.

Then one day I really had the chance to shine. Our teacher was in a pretty serious mood that day. Spring break had passed and most of the students were starting to forget about schoolwork and think about summer vacation. Grades were down and homework assignments were late. In an effort to get us back on track, the teacher began to quiz us with questions from our studies throughout the year. She sat at her desk, asking questions at lightning speed and expecting fast replies. Whenever a student would give an incorrect answer, she would remark, "Wrong!" and move on to the next student.

When my turn came, I answered quickly and correctly. Then it was Betsy's turn. "What year did Columbus discover America?" the teacher asked.

I stood still, sensing Betsy's terror. I knew she couldn't possibly remember the answer. The day we learned that lesson, Betsy had been too busy jabbing me to have heard anything the teacher said. But I knew the answer. And I wrote it down on a piece of paper and slipped it over the side of my desk where the teacher couldn't see.

Startled, Betsy looked down. "1492!" she answered in triumph.

I had saved the day.

In the days that followed, something interesting happened. Betsy started to open up to me. Her parents were recently divorced and her dad was somewhere where she said she couldn't visit him. Also, her mom had become ill and was awaiting surgery. I could see the pain in her pale blue eyes and, for a minute, I felt sorry for her. Betsy's teasing soon stopped altogether.

On the last day of school, Betsy turned to me. "You're really nice," she said. "I don't know why I was so mean to you."

But, by that time, I had figured out why she had been so cruel. She was so unhappy at home that she took out her frustrations at school—on me. However, when I was kind to her the teasing lost its appeal.

We parted that June day and I never did see Betsy again. Apparently, her mother's illness was serious and she and her sister were sent to live with grandparents in another part of the state. While I hoped Betsy found happiness there, I couldn't say that I missed her. Honestly, part of me was glad that she was gone. But a bigger part of me was even gladder that I had listened to my mom and turned on the kindness. It was just what I needed. And probably just what Betsy needed, too.

~Monica A. Andermann

The Best Way to Get Even

Remember, happiness doesn't depend upon who you are or what you have;
it depends solely upon what you think.
~Dale Carnegie

"Hey Carina," Candy quipped. "Where do you get your clothes? The reject bin at the Salvation Army?"

"Ewww!" her friend Jackie added. "Your bangs aren't even curled! Your hair is so shapeless!"

I had gotten used to the needling of bullies. By the eighth grade I was a seasoned veteran.

I was not going to dress or look a certain way just to make them stop bullying me. No one was forcing them to look at my clothes and hair. The curled bangs of the early 1990s made my female classmates look like electrocuted peacocks. It wasn't my style, and as for the clothes—it was out of my control where my parents could afford to shop.

Even though I refused to conform I was still angered by the way Candy and Jackie had humiliated me in homeroom. How empty were their lives that their only agenda was to make me miserable? I barely knew those girls, nor cared to, yet they seemed to be wholly fascinated with me.

Their harsh words followed me to every class, rode home with me on the bus, and took a seat at the dinner table.

"There will always be mean people, Carina!" my father explained to me later that evening. "You can only control how you react to it."

It was ironic that the kids were teasing me about my clothes, for my mom had just bought me a brand new beautiful dress that day. I remember marveling over it in spite of my pain. That was when there was a knock at the door.

"It's a UPS truck, " Mom said, staring out the window. "What could they be delivering?"

"Christmas is in three weeks," I reasoned. "Maybe someone sent us a gift."

My father answered the door. I remember him looking at the large package and saying, "It's for Carina."

Surprised, I looked at the return address: Young Authors of America. I had entered a writing contest. All of the junior high children at my school were required to enter. Inside were a bunch of letters, and four copies of a book. "I won!" I screamed after reading one of the letters. "I won!"

My poem was in that book. I was also given a bunch of press releases for my school and the local newspapers.

A big fuss was made about me the next day in school. On the PA system in homeroom, right in front of Jackie and Candy, it was announced that I was the only child in the school's five-year history of participation that had ever won that national writing competition.

Teachers and students congratulated me. The next day, Candy and Jackie told me how beautiful my new dress was. "Thanks," I replied. "I'm wearing it for my interview today. They're putting my picture in the newspaper. Have you ever made the paper?"

The girls blushed, and admitted that they hadn't. "I'll tell you what it feels like when I'm finished," I told them.

This story makes me very proud. I defeated those girls not with violence, or insulting words, but with two weapons that are far more threatening: success and excellence. Candy and Jackie could insult, degrade, and humiliate me; but one thing that they could not do was win that contest. They had entered it the same as I had. Funny, I guess Candy and Jackie only had a way with words when it came to abusing, and belittling people. They could keep that gift. I liked mine a whole lot better!

~Carina Lamendola

Bullies on the Bus

The man who does not value himself cannot value anything or anyone.
~Ayn Rand

was always the shy one. When a group activity was going on I didn't insert myself into the middle of the action, I sat and watched, waiting to be asked to join in. Sometimes I was asked and sometimes I wasn't.

I had a nice group of friends in school so it wasn't like I was a loner. There was always a nice group of people at my lunch table. School was never an issue. In my neighborhood, the kids that I became friends with were a grade ahead of me. This wasn't a problem until I was in eighth grade, still attending middle school, and they started ninth grade at the high school.

Suddenly, the bus rides were lonely. I sat by myself in the middle of the bus gazing out the window as we passed my friends' houses. Because they were in high school they caught a much earlier bus. I had to ride with the younger kids who were dropped off at the elementary school next to my middle school.

For some reason I became the target of three fourth-grade girls. They got a kick out of piling into the seat behind me and pulling my hair. One would taunt me with mean names. I ignored them or told them to quit, but the bullying continued.

As the season changed to winter and the school bus windows fogged up, I'd walk to my seat only to see one of them had drawn all over the window and made ugly pictures of me. I smeared the drawings and ignored them.

I noticed one of the girls, the one who always called me names, held slightly back from the group. It was as if she was being peer-pressured to be one of the bullies. Since my tactic of ignoring them wasn't working, I started making eye contact with her and smiling even if she was saying cruel things. That was my only retaliation. I wanted her to know that I knew she didn't want to be doing this.

It started to work. Some days she never made a comment to me. Other times she would shut right up as soon as I looked at her. I think my smiles confused her, as they were not the reaction she was expecting. The other two continued with the hair pulling and the drawings and making fake fart sounds and then trying to say I was stinking up the bus, when no one was actually farting and nothing smelled.

I got through the bus rides by reminding myself that the next year they would not be on my bus and by the time they were I would be driving myself to school. They were only a temporary problem, mean girls who didn't deserve my attention.

Still, one can only take so much. One day, as they sat behind me calling me names, I started doing the math in my head. When I was a senior in high school they would be freshmen. Everyone knew about Pick on Freshmen Day. It was a rite of passage I would be spared because when I was a freshman my good friends who were older than me would protect me.

I spun in my seat and glared at the two girls behind me.

"Do you think you're funny?" I demanded to know in the sternest tone I could muster.

"We're funny, you're not!" shot the one that I'm pretty sure was the leader.

"We'll let's see who is laughing when I'm a senior and you are a freshman and Pick on Freshmen Day comes."

I spun back around in my seat and secretly smiled. All was quiet behind me and the truth of what I said sunk in. Suddenly the leader burst into tears and made her way to the front of the bus. She cried to the bus driver that I was going to beat her up and she was afraid of me.

The only advice the bus driver offered was to stop picking on me.

Victory!

The bullying stopped, for me anyway. The girls started sitting in the very back of the bus, except for the one I pegged as the weakest link. She moved up front.

One day as I was getting off the bus she stopped me to apologize, saying she never meant to hurt my feelings. It turned out that once they stopped bullying me, her so-called-friends started bullying her.

I told her I understood and that is why I was always kind to her even when she was being mean. It wasn't that I didn't want to fight back; it's that sometimes you have to do the right thing even when no one is looking.

She got the message. And I never did participate in Pick on Freshmen Day. No one likes to be bullied.

~Valerie D. Benko

The Rumor Court

It isn't what they say about you, it's what they whisper.
~Errol Flynn

I could hear them whispering. I could see the looks they were giving me. They had believed every lie about me.

When I joined the volleyball team, I didn't plan on running into two girls who would make it their mission to make my life miserable. But when an old friend who hated me joined the team I knew I was in trouble. She immediately befriended a spiteful, self-centered teammate, Sierra, and together they began to spread rumors about me.

"She's a bad influence. She parties every Friday night, drinking and smoking."

"You know, she's a drug dealer."

"She acts like she's such a good girl, but I've seen what she's like. She's a hypocrite."

Not a word of it was true, but people believed it anyway. On top of that, they would harass me at practice when the coach wasn't looking. By this time, my parents told me I should just stop playing volleyball, but I loved it too much to quit and I didn't feel I should give up.

I was really hurt and angered by the thought of everyone talking about how I was such a horrible person. I felt so alone and abandoned. At times, I even felt like I was being punished for mistakes I hadn't made. I just wanted to lash out and give those liars a taste of their own medicine.

One day, I confided in a friend, Cassidy, and explained the whole story. I told her how angry I was and how I planned to get back at them. At first, her only reply was a quote from a poet about showing beauty and courage to the things that frighten us, because in reality they're really helpless things that need love.

That only confused me. I knew what Cassidy meant; she wanted me to be nice to those awful girls and show them love, but I was too angry for that. "They'll receive love when they give it in return," I told her.

Cassidy shook her head and replied, "An eye for an eye makes the world blind. You can't treat people with love only when they've earned it."

"But why should I show love to someone who clearly is no good?"

"Everyone has good in them," she continued. "Often, girls try to make you feel this way because they don't have confidence in themselves, so they try to make themselves feel better by putting you down. You never know what might be going on in someone's life that makes her want to treat you like this. You should consider what may be going on in their lives before you rush to judge them."

"But how is courage supposed to help me?" I asked. "I don't know how to express my courage without rage. How could rage ever turn into something beautiful?"

"Courage isn't always fighting," Cassidy explained. "It's not always standing up for yourself. Courage is doing what you know is right, even if everything, even yourself, fights against it. Sometimes it's having the courage to treat someone with love, even if you don't think you'll get anything back."

After I left, I started thinking about what Cassidy had said. I still wasn't sure what I was going to do or if I was going to follow her advice. I didn't have much time to consider it, because I had another practice with them soon after.

Sierra and I were both sitting on the bench, waiting to play.

While we were waiting, Sierra's dad came up and told her to come with him. They walked to a different room, but I could still see them from where I sat. I saw Sierra's dad start yelling at her, and he seemed to be really mad. Suddenly, he slapped Sierra in the face. She started crying and went to her mom, but her mom didn't do anything. Finally, Sierra went running to the bathroom in tears.

In that moment, I knew I had to go to Sierra, whether she hated me or not. I followed her to the bathroom and went inside. We didn't say a word. Then she hugged me and cried on my shoulder, and it seemed we almost understood each other. I thought back to what Cassidy had told me, and it finally made complete sense. I really could show love to someone who hated me.

Soon after, the rumors stopped. The girls and I began to work together peacefully again. I soon found that Sierra no longer treated me as an enemy. I have learned that, in the end, there are few things that cannot be fixed with love and understanding.

~Christy Box

Don't Fight It, Just Write It

Stay strong. Stand up. Have a voice.
~Shawn Johnson

As a little girl in elementary school, I was unusual in many ways. I was born in a Caribbean country called Trinidad and Tobago. I loved to wear flashy clothes that were not the latest trends. I was very shy and became frightened easily. I wore glasses. I had imaginary friends, and I was very, very good at language arts. All the things that made me unique also made me a target for bullies.

In second grade, another student caught me talking to my imaginary friend in the library one day about my love for books. She told everyone I was talking to myself. The rest of the class had a great laugh at my expense. After I walked into my third grade class wearing glasses for the first time, everyone started calling me four-eyes and nerd.

When I gave a presentation in fourth grade about where I was born, no one had ever heard of Trinidad and Tobago, so they made fun of me and called me an alien from outer space. A group of boys used to point at me and laugh at my brightly colored clothes every day. And a girl I really wanted to be friends with told me if I didn't do her Language Arts homework for her every day, she would never speak to me again.

Sometimes I came home feeling very sad, and I was afraid to tell anyone about what happened or how I felt. So I would go to my room, take out some paper, and write a pretend letter to my imaginary friend whom I called Star. After I felt better, I would crumple up the letters and throw them away as a symbol of starting fresh. Soon, I ended up writing every day in a notebook, and it became my personal, secret journal that I hid under my bed. My journal entries would all begin with "Dear Star." I realized that writing helped me feel better because I also wrote about happy things as well. In my notebook, I wrote in all different colors and even drew funny pictures sometimes.

As time went on, every time someone hurt my feelings or something made me sad, I would come home and write about it to Star. Eventually, I realized that I was good at writing, so I started writing stories like the ones I would read all the time from the library. I started turning my bullies into mythical creatures and silly characters in stories where I could control what happened. If the guy who laughed at my clothes wore a green shirt that day, I would come home and write a story about a green monster who I turned into a butterfly with my magic wand. If they laughed at my glasses, I would write a story about a girl who had magic glasses that gave her the power to see through walls like Superman.

But even though I would write these cool stories in my room, it didn't stop the bullies from picking on me and I was too afraid to stand up to them. I knew I had to do something because I did not like crying every day. I decided to use my writing ability to reach out for help. One day, I wrote a letter to my teacher about what I was going through, the same way I would write to Star. She talked to me kindly one day after school and told me my letter made her cry and that she was proud of my courage and creativity. She called my parents to explain that she would make sure the bullying stopped. She took charge of the situation because of my letter and had a serious talk with my bullies and the entire class.

My bravery in telling the truth through a letter inspired my teacher to ask all the students to write letters to her about their feelings regarding bullying. She was amazed by the feedback she got from the letters. It was useful because she did not know how much bullying was going on right under her nose. After that, she came up with new activities for us to play together so we would get to know each other better. She made us talk about things we were good at and taught us how to point out the good things about fellow classmates. She developed stricter rules for conduct that included bullying clauses. This made my life a whole lot better. Through writing, I made a difference.

Today, I am a professional writer, editor, and author. I've written for newspapers and magazines. My stories, both fiction and nonfiction, are inspired by all the great and not-so-great things that I have experienced, and continue to experience, in life. Writing about my feelings not only helped me survive childhood bullying, it has become my career and my favorite hobby in the world.

The lessons I learned from this childhood experience have benefited me my entire life and made me a better person. First of all, don't be afraid to tell the truth. Always try to find the good qualities in other people. And if you are afraid to speak out about something that is bothering you, then write it.

~Neesha Hosein

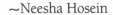

Monkey Arms

Never be bullied into silence. Never allow yourself to be made a victim.
Accept no one's definition of your life; define yourself.
~Harvey Fierstein

I couldn't wait to go to school that morning. I was wearing a new short sleeved, lacy blouse under my tunic and I was dying to show it off. It made me feel so grown up and feminine, so much older than my eight years, and I wanted everyone to see and admire my pretty shirt.

I heard the laughter before I rushed through the gate. I followed the sound to find my classmates standing in a circle. At first I thought someone had brought in the year's first skipping rope, but as I approached, I saw that a girl who sat next to me in school was standing in the middle, surrounded by some older kids.

"Monkey arms," someone shrilled. "Suzanne has monkey arms!"

The voice belonged to a boy named Norman. His twin sister Maryann echoed his chant. I ducked into the crowd quickly, not wanting them to notice me. They were the "rich kids", the ones everyone looked up to, yet also feared. They always bullied the poorer students, and I was one of those.

I peeked over someone's shoulder to find Suzanne hugging herself and crying. I saw that she was wearing a blouse similar to mine, but even from where I stood I noted that her arms were indeed quite hairy. I felt my sympathy rise. My first instinct was to reach out to her, to protect her.

"Monkey arms!" Norman jeered again. "Your momma's a gorilla and your daddy's a baboon!" he mocked.

He looked around with a malicious grin to see if everyone was impressed with his insults. His eyes settled on me angrily. I stared back. He nudged his sister, and Maryann followed his glance.

I wanted to say something that would defend Suzanne, but my mouth went dry. The other kids began to parrot his nasty words. I was the only one who hadn't joined in, and Norman glared at me threateningly.

I was young, but I knew how things worked. If I didn't go along with him and Maryann, I would become their next target. Everyone always followed their lead—or paid the price.

Norman continued to stare me down. I knew the taunts were growing louder, but they were drowned out by the sound of my hammering heart. He stomped towards me and grabbed my arm, his fingers pressing tightly into my skin.

"You must be related to Monkey Arms," he hissed. "You have a chimpanzee haircut. I'll bet your mother cuts it because you're too poor to afford a real haircut."

I lowered my eyes in mortification. My mother did cut my hair for that reason, just like she cut her own, my three brothers' and my father's. When I looked up again, I noticed some of the kids had turned their attention to us. I panicked. If I didn't distract them, Norman would start making fun of me too, so I did the only thing I could think of.

"Monkey arms!" I yelled, breaking away from his grip. "Suzanne has monkey arms!"

Within seconds, Norman went back to ridiculing Suzanne again, mimicking her twisted, miserable face, and pretending to wipe tears from his cheeks with his pudgy hands.

"Boo-hoo-hoo," he snickered. "Wahhh."

When Suzanne tried to escape the tight circle around her, he barred her way. She ran to the other side, only to have Maryann stop her. Finally she came my way.

"Block her," Norman yelled, and to my shame, I did, shoving her back. She looked at me pleadingly, her cheeks wet, her eyes red and puffy. I turned away so I wouldn't have to see her pain, wishing the earth would swallow me up. Just then, the bell rang. Relieved, I tore off to line up with my class.

Everyone seemed to forget the episode—everyone except me. I could see that the twins were already teasing another small kid, grabbing his schoolbag and tossing it back and forth while he tried in vain to get it back.

Once we were all in class, I pretended to be absorbed in my math book to avoid Suzanne's sad face. From the corner of my eye, I saw her fighting tears all morning, yet I said nothing to her. Instead, I remembered all the times she'd shared fresh cookies with me at recess, or slipped me a new pencil because mine was too short to write with and I couldn't buy another until my father got paid.

Finally it was time to go home for lunch. I dragged my feet to return to school after eating the cheese sandwich my mother slid my way before hurriedly going back to her many chores.

When class resumed, Suzanne wasn't there. Instead of the usual reading lesson, our teacher, Mrs. Brennan, tapped her desk with her ruler and began to speak to us in serious soft tones.

To her credit, she never once singled out any of us who had taunted Suzanne earlier that day. Instead, she quietly explained how cruel it was to tease someone about something they had no control over, whether it was a large nose, big ears, a handicap or anything else they could not change. She pointed out that we could no more help the way we were made than we could stop the sun from rising.

As she continued to give examples, my throat constricted with shame at the way I treated Suzanne. I wanted to tell her I was sorry. I promised myself that I would apologize the very next day, and vowed never to let anyone bully her or me again.

Suzanne didn't return to school. A week later, we heard she went to the hospital the day of the schoolyard incident. She'd slashed herself horribly while she was trying to shave her arms with her father's razor. Not only were her arms scarred for life, but she'd severed some veins and almost bled to death before her mother found her.

The day we started summer holidays, I finally gathered my courage and walked to Suzanne's house to beg forgiveness. I found the house empty. A "FOR RENT" sign hung in the window.

I never saw her again. Years passed. I tried to find her, but my efforts were fruitless. As an adult, I even tried Internet searches with no results.

I still have the last pencil she ever gave me. I keep it as a constant reminder that ugly words, once said, can never be unsaid, and that wanting to be part of the crowd is only a good thing if the crowd itself is a good one.

That was the last time I ever succumbed to peer pressure, and I never again ridiculed anyone about a flaw or handicap.

Suzanne will never know that she made me a better person. Whenever I find myself about to criticize someone, I remember a helpless little face streaked with tears, and I bite my tongue. If only I'd bitten it then. If only I could have found my sweet little classmate one more time to say the words that really mattered: "I'm so sorry, Suzanne."

~Marya Morin

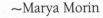

Chapter
6

Think Positive for Kids

Appreciating Family

Already Mom

Adoption is when a child grew in its mommy's heart instead of her tummy.
~Author Unknown

"I don't get it. Why are you adopting us?" The entire family, all six of us, had gathered in the living room to have one of our family discussions. Mom looked serious as she tried to explain.

"Your father and I were talking with Mr. Peterson, our lawyer, and the truth of the matter is he said it would be best if I legally adopted the three of you."

"The three of us?" I asked.

"Yes. You, Lisa and Robbie."

I looked at my older brother Robbie, who seemed to understand what she was saying.

I looked at my older sister Lisa, who nodded in agreement.

I looked at my little sister Jenny, but she just looked away.

The four of us kids sat while Mom explained, "Look at it this way. You know I am your mother, right?"

We all nodded.

"And I know that I am your mother. But we have to make it legal so everyone will know. We need to go to court and have a judge rule on it. When we go to court and the judge says I am your mother, the entire world will know."

I guess I appeared clueless because my big brother, who was already in ninth grade, said in his usual rude manner, "It's like this—if Dad croaks and some other relative wanted to, they could say that Mom wasn't blood and they would have the right to take us away from her."

At last the light went on. I finally understood.

My birth mom died when I was eighteen months old. My dad remarried six months later. When my "stepmom" married my dad he had three kids: me, two years old; my sister, Lisa, four; and my brother, Rob, five. Four years later my sister Jenny was born. I was so young when my mom passed that I never considered my "stepmom" anything but my mom and my "half-sister" anything but my sister, so this whole legal thing confused me.

"We have an appointment Thursday to go to court and talk to the judge," Mom said.

"But that's a school day," Lisa said.

"Well, guess what? We are taking the day off!" Mom replied.

"P-a-r-t-y!" was all Robbie could say as he danced around the living room.

"Listen up everybody. When we meet with the judge he will ask each of you questions about me, our family, and our home life. He will ask you if you feel that I take good care of you. Do you feel safe? Do you love me?"

I looked at Jenny, who had her head down.

"I'm going to tell him how mean you are and that you lock me in my room and..." Robbie teased.

Mom just shot him a look... that look.

"Okay. Okay, I'll behave," Robbie said.

Minutes later I looked over and Jenny was gone.

"What's wrong with Jenny?" Lisa asked.

"Why? Where is she?" Mom asked.

"She ran to her bedroom," Lisa said.

We all went to Jenny's room and found a sobbing bundle hidden under a heap of blankets and stuffed animals.

"Pumpkin, what's wrong?" Mom asked, as she gently lifted the covers off our hysterical sister. Jenny was crying so fiercely that she could barely breathe, let alone tell us why she was so upset.

Finally, after some deep breaths she stopped and just stared at us. "I thought you loved me," she finally squeaked out.

"I do. We all do. Why would you say that?" Mom asked.

"But you don't love me as much as you love them."

This time Mom was the one who looked confused.

"You know I love you. I love you all."

"But you don't love me enough to adopt me."

For the first time that afternoon there was complete silence as we all tried to understand what Jenny had just said. Then it occurred to us. With all the family meetings and discussions, we never realized that Jenny, as young as she was, didn't understand that legally she did not need to be adopted.

Mom smiled as she took Jenny on her lap and explained that Lisa, Robbie and I were born from a different mother but that we were a part of her heart. Jenny was her birth daughter, born of her body. She was already legally hers so she did not have to be adopted.

We all hugged her, except Robbie who messed her hair and called her a doofus.

That Thursday we all drove to the courthouse. Mom made us dress in nice clothes. Robbie kept pulling on his tie. Lisa kept pulling on her dress. I kept pulling on my hair as we waited to meet the judge.

When it was our turn to appear in front of the judge he asked each of us if were happy and if we wanted Mom to be our mom forever. Of course Robbie had to be smarty-pants and say he'd think about it, but quickly laughed and said "Yes, of course." When the judge asked Jenny what she thought, she looked at all of us, smiled, and said, "I'm happy that we are all adopting each other." So, together we raised our right hands and swore that what we had told him was the truth and nothing but the truth.

~Jeanne Blandford

Learning from Mother Nature

You know children are growing up when they start asking questions that have answers.

~John J. Plomp

Parents don't like to talk about some things. Some things are uncomfortable to talk about. Other things are sad to talk about. But most of these are things that we cannot avoid. Someday we'll have to learn about them, because they are a part of life, whether our parents like it or not.

It's not like parents are bad at what they do—they just want to protect us from scary and sad things for as long as they can. But there are some things a kid just wants to know about. So we find ways to learn, even if our parents are uncomfortable talking about these things.

Much of what I wanted to know I learned working as a farm girl at the nature center near my home. To me, this was my home away from home, my safe place. It was my place to go when I wanted to think, to dream, or just leave the everyday normal. I walked into that farm and I was no longer in a bustling suburb of New York City. I was in a place filled with green and animals and the rhythms and sounds of nature.

My boss at the farm was a kind lady, and she knew a lot about animals. She knew when they were happy, and when they were hungry, and when they wanted to play. She was like a mother to the whole farm. She even knew when the animals were sad or when they weren't feeling well.

One of the hardest days I ever had happened at that farm. One of the baby pigs was not eating right. I didn't know what was wrong, but my boss did. She was kind to the piglet and rubbed its belly while she told me what was going to happen. She told me that the baby pig wasn't born right. It had a problem with its mouth and it would never be able to grow up. She showed me the inside of the baby piglet's mouth, and how the food it was eating wasn't going down right. She let me stay with her while we made the hard decision to put the piglet down.

Watching that piglet fall asleep for the last time was one of the hardest moments in my life. I cried the whole time, even after my boss explained to me that it was the humane thing to do. If we hadn't done what we did, the baby would have slowly starved. Neither of us wanted that. I learned so much that day, and I cried just as much. But I also learned how to do the right thing, even though it seemed wrong.

I went home and talked to my mom about why the little piglet was not going to make it, and the whole process that my boss and I went through to make sure that it was not in any pain. My mom cried for the baby, but I made sure to tell her that it was the right thing to do.

That was the beginning of spring, and the beautiful thing about spring is that it is the time of new life. The week after the piglet died I got a call late at night. Our other mama pig was giving birth and my boss needed help. I ran through the woods as fast as my ten-year-old legs could carry me. My parents and my little brother came too.

We made it to the mama pig just before the babies started to pop out. And boy did they pop! My boss gave me a big responsibility. My job was to grab the babies after they came out and keep them warm and safe. She explained to me that Mama Pig was so excited, and so much bigger than the babies, that if she sat down she could squash one of the babies! I knew I needed to keep them safe. One by one the babies arrived, and one by one I cleaned them off, put them under the heat lamp and kept them safe. Mama Pig had ten babies that night. And I kept all ten safe.

I remember being so proud. I felt like I had helped make up for what happened to the little piglet with the mouth that wouldn't work. I felt like I made something right by keeping those babies safe. I talked to my mom and dad about it. I told them that there are reasons for everything, and one of the reasons that I lived behind the farm was so that I could be there to help the mama pig and her babies.

The farm taught me about birth, growth, life, and death. I learned some hard life lessons. But I was a lucky one. I had to watch my animal friends grow old, but I was also right there when they were born, when they learned to walk and when they took their first runs—usually all in the same day! Nature is amazing, and Mother Nature is one of the best teachers I ever had.

All of these things that I learned at the farm I discussed with my mom and dad. It turns out they actually liked talking about these things with me. They had just been afraid I would get scared if we talked about them. They were nervous, but what I learned at the farm gave them the little push they needed.

~Emma Blandford

History in the Making

Great things are not accomplished by those who yield to trends and fads and popular opinion.

~Jack Kerouac

They made me do it. I really, really, really did not want to do it... but they made me. At Turn of River Middle School you were required to enter a submission into the National History Day competition if you were in the highest learning group. I was in, lets just say, not the highest group. That being said, I did not have to partake in this competition, and truthfully I didn't want to. It just seemed like it would be boring and much too much work. Besides, I would be the only kid in my class who had to do it.

You see National History Day is not really just a day. It is a year-long commitment. It's an academic competition focusing on a specific topic for students in grades 6 through 12. It's a year of reading and researching and writing. It looked like a year of sheer torture!

It's a commitment my parents made me do. Well, to be fair, they very strongly suggested that I do it. But I don't believe I really had a choice if I wanted to live at home happily.

For the competition I had to come up with a historical event or person that was related to that year's theme. Each year, more than half a million students from all over the United States submit entries as an individual or a group in one of five categories: documentary, exhibit, paper, website, or performance.

I choose documentary because I thought it would be the easiest. Just pick up a camera and shoot someone talking, right?

Wrong.

The theme that year was "From Hateful to Hopeful." Earlier that year I went with my parents to a benefit concert in New York. The concert performer, Rob Mathes, was there to support "Through the Eyes of Children: The Rwanda Project." It was a showing of photographs taken by orphans depicting the country and people of Rwanda after the horrific genocide in 1994. The pictures and children were beautiful and uplifting. I was moved by it. I had found my documentary topic.

Starting out on my History Day journey, I learned a great deal about how to make a documentary and what goes into it. Writing, choosing images, colors, interviews, editing, music selection, and much more. It's very complicated—like a giant puzzle with many pieces. I had to learn how all the pieces fit together. I struggled a lot with it.

After I finished my work and it was time to compete I was very proud of what I had done. The work that went into it, the message I was sending, the overall finished product made me very happy. I started out on the district level, moving up to the regional level, and then made it to the national level. I had a newfound confidence and was going to Maryland to compete in the finals!

When I got to Maryland, I had to talk about my project and explain why I chose it. But like any good adventure, it's not the destination, but the journey. On my journey I was told, after competing on the regional level, that the judges and History Day representatives were shocked that I had made it past the district level. They thought the subject matter was too shocking. They were accustomed to papers on presidents or documentaries on U.S. history. They did not expect a documentary about genocide in another country to be shown in this competition.

One of my favorite questions after I had shown my video was, "Why did you choose that color red for your background?" My response silenced the room: "It's the color of blood." That's the impact

I wanted to have on every person who saw my documentary. That is what I am most proud of. The emotional response my work had on people. Many of the judges cried at the showing of my video.

Although I did not win an award at the national level I am still very proud of what I created. Through this experience I learned how to organize my thoughts, research, interview people, film and edit. I learned that creating something visual could help lift people's spirits as well as educate. My documentary was even selected to be a permanent part of the Holocaust Museum in Houston, Texas.

Even through all my whining and complaining while I learned the process, I had a great experience that changed me—not only my work ethic and perseverance—but also my willingness to do something different and not cookie cutter. I was told that my video would not make it past the first round of judging, but I made it all the way to the national level—all because I had a family that believed in me and helped me to believe in myself.

~Tucker Blandford

Easter in Ruins

Sometimes being a brother is even better than being a superhero.

~Marc Brown

I was eight years old the first time that I felt sympathy for my sister. I was a terrible brother. I didn't do anything outright dangerous to my sister, but I teased her mercilessly, generally made her feel terrible, and certainly did not contribute anything positive to her self-esteem.

I didn't really care. It was part of who I was. I didn't know, then, that it was also shaping who she was.

Then along came Easter, one of our favorite holidays. Not because we were devoutly religious and we understood what the holiday actually meant—we were kids, after all—but because that mystical white bunny came and left us baskets full of candy, toys, and useless green filling.

My sister and I thought we were special because the Easter bunny would always hide our baskets. I'd asked my friends at school and barely any of them ever had to find their Easter baskets. They were just there waiting for them when they woke up.

How boring.

Easter morning arrived and it was time for us to spring into action.

"Michelle," I whispered, peeking through the brown plastic door that separated our rooms. It latched closed with a small magnet that worked for approximately two days after my father had installed the door.

"Michelle," I said a little louder this time. "Wake up. It's Easter. We have to go find our baskets."

She rolled over in bed and pulled down the covers just far enough to peek her eyes over her blanket at me, like a crocodile looking up from a murky swamp.

"Michelle!" I whispered more intensely. "Let's go!"

I pushed the plastic door to one side of the doorway and slipped into my sister's room, sat down on the bed, and shook her hard.

Even at age six, my sister was a late sleeper. She had absolutely no desire to stumble out of her bed at the crack of dawn to open presents, hunt for Easter baskets, or do anything other than close her eyes and fall back to sleep.

I, however, was impatient. And a terrible brother.

"Now!" I shouted before slapping my hand over my mouth. The last thing I wanted to do was wake up our parents, only three rooms away in the small first floor apartment.

After a few minutes, my sister finally relented, pulled herself out of bed, and started looking for her socks.

"Mom and Dad are still sleeping," I warned her as we crept through our rooms and out into the kitchen. "If we're quiet, we can find our baskets without waking them up."

It didn't take long for me to find my basket. It was sitting right behind my father's favorite recliner, overflowing with chocolatey goodness and it was obviously mine because it contained the latest issue of my favorite wrestling magazine.

My sister continued searching in every room while I dropped my bounty off at the kitchen table and started separating candy into categories: Chocolates, jellybeans, malted chocolate eggs.

It had to be at least twenty minutes before I looked up from my potential sugar rush displayed on the table to see that my sister was still looking for her basket.

"I can't find it," she said. She looked upset. "I looked all over. Can you help me?"

I had no interest in helping my sister find her Easter basket, so I started to head back to my loot on the table.

"Please?" she asked again. "I can't find it."

I decided to help my sister find her Easter basket, but don't get the wrong idea. It wasn't because I felt sorry for her. Not at all. It was because I'd now been issued a challenge. I had a mission and a case to solve. The Case of the Missing Basket.

"Okay," I said. "Let's keep looking."

We started searching through the cabinets where my mom kept her pots and pans.

By now, our parents were awake. Dad headed straight for the bathroom, while Mom tossed her gray, wool robe over her shoulders and made a beeline for the coffee maker.

"Looks like the Easter bunny came!" she said, looking at my treasures covering the kitchen table. "You found them already? He must not have done a very good job hiding this year."

"I found mine," I said and nodded towards my sister standing in the doorway between the kitchen and the living room.

Mom spun around and looked across the room at my sister.

"Where's yours, Michelle?" she asked.

And that's when my sister started to tear up. She wasn't fully crying yet. Michelle was as tough as sisters come, even at six years old. It was as if her six years of dealing with all my teasing had already hardened her to this cruel, cruel world.

"Let's keep looking," Mom said, grabbing my sister's hand. "I'm sure it's here somewhere."

My sister smiled and pulled our mother into the living room, where they started looking under the couch cushions and behind our television.

Nothing.

"You know," Mom said suddenly, "we haven't looked in any closets."

She pointed across the living room to the hallway closet with the doorknob that never quite held the door closed.

Michelle shot across the room and swung open the closet door.

She got down on her knees and started rifling through the shoes and bags and mismatched gloves on the closet floor.

Nothing.

I heard her sniffle just slightly as she sat back on her heels, defeated.

"Look up!" I said. "Up above the jackets!"

Mission accomplished.

"My basket!" she yelled. "Mom, my basket is up on the shelf! Can you get it?"

Our mother smiled and pushed her way into the closet just far enough to reach up into the dark recesses above the coats and plastic bags and snowsuits hanging below. Way up on the shelf where we usually kept our car washing bucket and soap was my sister's Easter basket.

"Here you go, honey," she said, as she handed Michelle her basket, too excited (or relieved or tired) to notice anything strange before passing it off. "I told you the Easter bunny didn't forget you."

And that's when it happened.

My sister. The rock. The tough girl that I, until that day, had never seen break down. Michelle started crying. And when I say crying, what I mean is tears streaming down her face into a messy puddle in her Easter basket.

My sister's Easter basket was empty. Not completely empty. But it was empty all the same. All that remained were the half-chewed remains of Kit Kat wrappers and nibbled pink Barbie boxes. The only thing still intact? The fake green grass in the bottom of the basket.

Mom called my dad into the room and pointed to my sobbing sister and her sad little basket. "Mice!" Dad said as he started tearing the closet apart. "I'll get them..." That was the last thing we heard him say before the sound of winter jackets, a dustpan, and the vacuum hitting the floor overwhelmed the room.

By now, Michelle had stopped crying. She'd dropped her basket on the floor, wiped her tears, and retreated to her room.

"Just leave me alone," I heard her say as Mom followed her to the door. "Leave! Me! Alone!"

That was my tough little sister, the one I had trained to be strong and not reveal her feelings through my relentless teasing. She wasn't going to shed any more tears in front of us.

But as I sat at the kitchen table flipping through the March issue of my magazine, snacking on an Almond Joy, I suddenly felt something I'd never felt towards my sister before. I felt sad for her. I felt it go through my body like a chill. I felt exactly what I thought she felt. Complete and utter sadness. Only, I wasn't nearly as tough as she was.

I dropped my magazine, reserved one Reese's Peanut Butter Egg (my favorite) for myself, and put the rest of my candy back in my Easter basket on top of the green plastic grass.

I walked slowly into my sister's room, where I found her sniffling quietly under her covers. "I'm sorry, Michelle." I said quietly. Maybe even too quietly for her to hear it.

I took one last look at fully stocked Easter basket and then I left the whole thing right there at the foot of her bed.

I went back to the kitchen to get my magazine, and then got back into my bed to read.

And then, through the thin plastic door between our rooms, I heard the faint sound of candy being unwrapped.

I smiled, lay back on my pillow, and put on my headphones.

That was the last time I ever saw my sister cry.

~Scott Neumyer

56

Three's a Crowd

Family life is a bit like a runny peach pie —
not perfect but who's complaining?
~Robert Brault

t was easy to like my dad's girlfriend the first time I saw her, because she had a puppy. My brother and I first met Helene, and her Pug puppy Hercules, at her aunt's lake house when I was ten years old. I ran back and forth in the yard, Hercules nipping at my heels and rolling in the grass. "This won't be so bad," I thought.

When my parents separated, I was seven years old and pretty much okay with it. My parents fought a lot when they were together, and it was fun to stay at my dad's new apartments. The first one had a trampoline in the back yard and the second one had washing machines that took quarters and a pool downstairs. Plus, my dad always bought the cereal with the most sugar in it and Mom only bought Cheerios. It seemed like a good situation to me.

But then Helene entered the picture. I guess I didn't think my dad would be alone forever, but I hadn't thought much about it. I was more preoccupied with dragging my books to school every day and the fact that I could never get my hair straight like everyone else. One day, my dad took my little brother and me out to get fast food and told us that he and Helene were going to Tahiti to get married. I had chicken nuggets and French fries at the time, so I was okay with this too.

Once I was in high school, I wasn't so okay with everything.

Helene and my dad may have had the best cereal, but they were really strict about things I didn't appreciate. They didn't like the way I wore my make-up, and they wouldn't let me wear sweatpants to school. Helene got mad at me when I forgot things at my mom's house and we had to drive to get them. She had also started hugging me and telling me she loved me, and it felt weird because I hugged my mom and told her I loved her. Could I also tell Helene I loved her? I really wasn't sure. It felt like a betrayal.

Helene soon had a baby, and things were turned upside down. Having friends over meant staying quiet while the baby was napping, and wading through pacifiers and baby bottles to get to the snacks in the kitchen. Who was she to walk into my life and tell me what to do? Why did she have to ruin everything?

When I went to college, I had a big fight with my dad and Helene. I didn't talk to them for almost a year, and I can't even remember why, but I was very mad at them. After years of feeling lost, shuffled between multiple houses, feeling like everyone had a lot of rules for me to follow and not a lot of reasons for me to follow them, I blew up. I guess we all did.

But one morning, I found myself eating waffles with Helene at restaurant in New York City. She was there to talk to me on behalf of my dad, who wanted to work things out. But we didn't really talk about my dad. We talked for hours, and when we got up to leave, she hugged me and told me she loved me. For some reason, it didn't feel weird anymore.

Now I'm an adult, and my stepmom and I are very close. We're not perfect, but I finally feel like I've figured it all out. I love my mom. I love my dad. I love Helene. It's more than okay—it's an amazing bonus in my life. It's easy to feel like three parents are too many when you're younger, but now I know I'm very lucky. Every time I visit my dad's house, Helene has a bed made up for me, a meal waiting, and a sympathetic ear available. She is a great listener, and she's always on my side.

In the end, the silver lining of my parents splitting up wasn't the trampoline, or the cereal, or even the pool. It was having Helene, and my two new little brothers, become part of my life.

~Madeline Clapps

57

Me and My Hairy Legs

A mother is one to whom you hurry when you are troubled.
~Emily Dickinson

The summer before fifth grade I should have been outside playing soccer and swimming in the pool. Instead, I found myself at "math camp." Despite my natural talent for numbers, I didn't really question spending several weeks of my summer cooped up in a stale-smelling classroom without air conditioning. Why would I since all of my friends were there too? We were going through an accelerated math program because we fell into the group of students that the teachers had chosen to move ahead.

At the time, I had two close girlfriends, and sometimes people would mistake the three of us for sisters because of our fair skin and dark hair. Even though we were all skinny, I was the lankiest of all, with gangly arms and legs that were great for keeping up with the boys when running and swinging from the monkey bars. I'd just swapped out my glasses for contact lenses, so I no longer fell into the four-eyes category of kids. Being able to see the chalkboard, and more importantly, playing soccer without glasses bouncing on my face, felt awesome. But there was something else that set me apart from the rest: my Italian heritage.

I took after my dad, who was second generation Italian. Like him, I had bushy eyebrows that connected in the middle. My arms and legs were covered in long dark hairs especially visible when I didn't have a suntan. Even though I was conscious of the fact that I had more hair on me than my friends, most of the school year I was protected by pants and long sleeves.

After consistent pleas to my mom, I had finally been allowed to tweeze the space on the bridge of my nose to get rid of my embarrassing uni-brow. A few weeks earlier, one of my friends told us that she had used her older sister's razor to shave her legs. Even though her hair wasn't as prominent as mine, I had asked my mom if I could shave. She said that I was still too young. I pouted but didn't protest. I knew that there would be no persuading her.

The summer continued as usual, with mornings spent in the classroom, a short lunch break, then more schoolwork in the afternoons. Even though the girls and boys mixed during class, at lunchtime we split into separate groups. My friends and I decided to learn how to play poker. We all loved playing cards and loved our candy even more. So we decided to use lollipops as money and would play until we were told to come inside by the teacher.

One day, the boys had asked to join our game, but we wouldn't let them. So they went off on their own. When it was time to come back inside, the boys started to taunt us with remarks that we weren't as cool as them. Back and forth between the girls and boys, the banter continued. It escalated too quickly for my liking though. A sinking feeling in my stomach warned me that someone's feelings were going to be hurt, but I had no clue that they would be mine.

"Well, you have hairy legs!" one of the boys shouted across the hallway, pointing at me. The room went silent, and I ran to the bathroom fighting back tears. I couldn't help crying and dreaded having to go back into the classroom to sit through more math knowing that all of the boys thought what I thought: I had hairy legs.

When I stopped crying, I went back to the classroom to my assigned seat. I covered my legs with my sweatshirt and didn't pay attention. All I wanted to do was go home to my mom.

That night when I got home I was afraid to tell my mom. She had been so against me shaving that I feared she'd say no again. But she could tell something wasn't right with me. I told my mom what happened at math camp that day and cried. Even though she had been adamant about not letting me shave my legs yet, she took me to CVS to buy an at-home waxing kit. After dinner, we sat on the floor of the family room ripping the hairs from my legs. Even though the sting of the hairs being pulled from my legs hurt, it felt nothing like being teased for having hairy legs.

The next day at school, I didn't cover my legs with my sweatshirt. And no one teased me about my legs being hairy. And the girls and boys played separately during lunchtime. Everything went back to normal, and I didn't have to cry about having hairy legs again. It was all thanks to my mom.

~Amanda Romaniello

Bare Feet in the Waves

Rejoice with your family in the beautiful land of life!
~Albert Einstein

Even though I loved the ocean, I dreaded seeing my cousins each summer when our two families reunited at the beach. Brian and Lonnie knew things I would never understand, or at least they acted like they did.

After eating a picnic lunch with our families, my big sister, cousins and I went to the snack shack to buy ice-cream cones. The day was hot and the ice cream dripped down my hand before I could eat it all. The sweet, sticky treat melted into glop and finally fell into the sand. My sister reached out with her napkin but before I could take it Lonnie pointed to me and said, "Like a baby." I was eight years old—hardly a baby. My sister, looking confused, handed me the napkin and whispered harshly, "Can't you be more careful?" Brian smirked and rolled his eyes.

"Come on," Lonnie said, "let's play people-watching."

Every summer Brian, Lonnie and my sister played this game on the crowded beach, and though they let me tag along, I never understood how to play. I hoped that this was the year I would finally get it and fit in. As we took off I turned back and saw the grown-ups eating watermelon and laughing. While I was watching I noticed my dad get up and walk down to the water. He stood there, looking out over the waves like there was something there to see. Why did he do that? What was the point? When I turned back, my sister and cousins were way down the beach.

"Wait up!" I called, but they didn't hear me, or at least they didn't turn around. I had to run to catch up, hopping over towels, avoiding coolers, and slowing down so I wouldn't knock over any little kids. When I finally caught up, my sister and cousins were deep into the people-watching game.

"See that girl over there," Lonnie said. She pointed to a teenager in a red, two-piece bathing suit who was holding hands with a small little boy. They were jumping up and down in the surf, laughing. It looked like fun. "She's his babysitter but she doesn't really like him."

"That's cause he stinks," Brian said. "I can smell him from here." I sniffed the air but all I smelled was the salty ocean breeze.

Again they took off fast. When I caught up I could hear them laughing, but I missed the joke.

Just then I saw a girl about my age run into the water at super speed. Inspired, I pointed to her and said, "That girl over there is running from a wild tiger. The tiger can't swim so the girl jumped in the water to be safe. The tiger escaped from the zoo but nobody knows because he was sneaky. He crept into the back seat of a car when no one was looking and ended up here." As I told my story I watched the girl, who was riding the waves now with a giant smile on her face. It looked fun. "You guys want to go swimming?" I asked, but when I turned to my cousins and sister, they were way up the beach. Did they even hear my tiger story?

Running to catch them I saw my dad in the exact same spot, just standing at the edge of the waves, but now I noticed that his feet were submerged in the sand. I ran over and stood next to him trying to wiggle my feet into the wet sand so they would be like his, but it didn't work. The sand beneath my feet was hard.

"How did you do that?" I pointed to his feet.

"Just stand here for a while and you'll see," he said.

I didn't want to stand there for a while. I had to catch up with the others. I needed to hear what they were saying. Or did I? They weren't being very nice and they kept leaving me behind. And yet, if

I didn't find them, what else was there to do? I wasn't about to stand with my dad all day. Yet as I was standing there, something happened. As each wave passed over my ankles and receded back to the sea, it dragged the sand along, pulling it away from under my heels. And as the sand got sucked away, my heels sunk down.

"It's happening, Dad," I shouted. The next wave did the same thing; it pulled sand from under my feet and dropped sand on top of them at the same time. "My feet are being buried in the sand!" But my feet were nothing like my dad's because his were buried up to his ankles. That would take forever. There was no way I was about to stand there that long. I had things to do.

Just then my sister and cousins walked by. Lonnie pointed at my dad and laughed. I was glad my dad didn't notice. "Come on," Lonnie yelled to me. "We don't have all day. If you want to play with us, now's your chance!"

I was about to pull my feet out from the sand to join them, but just then another wave came. This one was big, up to my knees. It almost knocked me down! When it receded it pulled so much sand from beneath my feet, more than any wave yet. After it was gone I noticed that the tops of my feet were completely covered. My dad looked out at the waves and I looked at my cousin.

"I'll stay with my dad," I said.

My cousin looked at me like I had just said, "I'll stay in school for the summer," but I didn't let it bother me. They left to play their game while I stayed with my quiet dad, choosing him and the waves and the sand. Smiling, I let the water splash over my feet again and again as I breathed in the salty air and listened to the crash of the surf, the call of the gulls and the gentle breeze that washed over my dad and I, that awesome day at the beach.

~Lava Mueller

Proud to Be Your Sister

Sisters function as safety nets in a chaotic world
simply by being there for each other.
~Carol Saline

Dear Alex,

There was never a certain time in my life when I found out you had special needs. The fact was always there, even if I didn't understand what "special needs" meant. Somehow, I just knew that you were different. Back at age four, it didn't matter that you couldn't play with me or that you had so many doctors. I thought it was cool that you went to a school with so many "fun" things to do. I was jealous that you got to have OT and PT every week.

As I got older, I realized that your special school, doctors, and therapies weren't such an awesome thing. I began to understand that you weren't just special. You were a special needs child.

Brain damage. ADHD. Legal blindness. Epilepsy. This is how the doctors describe you. But I have always seen more. I saw you speak for the first time at three years old. I saw you being rushed away in an ambulance at five in the morning. I saw you trying a new food and spitting it out. I saw you smile at me and it was that moment that I realized what a great brother I had.

When we were little and shared a room I never slept in my own bed. Do you remember, how as soon as Mom and Dad would shut the door, I'd climb into bed with you? We'd stay up for hours, playing our silly little word games, and I'd teach you how to say new things. I cherish those nights when we became more than just two siblings. When you became my best friend.

It could be a coincidence that Anna and Maddy shared a room and you and I shared one. But it was the best coincidence that has ever happened to me.

You were always afraid of so many things. The birthday song, fire, cameras, juice, fruit, clapping... I could go on and on. You are still afraid, trapped in a world of blurry color and unfocused light. I wish I could pull you out... but I can't.

Now that I'm older, I hear people using words like "retarded," "cripple," and "moron," and it breaks my heart. It hurts that others do not understand how hurtful their words are, even if they don't say them directly to those with special needs. It makes me mad that, time and time again, people who have a loved one with special needs try to educate these clueless nimrods and these people go and say we're stupid. When I hear someone use these words, regardless of what they actually mean, I think of you. To them, you are a retard. And I cry. Because those people are cruel.

If my classmates could meet you, I know they would understand. I know it! But they can't meet you.

You can be annoying, sure. I mean, you break my stuff, shriek at the top of your lungs, and mess up the computer.

When you have seizures and have to go to the hospital, it scares me. I hate that you have to experience that, even though I know you're lucky you don't have them as often as some kids do.

What I'm trying to say, Alex, is that I'm so proud to be your sister. I'm proud of all you have accomplished, and what you will accomplish.

Thank you for being there for me, a constant confidant, when I couldn't tell anyone else. Thank you for your hugs, thank you for telling me you love me, thank you for all the morals you have taught me.

You're beautiful.

Love you forever, Like you for always,
Kathryn

~Kathryn Malnight

60

Sharing My Friend

Forgiveness is not an occasional act, it is a constant attitude.
~Martin Luther King, Jr.

Cindy was my best friend. My mom called her a nuisance, but to me, she was a dog with a personality. At eleven, I fell in love with the tiny, curly-haired dog. Cindy was smart, too. I taught her tricks. She would sit by my feet and when I put a stick or piece of carrot by her mouth, I'd say "chew" and she would stand and obey. She loved going for walks with my friends and me. She danced around us as if listening to our conversations about school and clothes and movies we'd seen.

Sometimes, I sat with her in the front yard, letting her explore the soft grass. I'd tell her about my friends, the boys I liked, the test I was about to take in History. Cindy would sit and stare at me as if listening to everything I told her.

Then my uncle, my mother's younger brother, came to live with us. He and his wife slept in my room and I slept on the couch. My mom didn't want Cindy's curly fur all over the living room furniture, so she slept in the utility room in her plush bed. Instead of being beside my bed as usual, she was out of my aunt and uncle's way. I resented their presence and kept Cindy outside with me as much as possible.

But one afternoon, I went to get her from the back yard and she wasn't there. The back gate was partly open. Had Cindy been searching for me?

I looked everywhere around the neighborhood, knocking on doors and asking everyone if they'd seen her. I called her name, my friend who always came to me. This time she didn't come.

"Sorry," my uncle said. "I guess when I went through the gate to check something in my car, I forgot to close it completely."

I didn't want his apology. I cried and searched.

I prayed for her safe return. Then one morning, two days later, my uncle left after breakfast. An hour later he was home, Cindy in his arms.

"She'd been picked up by the pound. I thought I'd check and there she was. Must've pulled her collar off somewhere," he said.

Mom let me keep her beside me all night. I hugged her and told her about everything I'd done since she'd been gone. She licked my hand and listened.

It was two days later before she'd leave my side. She limped a bit, though we couldn't find anything wrong. But she was home.

My uncle felt bad and offered to buy me another dog to keep Cindy company outside. I knew he and my aunt were having a hard time. They didn't have much money. I wanted to hate him, but I knew it wasn't his fault he was living with us.

One day, I came home and found him sitting with Cindy in his lap and talking to her. I listened a moment and wondered how long he'd been telling her his troubles. I guess he was smarter than I thought. Cindy stared at him, looking into his face as she'd always done with me when I talked to her.

I watched them. I thought that maybe Cindy and I could give him another chance.

"Want to feed her?" I asked.

He nodded. I gave him the box of her favorite treats. He fed her and stroked her small head.

"She's a good listener," he said.

I smiled. I already knew that. I guess if Cindy forgave him, I could too.

~Kathryn Lay

61

Life After Camp

The soul would have no rainbow had the eyes no tears.
~John Vance Cheney

Zach died the summer before I went into seventh grade. He was fifteen and he'd had leukemia for a while. He lost all the hair on his head, but his eyelashes grew longer and longer until they needed to be untangled.

We were at camp when it happened. It was my fourth year of camp, but only my first year with the middle-school age group—one magical week of overnight camp in the woods of western Maryland. We were the smallest group on record—fifteen kids, five counselors.

Jeannie got a letter from her mom midway through the week. She read it to us from her top bunk. Zach was feeling better this week. Her mom was hopeful. Couldn't wait for Jeannie to come home and see her brother.

Jeannie smiled, relieved, and we were all relieved with her. She threw herself into the rest of the camp activities with abandon, the weight of her brother's illness temporarily lifted.

On Thursday, Jeannie's uncle showed up. It was hard to hide him; with only fifteen campers we were almost always in one big group. Jeannie disappeared with him for a while. The rest of us spoke in whispers, feeling the change in the air. Finally, the camp director called us all together. We stood in a circle, arms around each other, a whole-camp hug.

"Jeannie's brother Zach passed away this morning," the director told us. We huddled closer together, blinking. "I know everyone is upset," she continued as we fought back tears. "But right now Jeannie needs us to be strong for her."

Jeannie showed up in time for dinner. We sat about awkwardly, offering hugs, trying to think of the right thing to say. Most of us had never had someone close to us die—maybe the odd great-grandparent, but never an immediate family member. We struggled to be supportive. We waited to find out when she'd be leaving camp for the funeral.

But Jeannie was stronger than any of us had imagined. She cried, and she let us cry with her. She told us that Zach was in a better place, no longer suffering. He didn't need doctors and nurses and eyelash untanglers anymore. She had made her peace with his leukemia, and with his inevitably early death, some time ago. And she did not want to remember him as the shell that he had become in his illness. She wanted to remember him as her mischievous older brother, who loved life. She wanted to remember him at one of his favorite places—at camp.

Her uncle drove home alone that day. Jeannie called her mother, who agreed that the best way to honor Zach was to honor him from a place full of life, surrounded by a loving group of camp friends. And for the rest of our time at camp, we honored Zach with life. We sang his favorite camp songs, made s'mores, and told stories and bad jokes. We listened to the sounds of the forest, got carried away with laughter, and danced late into the night around the fire.

At closing circle on Saturday, Jeannie spoke about how she felt closer to Zach at camp, with us, than she did anywhere else. We cried again—for Zach and how unfair it was that he was gone, for Jeannie and her strength, and for the end of our week together.

Finally, we all stepped out from the circle, campers and counselors. We walked down the hill to the Big Meadow, where our parents hugged us and hauled our bags into the trunks of their cars. Like every other year at the end of camp, we brought home dirt and daddy-long-legs, friendship bracelets and promises to write. But that year we also took home the resolve to live. We went back out into the world to honor ourselves and everyone else in our lives with life.

~Amy January

Taking Care of Family

> *Unless someone like you cares a whole awful lot,*
> *nothing is going to get better. It's not.*
> ~Dr. Seuss

"Drienie! Miemie! Lourens!" Mom's voice cut through the lazy Sunday afternoon. "I want you to quickly go and take your baths and then dress nicely! We're going to visit your cousins in Ellis Park."

At the first sound of Mom's voice we did not move. Sunday afternoons were easygoing and free of work and responsibilities—but when we heard the last part of the sentence, after all the instructions, we moved fast! We did not see the Ellis Park cousins as much as we saw the rest of our cousins who lived in our neighborhood. The Ellis Park cousins lived an hour away on the other side of Johannesburg—the "not so nice" part of town—and we were eager to see them.

On our way to Ellis Park we stopped at a food shop and Mom bought enough food for dinner for ten people, plus a lot more. We did this every time we went to visit these cousins. I often wondered about the food that we took with us when we went to visit our family in Ellis Park. Our visits were never planned ahead and my aunt did not know we were coming. They could not afford a telephone. How did my mother know they had not already eaten? But every time we arrived there Mom was greeted by my aunt's grateful smile.

As we entered Ellis Park, my sister, my brother and I observed the world slowly passing by our car windows. Even though we'd been there before, it still amazed us. Poorly dressed, dirty children played outside on overgrown sidewalks and messy front yards that were strewn with broken bicycles, toys and other junk. On some of the front verandahs, men wearing dirty shirts with unshaven faces sat drinking out of cans. Women sat on front doorsteps with expressionless faces. Some of them followed our progress down the street until we came to a standstill in front of our cousins' house.

As soon as the car stopped we sat up excitedly. We were here! Dad warned us to be careful getting out in the street and when we were all out he locked the car and took some of the food from Mom. We kids ran ahead, eager to see our cousins.

The front gate hung from a hinge. As we ran up the steps we noticed our uncle sitting on a chair on the verandah. He looked at us through half closed eyes, holding a glass of dark liquid in his hand. We stopped in our tracks, not quite sure what to do. We never knew whether we should hug him or just walk past him. He never seemed to recognize us.

Mom came up the stairs behind us and walked toward our uncle. She told us to find our cousins. We did not need a second invitation. We ran to the front door shouting their names. Happy replies greeted us. I looked back and saw Mom hugging our uncle, a soft smile on her lips.

We disappeared into the house with our cousins and discussed what games we were going to play, leaving our parents on the front verandah.

Later we all feasted on the wonderful meal Mom provided. Our uncle did not join us for dinner. I gathered he was still sitting on the front verandah.

Our aunt filled a plate of food and put it in the fridge. "He'll eat later," she said softly.

We ate and laughed and enjoyed one another's company. Mom and our aunt cleaned up and called us to come and get our candy. We disappeared again with the special treats, leaving our parents to have a cup of coffee at the kitchen table.

Mom explained to us once that her brother had an illness called alcoholism and that he couldn't help himself. But, we knew that our parents did not approve of our uncle's ways even though they loved him. I also knew that because of my uncle's illness, my cousins lived in a poor part of the city and because of my uncle my aunt had to struggle to make ends meet.

I always had a feeling of the utmost thankfulness when we were hanging out the windows waving to our cousins as we left. I was thankful for my father who did not have an illness and thankful for a mother who shared what we had with our aunt and cousins.

I learned early in life that family was family—whatever their shortcomings, whatever their problems, we were bound together by blood and love that surpassed all else. Our parents showed us how important family was. They showed us by always being there for family whenever they were in need.

Many years later our uncle stopped drinking. He told his family how devastated he was to think about all the years he missed in which he could have had a normal, happy life with his children and his wife. We all could not believe the transformation that took place. Our uncle was a completely different person with a great sense of humor. My aunt was also a different person and seemed so much happier. For the first time they lived in a lovely home and went away on fishing trips and enjoyed each other's company.

~Drienie Hattingh

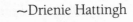

Think Positive
for Kids

Making Real Friends

True Friendship

My best friend is the one who brings out the best in me.
~Henry Ford

"Stinky Ricky," the school kids chanted on the playground, loud enough for him, but not loud enough for the teachers to hear. Ricky stood and fidgeted outside the group, waiting to be invited into a game, but the invitation never came. So eager he was to join in the fun that he kept his hand raised long after the teams had been chosen. He eventually moved to the sideline for the duration of the game, but he still clapped or jumped up and down whenever a kid scored a point, showing his good sportsmanship. Maybe they'd let him play tomorrow, I thought.

When the class bell rang and the kids scurried inside, giggling and playfully shoving one another, I watched as Ricky stooped and picked up a stray marble, holding it up to the sunlight, smiling at his newfound treasure before sliding it into his pocket.

Once inside the classroom, things didn't improve much for Ricky. Kids scooted their desks as far away from his as possible without being too obvious to the teacher. "Ricky has lice," a girl whispered. "It smells like he peed his pants," another said. A boy's foot jutted out from underneath his desk when Ricky walked by to sharpen his pencil, causing him to stumble. The class erupted in laughter.

"What's so funny?" our teacher asked, turning away from the chalkboard to find Ricky standing.

"Nothing," Ricky blurted, flustered.

"So you think you're the class clown, Ricky?" she asked, which led to more laughter.

"No, ma'am," Ricky said before slipping back into his seat.

Why didn't the teacher see what was happening? I stayed after class with plans to come to Ricky's rescue, but I chickened out. So I started to secretly offer him support: a smile when I passed him in the hallway, a nod when he returned from attempting a math problem at the chalkboard, a whispered "hi" before class. After school, when riding my bike past his rundown house, I waved to him, and he waved back with enthusiasm.

But then something awful happened. Ricky started to follow me around school. He thought we could be friends. Didn't he know that I wanted to be nice, but not the kind of nice that would lead to me being teased like him? I had to fix the problem before my classmates noticed, so I started to ignore Ricky like they did. He did smell, after all, and he wore the same clothes each day. His glasses were scratched and lopsided on his dirty face. He had trouble reading out loud and failed most of his tests. It wasn't his fault that he was poor and had difficulty learning, and I felt sorry for him, but we couldn't be friends. No way. We had nothing in common, I told myself. But I suspected that might not be true.

Each day in the cafeteria, Ricky ate alone. While he sat and picked the crust off his bologna sandwich, we shuffled past with our hot lunch trays. A boy walked by and swooped up Ricky's bag of potato chips and a game of keep-away followed until tears left a white streak down Ricky's dirt-stained cheeks.

"Cry baby," a boy called out before crushing the chips and tossing the bag back to him.

I wondered if Ricky cried because it was the only meal he would get that day.

Surprisingly, Ricky once found the courage to sit with some boys at a different lunch table. But once he sat down, all the kids moved to another table and left Ricky alone once again. My heart ached for him at that moment, and I felt guilty for not joining him out of fear of being shunned.

The next day, after getting my lunch tray, I tried to walk past Ricky to follow my friends to our usual table, but my feet wouldn't budge. My moment of truth had arrived. I stood before Ricky, and we made eye contact before I slid onto the bench. "Hi," I said, and he smiled.

"What is she doing?" I heard one of my friends ask another.

"Cathi, come on," a friend called.

I ignored their calls and ate lunch with Ricky that day. We ate in silence but kept each other company nonetheless. The next day, I endured taunts from some of the kids: "Cathi and Ricky sitting in a tree," and "Cathi loves Stinky Ricky." But I stood firm in my decision to befriend Ricky, knowing I couldn't let him down again. Soon, the teasing stopped when I refused to give in to peer pressure.

Ricky and I began talking at the lunch table, at recess, and after school. My girlfriends never understood my loyalty to Ricky, but they didn't disown me either. They just thought it odd. They didn't know that Ricky and I were more alike than we were different.

I could never tell my girlfriends that the harsh treatment Ricky received at school was how I was treated at home. Since I couldn't tell them the truth, perhaps they weren't really good friends after all. But Ricky knew we led similar lives, just in different places; he went home to escape school, and I went to school to escape home. Maybe the reason I could extend myself to him was my understanding of those who were mistreated. Over the next few years, Ricky and I shared our fears and our disappointments, and our hopes and our dreams. But most of all, we shared a true friendship.

~Cathi LaMarche

The Pops

When you choose your friends, don't be short-changed by choosing personality over character.
~W. Somerset Maugham

The entire mood of the room changed. It was them. We all watched in awe as they took their seats at the lunch table across the room. The "Pops" had arrived. Like every other day, I nibbled on my chicken nuggets while conversations buzzed around me. Every so often, I would look at the other table. The "Pops," the name we had given the "popular" girls in our grade, would sit in their big group talking and giggling. Each one of the Pops was like a celebrity. They were just so cool and amazing. I made a decision at lunch that day. I would become one of the Pops.

My campaign took a lot of strategizing. What clothes would I wear? What things should I say? How should I do my hair? I realized that none of the Pops wore glasses, so I stopped wearing glasses when I was in the same room as one of the Pops. I only wore clothes that I felt the Pops would like — the rest of my clothes were banished to the back of my closet.

Weeks passed and I was having no luck. None of the Pops even noticed me! I felt like my efforts were pointless. I was never going to sit at the popular table! But then I got my chance! During music class, we were put into groups and Maggie, one of the Pops, was in mine. Somehow, we got into an argument about who would be doing what, and I was furious at her. A few hours later, it hit me. I would apologize to Maggie and invite her to eat lunch with my friends.

And that's just what I did. I went right up to Maggie and apologized about the argument in music class. When I invited her over to our table, she surprised me by saying, "Jess, why don't you come eat lunch at our table?" I felt like I had just won the lottery! This was the most unbelievable thing to ever happen in my whole life! I was going to eat lunch at the popular table!

After waiting in anticipation for an hour, lunch finally came. I grabbed a seat next to Maggie while the other girls arrived. This was going to be so awesome! I wondered what we would talk about? Maybe they'd even invite me back! All the Pops came and sat. And I realized that being at the popular table wasn't all it was cracked up to be.

The rest of the girls didn't say much to me. All of them talked about a whole bunch of stupid things, and were making loud, obnoxious noises nearly the entire time. I kept looking over at my friends at the other table, all having a good time as usual. And here I was with the Pops, the most spectacular of people, and I was miserable! These girls were just plain mean and annoying.

The next day, I put on my glasses and one of my "un-popular" looking shirts. When lunch came, I strode right over to my regular table with my friends. After I sat, I looked over to the popular table, where all the Pops sat acting dumb and being irritating. A huge smile came across my face. It was so nice to be back at my own table instead of with them! What even makes them popular anyway? I realized that my table, with my friends, was the real popular table.

~Jess Forte

Playing Chicken

For attractive lips, speak words of kindness.
~Audrey Hepburn

When I was in grade school I had one really great friend. We lived on the same street and liked to do the same things: bike ride, roller skate and build forts in the empty treed lots around our house.

Monica was a tall girl who had moved from the United States to our little patch of Vancouver Island, Canada. This made her a star in my eyes. Minnesota sounded so foreign, a place where magical things happened.

We became fast friends and were inseparable most of the time, almost as though we were joined at the hip. When we weren't actually together we would be on the phone talking about someone or making plans for this or that. One day in grade four, the strength of our friendship was tested.

As luck had it, that year we were put into two separate classes, something that neither of us was pleased about. We even tried pleading with our parents about the situation but it turned out that our parents were for the separation, saying that it would make us focus on schoolwork more.

I was stuck in a classroom with some of the more "popular girls." They had the best and latest clothes, toys and went on big vacations. I can remember being so jealous of them sometimes, and it would only make me more lonesome for Monica. I tried to be nice to them, thinking perhaps that once I got to know them they would not be as bad as I imagined, but they just looked down their noses at me. I knew most of them were brought up in the same neighborhood and that would have been another reason why their bond was so strong, but it didn't take the sting out of the rejection.

Which is why what happened on the schoolyard took me so off guard.

Monica and I were down on the bottom playground where a balancing beam stood two and a half feet from the ground. We liked to play a game called Chicken on the beam. We would each walk in from one end, meet in the middle, and see who could knock her opponent off the beam with her arms. We were having a great time trying to knock each other off when we heard "Well if it isn't Laurel and Hardy." Jennifer, the most popular girl in the school, always referred to us like this. I had to ask my dad who they were and he told me about the classical comedians of the black and white era of American television. I looked them up. They were two men who dressed up in suits and did slapstick comedy. One was tall and lean—that was in reference to Monica, and the other was short and stout—in reference to me. The names at first didn't bother me at all because I didn't understand the insult, but once I knew who they were and watched some of their acts I got what Jennifer was laughing about.

Monica and I stopped our mock "Chicken Fight" and hopped down. "What do you want, Jennifer?" I asked, knowing full well she hated being called by her full name. She came over to me and smiled; her friends circled and crowded around.

"We've noticed you," she said, pointing at me. "We want you to join our group. There is a sleepover this weekend at Stacey's house and you are invited, but only if you give up your friendship with Laverne here." She finished pointing at Monica.

I started to get really angry by this point; she had just insulted us again about our height differences and insinuated that Monica was somehow flawed. Why would she think I would give up my best friend for her and her band of ridiculous girls that clung to her every word? I wanted a friend of equal footing, not some girl who wanted to be the queen reigning over her subjects.

I looked at Monica and tears were welling up in her eyes; she had this look on her face that said I should do it and she would not be mad. Monica turned to leave. I looked at Jennifer who, by now, had a victorious grin.

"Wait!" I called out to Monica. "Where are you going?"

"What do you mean? You can't be friends with me if you want to be friends with them."

"Who says I want to be friends with them?" My smile grew larger as I saw the shocked expressions on Monica's face and on the faces of the other girls.

"I would not take a thousand of them over our friendship. They have no idea what true friendship is; if they did they would never have asked the question," I told Monica. The smile was restored on her face.

I went over to where Jennifer was standing. "You have made me realize something. You aren't happy. You might look happy on the outside when others are watching you, but that is only so they won't know how lonesome you truly are. There is nothing like a good friend to turn to when things get tough, or when you have something great to celebrate. Hopefully sometime soon you will find this out."

Then Monica and I left them standing there, silent, and headed back to class. The popular girls had played Chicken, and they had lost.

~Tracie Skarbo

The Case of the Vanishing Sunglasses

Character is much easier kept than recovered.
~Thomas Paine

My eyes scanned our living room, a place where, in just a few short minutes, my best buddies would convene, with sleeping bags and nail polish in tow. I then peeked around the corner at my mother in the kitchen, putting the finishing touches on my fluorescent-colored cupcakes. The anticipation within my gut had reached a peak, and I couldn't help but let out a little squeal of excitement and perform a brief happy dance. When you're a fifth-grader, the only thing better than celebrating your birthday is celebrating your birthday with friends at a slumber party: eating cake, wearing PJs, and listening to all the music your ears can handle.

Then, the flash of headlights in the driveway was followed shortly by the chime of the doorbell. It was time!

My best friend Jaime was the first to arrive, and then came Dawn, Tamika, and Angie. As we waited for Nicole, we killed time by admiring Angie's new sunglasses. Angie was the first in our clique to score a pair of cool sunglasses from her parents. We ambled to the bathroom to ooh and ah over them as if they were encrusted with Harry Winston diamonds. I was in the midst of trying them on—while cocking my head to one side and pursing my lips in front of the mirror, I might add—when my mom interrupted us to announce Nicole's arrival. As a welcome gesture, I removed the sunglasses, placed them on the bridge of Nicole's nose, and gave her a heartfelt hug. We then meandered to the basement for a board game and karaoke marathon.

That was the last time we each recalled seeing Angie's sunglasses.

Fast-forward to the next morning when all of my friends, in a sleep-deprived haze, scrambled to organize their belongings before their parents picked them up.

"I can't find my sunglasses," Angie said as she rooted through her duffel bag. The panic in her voice was palpable. "I know I put them in here...." What ensued was a frantic search followed by finger-pointing and tears. I summoned my mom for an intervention.

"Calm down, girls," she said. "Let's retrace our steps."

My mother's advice led us all to the bathroom, and we all proceeded to search the cramped quarters, bumping into each other in the process. The investigation was going nowhere, and things really took a downturn when Angie unabashedly turned on Nicole.

"You took them," Angie accused. Nicole's response to Angie's words was visceral: her eyes welled with tears and her shoulders bowed under the weight of her friend's accusation.

"I didn't," Nicole said softly, shaking her head in protest. Although her reply was barely audible, her eyes spoke volumes. "I put them by the sink! I didn't steal them, Angie, I swear."

The futile search for the sunglasses continued until parents arrived to retrieve their daughters. Angie was the first to leave. She gave each of us a hug goodbye—everyone except Nicole. "I know you stole them, Nicole. And I won't forgive you for it," Angie declared. Angie's harsh words hung over us like a cloud and served as a warning to us all: Take Angie's side or else. The battle lines had been drawn.

But I was torn. Not because I considered both of them friends, but because I felt in my bones that Nicole was telling the truth. I had no way of proving it and I had no idea where the sunglasses were. I only knew Nicole to be a good friend and an honest person. The next morning at school, I told Angie that I would remain her friend—but that I was standing by Nicole, too. Predictably, Angie didn't take kindly to the news. By sticking my neck out for Nicole, I had become an outcast.

After a week or so of being a social pariah, there was still no sign of the sunglasses. I was brushing my teeth before bed when something prompted me to look behind the bathroom sink, between the wood planks that concealed the pipes. This was an area that, in our haste, would have easily been overlooked during our initial search. I peered down… and there they were. Although we had all seen Nicole put the sunglasses on, no one saw her take them off and place them near the sink. I nearly choked on my toothbrush I was so overjoyed! But my knee-jerk relief was immediately squashed by the realization that Angie would now think I took her sunglasses. All I could do was hope that everyone would believe me. I was somewhat pacified, however, that Nicole would be vindicated.

I couldn't see how things could go wrong.

And, thankfully, they didn't. The next day, I revealed everything to Angie and Nicole. As I surmised, Nicole was thankful that the ordeal had finally come to an end, but she said she was even happier about the fact that I had stood by her.

It was Angie's response that had thrown me for a loop: She said that, after truly thinking about the situation, I was a good friend for standing by Nicole when she had been too quick to write her off. She also said that she was sorry that her actions had put a damper on my birthday party.

All was forgiven, and in a few days' time, we were back to normal and looking forward to the next slumber party; it was Dawn's turn. I remember her telling me how excited she was to host the gang at her house, and how she wanted her party to be just like mine.

~Courtney Conover

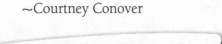

My Annoying Best Friend

Support your friends—even in their mistakes. But be clear, however,
that it is the friend and not the mistake you are supporting.
~Hugh Prather

The summer before seventh grade our family moved and I said goodbye to everything that was familiar. For my parents it was a good thing because it meant owning a home for the first time. I'll admit it was exciting and the house was brand new. But it also meant that I'd have to change schools and that put some butterflies in my stomach.

I tried not to think about the new school too much. Summer was vacation time and I had other things on my mind, like the boys in the neighborhood and how I was going to decorate my new bedroom. But as August wore on a nagging began in the back of my head. How big was this school and where would I fit with all the other kids? I wouldn't know a single person and I'd have to make my way in and out of many classes.

Mom drove me to the first day of school. I tried to put up a brave front and didn't want anyone to see her drop me off. Kids jammed the school grounds and long lists of names with room numbers were posted for homerooms. I discovered I had to get on a bus to another campus. Because the school was new and not completed there were a few classes that had to be taken at the old high school. I listened hard to the kids around me and followed them onto the bus. That's when I met Barbara. She sat next to me and looked almost as lost as I felt. We struck up a nervous conversation and soon learned we were in the same English and Social Studies class. Then I found out she lived only a few blocks from me and my hopes rose that she would be a new friend.

As I got to know Barbara some of the things she did began to annoy me. Yes, she was funny and we had a lot in common. She'd just moved and needed a friend, too. But she was very critical of others and sometimes of me. She made fun of my bushy, curly hair, my big glasses, and the clothes I wore. But I needed her to be my friend and it seemed as though the things we had in common outweighed the annoyances.

I soon realized I wasn't the only one who noticed Barbara's mean side. The girls in the "popular" crowd had also been exposed to her sharp tongue. One day, right after class was dismissed, one of the girls approached me while I gathered my books.

"Some of us were talking and we really like you," she said. "The only way you can hang out with us, though, is if you dump Barbara."

I don't know what stunned me more, being asked to join the popular crowd or that someone would actually ask me to dump my best friend. I stammered, "Oh, well, I don't know." Then I smiled and headed for the bus.

I didn't breathe a word to Barbara about what had just happened, but I wondered about our friendship. Were those girls only trying to make trouble between the two of us? Would they watch me dump Barbara and then dump me for laughs? I didn't know what to do.

That night I thought about what Barbara meant to me. We'd shared jokes, stayed at each other's homes for overnights, swapped sandwiches at lunch and so much more. She had her nasty days just like the rest of us. Once, she was so furious with our math teacher, she stormed out of class and yelled, "I hate his sweetest guts!" I was shocked, but I laughed, too.

I didn't sleep so well that night and secretly hoped the girl who'd told me to dump Barbara would have forgotten about it the next day. But she hadn't. When class let out she slithered up to me again.

"Well, are you going to dump her?"

From the corner of my eye I spotted two of the other girls from the group. They were watching me and giggling. I wondered if I was cool enough for them. And then something happened. I got angry. I didn't like being bullied like this. I didn't want to make the choice they were forcing me to make. So I tossed my head and said, "I don't think so. I like Barbara and we're good friends." Then I gathered my books and flounced away, shaking like a leaf. It was hard to say "no" to the popular crowd. But what a big relief!

Even though Barbara still annoyed me at times, I knew I'd done the right thing. I'd made my own decision about a girl who had befriended me when I badly needed a friend. Sure, she had her quirks like everybody else. So what? When she moved the following year I missed her friendship terribly. But what I kept has never left me, my self-respect.

~Susan Sundwall

A Great School Year

The most I can do for my friend is simply be his friend.
~Henry David Thoreau

I t was November of fifth grade. Well into the new school year, and here I was, starting a new school… again. Being the new girl was hard. It never got easier. Where was my class? Where was the cafeteria? Where was the library? Where were my friends? I didn't have any. At least not yet.

On my first day, my teacher, Mrs. McKinley, stood me up in front of the class and introduced me. I felt so embarrassed. I looked around at all the faces and thought about how I would get to be friends with all these kids. I stood there, not listening to what Mrs. McKinley was saying, but rather, daydreaming about having friends over after school for snacks and homework. Thinking about Saturday trips to the roller rink. Wishing for slumber parties with my new friends.

The first week of school was hard. Really hard. I sat by myself in the cafeteria. I got lost looking for the library. I was late to class. I didn't really like my new school. It was hard adjusting. Maybe this was not going to be a good school year.

The second week got a little easier. I found the library and made it to class on time. But at recess and lunch, I still sat by myself. I went home and explained to my parents that I didn't want to go back to school because I didn't have any friends and it was not going to be a good school year. "It's all right," they assured me. "You will have friends and you will have a good school year."

The third week, a miracle happened. All of us students were sitting at our desks in the morning, waiting for Mrs. McKinley. She hurried into the room a couple of minutes late… with another new student! A girl by the name of Holli.

Being a latecomer like me, Holli was seated in the back of the class at the desk next to mine. She sat down and barely made eye contact with me. She looked lonely. When she finally looked my way, I gave her a big smile. She sheepishly smiled back. I decided at that moment that Holli and I would become friends.

As soon as the bell rang for recess, I asked her if she wanted me to show her around. I explained that I was new to school also, and we should be friends. She agreed. We hung out at recess. I showed her where the library was. I showed her where the cafeteria was and where the line started. We ate lunch together on her first day.

As we sat at lunch we found out we had a lot in common. We both moved around a lot. We both liked scratch and sniff stickers. We both liked pink nail polish. We didn't like homework. We preferred chocolate milk over plain. We talked the entire lunch period without a break. Before we knew it, the bell rang and it was time to head back to class. We walked together. I went home that day and told my parents I'd finally made a friend.

By Christmas time, Holli and I were inseparable. We called each other almost every night. Our parents took us up to Montrose Avenue to go sticker and nail polish shopping. We occasionally went to each other's houses after school for snacks and homework. We went to the roller rink. All of my hopes for the school year had come true!

During one of the last weeks of school, I had a slumber party at my house with Holli and a few other girls. By now, Holli and I had made other friends, too, but we were each other's best friend.

We had a fun night. We listened to music, made popcorn and chocolate pudding. We danced and painted our nails. As the night was ending, and we were all lying on the living room floor in our sleeping bags, I thought to myself how lucky I was to have friends. I whispered over to Holli, "Are you still awake?"

"Yes," she said.

"I'm glad you're my best friend," I said.

"Me too," she said.

What a great school year this had turned out to be, all because I smiled at the new girl.

~Crescent LoMonaco

Chosen Last

Confidence comes from discipline and training.
~Robert Kiyosaki

Mrs. Martin looked up from the spelling tests she was grading. "Jeff and Kevin will serve as captains. Come to the front of the room, boys, and choose your teams."

Choose your teams. I hated those words. My sixth grade class at Cedar Hill Elementary played softball every day at recess. Every single lousy day.

The captains chose the athletic boys, then the athletic girls, and then the not-so-athletic boys. By the time they got to my friend Sandra and me, we were often the only ones left, probably because she and I always ran to the outfield and dodged any balls hit in our direction. When a ball did come our way, our teammates would scream, "Throw it to second base!"

I'd run after the ball and throw it with all my strength, but it never went far enough. Most of the time, the ball didn't even go in the right direction. My captain would yank off his cap and throw it to the ground.

I thought nothing was worse than being chosen last until a few days later, when Mrs. Martin made a startling announcement before recess: "Sandra and Judy will serve as captains. Come to the front of the room, girls, and choose your teams."

The toss of a coin gave Sandra first choice. "I pick Arlene."

No one made a sound. Every student sat still, staring at Sandra.

Why would my friend embarrass me like that? I knew she wanted me on her team, but she should have chosen the good players first. I walked to the front of the room, looking at the floor the whole way.

As soon as Judy chose Jeff for her team, Kevin and Joe moved to the edges of their seats. Jeff, Kevin, and Joe were the best ball players in our class.

Sandra said, "I choose Elaine." A few of the boys laughed.

Judy pointed to Kevin.

I whispered to Sandra, "Choose a boy."

When she called Joe's name, he threw his glove on the floor. The teacher stepped from behind her desk. "Joe, take your place with your teammates."

Our team was slaughtered.

After school, I walked up the road toward my house. An April breeze blew my hair as I kicked at the gravel. When I walked into our front yard, my mother scooted over so I could sit beside her on the white swing. She offered me a sip of her sweet tea and listened as I told her about my day.

When I finished my story, Mama didn't say anything. I knew she was thinking it over. She finally said, "You need to ask Leonard to teach you to play ball."

My brother, Leonard, was my hero. Fifteen years older than me, he had become like a father to me since the death of our dad the previous year.

"You'll be twelve next week," my mom said. "How about a bat, ball, and glove for your birthday?"

"You really think Leonard could teach me to play?"

"We've got all summer to find out."

On Saturday morning we drove to town. Mama and I listened as the salesman explained how to break in a new glove.

Leonard, Wanda, and their three sons visited on Saturday afternoons to help Mama with the heavy chores. During part of that time, my brother began to train me to be a ballplayer. If his construction work brought him nearby during the week, he ate a quick sandwich and spent the rest of his lunch hour working with me. Sometimes he showed up before he went to work. Mama would shake me awake and whisper for me to get my ball and glove.

Did I ever think about giving up? Yes, I did. I couldn't throw the ball more than ten feet and it still didn't go where I aimed it. Leonard encouraged me, though. "You used to dodge the ball when I hit it to you, but now you always try to catch it." By the end of June, I saw for myself I could throw a lot better.

When Leonard's red truck pulled into the driveway one Saturday morning, Mama said, "He isn't here to play, Arlene. We're going to build us a ballfield!"

The house sat toward the front of our two acres, so there was plenty of room. My brother mowed the grass and marked off an area. I picked up sticks while he dragged a bag of sand around the four sides of the diamond. When we filled a wheelbarrow with dirt to build up the pitcher's mound, Leonard's sons (ages five, four, and three) climbed on for a ride. My dog didn't understand what was going on, but he pranced around to show he was in favor of it. I don't know when I've worked as hard, gotten as dirty, or laughed as much as I did that day.

We played softball every Saturday afternoon with everyone we could round up. My mom was amazing. She couldn't run fast, but she could sure hit and catch. And, boy, could she ever pitch. She fired the ball across the plate better than Leonard.

When the calendar on the kitchen wall showed it was time to go back to school, I stuck my ball glove in a brown paper sack and took it to school with me. The teacher selected Jeff and Joe as captains for our first softball game. Jeff called my name close to last. I reached under my desk and pulled out my glove.

"Where did you get that?" Sandra asked. I pretended not to hear and lined up behind my captain.

I didn't follow Sandra to left field. Leonard had told me to stand a few yards behind the person playing shortstop.

Joe stepped to the plate and sent the ball over a faraway fence. That was always an automatic home run. Kevin picked up the bat next. He missed the first pitch and then tipped the second one out-of-bounds. The third time, he connected. The white round blur whizzed past the shortstop, just out of his reach, and right at me.

A voice inside me screamed, "Dodge that ball! Get out in left field where you belong!" I didn't listen. I positioned my glove. Smack! I caught the ball!

Someone yelled, "Throw it to first!"

I hurled the ball through the air. It went in the right direction and made it all the way to the first baseman. Jeff waved his cap above his head and hollered, "Double play!"

The next day brought another terrific moment. Kevin and Brent were captains. Kevin chose Jeff, Brent chose Joe, and then Kevin said, "I choose Arlene."

I was chosen third. That's right, third.

When I think about those long ago days, I smile at the memories of catching the ball and of being chosen third. My all-time favorite memories, though, will always be those softball games in my backyard.

~Arlene Ledbetter

The Nice Popular Girl

It's nice to be important, but it's more important to be nice.
~Author Unknown

My closest friend when I was little was Priscilla. She and I were friends through all of elementary school. Priscilla was always the most popular girl in our grade, not just our class, but in our whole grade. I remember one time when I bought a new pair of shoes, which she liked, and she went out and bought the same ones. Mine were black, but she said they were out of black in her size so she bought them in navy blue. All the other girls in our class saw her shoes and copied them, and within the next couple of weeks most of the girls in our sixth grade class were wearing those shoes, in navy blue. I was the only one with black ones. I remember thinking how bizarre it was that everyone copied her shoes, right down to the color.

I remember watching Priscilla in the lunch line too. We had a lot of choices in the cafeteria, and no one knew what was cool. Were we too cool to drink milk? Which were the right foods to choose? We were all so insecure. Priscilla just did what she wanted to do. One day I was in the line behind her and another girl who was trying to become Priscilla's best friend, replacing me, or at least I thought so. That girl didn't have milk on her tray but then she saw Priscilla take milk, so she put her juice back and took milk instead. Then Priscilla changed her mind and put the milk back. So the other girl put her milk back too. I was disgusted by this and thought it was ridiculous to copy someone to that extent.

Priscilla was popular with the boys too. We all had crushes on the same boys but they always ended up with Priscilla. Since we were young, that just meant that they officially "liked" her and talked to her at school. This was before texting, and boys didn't call girls on the phone at that age, as that would have been terrifying. But in school, these boys were officially with Priscilla. And she seemed completely comfortable talking to them, not nervous at all. When I "went steady" with a boy in seventh grade I was so embarrassed I could barely speak to him.

I know that the "popular" girls are often the mean ones too, but this was not the case with Priscilla. She was nice to everyone. There was a small group of semi-popular and very mean girls, but they were separate from Priscilla and me and our closest friends.

It was only decades later, when I found Priscilla 2,000 miles away by searching for her on the Internet, that I learned something shocking to me. Priscilla had no idea she was popular. She didn't know that the other girls copied her; she didn't know that her "boyfriends" were the boys that all the girls were crushing on. She was clueless, and it turns out she had been very insecure during those years. She was even afraid to talk to those cute boys. It was a real eye opener for me. The most popular girl in the grade was insecure, completely unaware of her influence and status among us.

It just goes to show, you never know what's going on inside someone else's head, even if it seems obvious.

~Amy Newmark

Those Who Mind Don't Matter

Never apologize for showing feeling. When you do so,
you apologize for the truth.
~Benjamin Disraeli

It's hard to be the new kid in school, not knowing anyone, not knowing where to go or who to talk to. You feel lonely and lost, like you don't belong. This is just how my friend felt when he moved here to California from Mexico, and into our school, the Vaughn Next Century Learning Center. Trying to fit in but not stand out, learning a new language and making new friends.

"Everyone listen up! I would like you guys to meet Jose. He is new here at Vaughn and to this state, so be nice and show him around," said Mrs. Espinoza.

No one talked; it was silent. They looked; some stared and whispered to each other. He was wearing loose gray pants and a dirty white polo; his shoes squeaked every time he walked. Everyone would giggle at the sound, but no one would talk to him. I wondered how he felt being here having everyone's eyes on him and being laughed at. I wanted to say hi but was too afraid to be made fun of for talking to "the new kid." Every day he would sit by himself and eat his lunch quietly, not saying a word, just focusing on his food, wishing that school would be over soon. Many of the students would pass by and make rude comments about him. He would just frown and look down at the floor. I wanted to say something but again I was too afraid.

When I got home I talked to my sister about Jose. I told her about him being new and about how the students at school treated him. Then I told her that I wanted to talk to him but was too afraid of what my friends' reactions would be. She said, "If they are true friends they will stick by you no matter what, understand and not judge you, because those who mind don't matter and those who matter don't mind."

The next day I knew exactly what I was going to do. I got my lunch and walked towards Jose with everyone's eyes on me wondering what I was about to do. I sat next to him. He didn't say a word, he just kept eating his food. I decided that I was going to have to start the conversation.

"Hola Jose, me llamo Gloria quires ser mi amigo?" He looked up at me with a huge grin on his face. I couldn't help but smile back. While we talked and ate our food together I realized that he was a very nice guy. We talked about sports, and what we like to do in our free time. We also talked about how different it is living here in California than in Mexico.

As days went on I kept talking to Jose. I noticed that I was losing some friends but some actually came to join us. Jose and I became best friends and still to this day we are best friends. From little kids in fourth grade to young adults in tenth grade, Jose has always been there for me since day one and is still there today. That's why you should never judge someone by the way they look or dress—they could end up changing your whole life.

~Gloria Yaxiri Plancarte

The Real Popular Table

A friend can tell you things you don't want to tell yourself.
~Frances Ward Weller

All I wanted was to sit with them. Jill had the best clothes. She looked like she walked straight out of a store window. Julie wore blush and lip gloss. Brett had the coolest haircut, plus she was already on the varsity field hockey team and we were only in the sixth grade! Crystal had a boyfriend, Aimee was a cheerleader and Shannon could boss people around and they'd do whatever she said. I sure didn't have that kind of power, but then again, I wasn't popular.

Everyone else called them the "popular girls" and at lunch I'd watch them from across the middle school cafeteria and wonder how on earth I could get a seat at their table. I imagined how much fun they had sitting there, the envy of the lunchroom, while I picked at my soggy PB&J at the table near the trash cans. This wasn't how I thought middle school was going to be at all. One day, I'd had the nerve to walk past their table and Shannon and Jill had started making fun of me, saying I smelled. Shannon called me a "scum." That was what the popular girls laughingly called all of the non-popular girls. They thought it was hilarious and it was even funnier when Julie pointed out that she'd seen my sneakers on the clearance rack at Dollar General. It was true though. My family couldn't afford shoes like the popular girls wore.

I had three friends. We knew each other from elementary school and rode the same bus, which was, of course, not the same bus as the popular girls because they all lived in the new, fancy subdivision outside of town. My friends were "scums" too. One of them was super smart, another super shy and the third was just super weird, but she could always make us laugh. They were the ones I sat with at lunch.

"I hate them," I sighed, slumping down into my seat beside my three friends and opening my lunch bag. "The popular girls are so mean."

"Well, we aren't mean!" said my weird friend, and she was right.

I looked towards the popular table. Aimee appeared to be in a fight with Jill, while the other four had ganged up on a nerdy, red-headed boy, who was easily the smartest kid in our grade and maybe even our whole school. He was practically in tears when they got done with him. He took his tray to an empty table in the far corner of the room to eat alone.

That was when it hit me. Why would I even want to be friends with people who were so mean? My friends were far nicer and from the looks of it, we had a lot more fun. None of us fought or made fun of people. We laughed, sang, joked, traded stickers and spent our lunch hour making up hilarious skits to act out and entertain one another.

"Hey," I said gesturing towards the lonely, red-haired boy, "Maybe I should ask him to come eat with us."

"Sure," said my friends.

He sat with us every day after that, which was great because he helped me with my science homework.

From then on, we made a point to invite everyone the popular girls made fun of to eat at our lunch table. Soon our table was filled and we had to add more chairs, all of us willing to scoot in just a little closer to make room for someone else. It may have been a little cramped, but at our table, everyone fit regardless of whether or not they were fat, dressed funny, came from a poor family, didn't shop at the trendy stores, played tuba in band, were obsessed with *Dungeons and Dragons*, or were funny looking. I started to look forward to lunchtime. Middle school was turning out to be a lot of fun after all.

Around Christmas, the popular girls banished Aimee from their group. We never asked why and it didn't matter when she came to our table and meekly asked to sit down. Of course we let her in and she looked relieved. I offered her an Oreo from my lunch bag and she thanked me.

"Wow, it's so nice to be away from them. I used to look at you guys over here and wish I could have as much fun as you," Aimee said.

"No way," I replied in disbelief. "I used to wish I could sit at your table!"

I looked around and realized how silly I had been. Almost twenty kids now sat happily at what was once the "scum" table. We were laughing, sharing, smiling. I glanced back at the popular girls with their perfect outfits and hair. There were only five of them now. They rolled their eyes and wrinkled their noses, pushed their food away. They teased a short girl and mocked a boy who was in Special Ed classes and the whole time they looked completely miserable.

Later, I looked up the word "popular" in the dictionary. It meant to be liked by a lot of people. Hardly anyone liked the popular girls at school. They didn't even seem to like each other or themselves very much. When I looked at my group of friends, which seemed to grow every day, I understood where the true "popular table" was in our middle school cafeteria and knew that I had gotten my wish after all.

~Victoria Fedden

Chapter 8

Think Positive for Kids

Making Good Choices

Badge of Courage

*Stand up to your obstacles and do something about them. You will find that
they haven't half the strength you think they have.*
~Norman Vincent Peale

I was in seventh grade, the first year of junior high, and desperate to "fit in." I tried to dress like the other girls, but it was always a struggle. I had no fashion sense, and that, combined with our budget, left me at a great disadvantage in "looking the part." Already I was seen as kind of a freak because I was in advanced math—eighth-grade advanced math—so that automatically set me apart. I joined the Girl Scouts, looking for some instant camaraderie, something my mother, who was a bit of a social outcast herself, saw as a great opportunity. There were the badges, after all.

The local Girl Scout Troup was small, nine girls, and it was co-run by two mom-leaders: Tina's mom, Mrs. Caspin, and Carla's mom, Mrs. Vilar. They were good friends. How exciting to meet up in a group after school to plan events! Honestly, though, I don't remember much of what we accomplished except for one episode that changed my life, which I'd like to share with you here...

Tina was a very popular girl. I remember she even lived across the street from the school, which I interpreted at the time to somehow mean she was even better off than her fancy clothes would suggest. After all, I had a mile-and-a-half walk to school each day. Tina had a friendly, if not warm, smile. She was skinny, with luxurious, shiny, long brown hair that she put up in combs on either side of her head.

I tried to pin my hair with combs, but it was never as pretty or as perfect as hers. I never could seem to measure up to Tina, so I settled on being her friend.

Carla was another story altogether. She was tall and already had a well-developed figure, which was embarrassing for her in seventh grade. She dwarfed Tina when they stood side by side.

Our annual Girl Scout camping trip was drawing near! It was time to earn those outdoor badges for fire-building, wood-gathering, leaf-collecting, outdoor cooking, even fishing, perhaps! I was excited to go on a girls' trip into the wilderness. I had camped with my family every year, in a large tent, but going off with a group of my peers would be a fantastic new experience for me. We had earned some of our money for this excursion from plant sales. For the rest, my mother had promised me she would foot the bill, so it was with a grateful heart that I turned in her check for the balance. This was going to be such fun!

The Tuesday before our Friday afternoon departure was a day like any other. I went to school, sat in class, and in off moments, pondered how it would be to sleep out under the stars three nights from then. One of the girls in my troop handed me a note during lunch. It said, "Meet us after school on the back stairs." The back stairs let out toward the athletic field and my walk home. "Sure," I thought, smiling. I wondered what was up, without suspicion. I felt included. I felt like I had friends. And for a young girl struggling to find her place in the school's social system, it was like a warm hug.

When the last bell rang, I went to my locker to organize myself for the walk home, and Sue, one of the other scouts, passed me, saying, "You going to the stairs?"

"Yep," I answered cheerfully. "See you there." I hurried to join my new friends. Three minutes later I opened the fire door onto a very strange scene. Tina was down half a flight of stairs with some of the girls from my troop. She was facing Carla, who shared the landing, on the other side.

"Oh, good, Sandy, you're here. So, Sandy… maybe you can tell Carla what we've decided, please."

I was completely baffled. What was Tina talking about? "I, uhm, I don't really know…" I stuttered. This was not at all what I expected, and furthermore, it felt awful. There was an expectation, or the scent of victimization, in the air. Tina glared at me for a moment. I must've looked pathetic because she quickly turned away and faced Carla again, who looked like a deer caught in headlights. "What we've decided, Carla, all of us, really…" she gestured (ironically) with wide open arms, "is that none of us want to share a tent with you this weekend." Her face held a smug smile.

There was a brief silence before Carla and I both said, "What?"

"It's not personal, really, Carla. It's just, well, we just really don't want you sleeping in our tents."

"I didn't…" I began, but it was too late. I was complicit, even though I wasn't. I wasn't there for Carla, because Tina had invited me—it was guilt by association. The fact was, I hadn't given any thought to who was sharing a tent with whom, but we had an odd number of girls, and only two-person tents, and if I'd had a preference, well, Carla wouldn't have been my first choice either, that's for sure. She was simply so different, and she didn't represent what I was trying to fit in with.

Carla turned on her heel and left with some dignity, simply because she avoided crumpling into a sobbing heap, as I'm certain I would have done. She was crying, but composed.

I picked up my books and left, muttering, "That was a rotten thing to do," though I'm not convinced I wasn't talking about what they'd done to me, or even what I'd ended up doing, remaining so quiet. The whole thing turned my stomach.

When I got home, I told my mother about it. She made some calls. Lectures were made, apologies were given, and fellow scouts looked fiercely contrite and repentant. I was not required to apologize, because it hadn't come from me, but I was still mortified by my role in it all. I'd been ambushed, just like Carla, but I had escaped mostly unscathed. Carla held her head high, but the damage was done, right? There was no coming back from that for her.

It turned out that Carla couldn't go on our camping trip, anyway, because her dad was taking her away for the weekend. I knew the truth. They had to find a way for her to save face, and who could blame them? I didn't want to go, either, but Mom had already paid, so I went and made the best of it. Carla's Mom, Mrs. Vilar, also came along, though I don't imagine it was fun for her, knowing the girls' meanness. She was nice to me, and I was grateful for that.

It was an uneventful weekend, but I had worked hard to do many of the activities our troop leaders had prescribed. When we were packed up and ready to go, Mrs. Caspin held a badge ceremony, and awarded me (probably the other girls, too, but I didn't pay attention to that) a ridiculous number of badges for things that seemed, at that point, so petty and meaningless. I even got a sewing badge, and I thought, "But I didn't sew anything!" I still had that bad taste in my mouth, for the embarrassment Tina had subjected Carla to, and my own shame at my involvement in the whole mess.

I made a decision on the beautiful drive home in a quiet car of girls. I resigned from the Girl Scouts after that camping trip. None of the badges I earned that weekend meant anything to me. Instead, the lesson I had learned was that *wanting* something doesn't automatically make it *good*. The friendships I had coveted were built on treacherous sand. After all, if Tina could be so very cruel to her mother's friend's daughter, the other co-scout leader's little girl (and put me in that uncomfortable position with no warning), what kind of friend would she be to me? I realized I just didn't need to "fit in" with the likes of those girls—nor did I want to.

I gave myself the Badge of Courage to walk away from them.

~Sam (Sandy) Sorbo

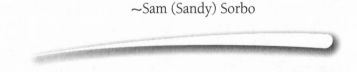

74

Guilty Nightmares

The fears you don't face control you. The fears you face, you move beyond.
~Dr. Wayne Dyer

When I was ten, I read all sorts of books. I liked funny books, serious books, books about a babysitting club, and even scary books. My mom paid attention to what I was reading, and while she let me read scary children's books, I wasn't allowed to read scary adult books. Of course, that made me very curious. Why wasn't I allowed to read those scary adult books? Were they too scary? Would they give me bad dreams? What were they about? When our babysitter took my little brother and me to the library, I realized that I could check out whatever books I wanted and my mother would never know.

I located one of the scariest-looking books I could find, with a frightening clown on the cover, and I thunked it down on the circulation desk, acting very brave and grown-up so the librarian wouldn't ask me if I was allowed to read such a scary book. She raised her eyebrows a little but she let me have the book. The babysitter said, "Are you sure your mom's okay with you reading that?" I shrugged my shoulders and said, "It's just a book." It wasn't exactly lying, but it was definitely deceiving.

That night, I read the first fifty pages of the book. I was too terrified to read any further! I didn't even want the book to be in my room anymore. The clown on the cover was much scarier at night than it had been earlier that day. I snuck into the living room, and I hid the book under our sofa. That night, and for many nights afterward, I had terrible, terrible nightmares. Sometimes I was trying to run away from a clown but my feet were too heavy so I could barely move. Sometimes I arrived at school only to find that my teacher was a clown and the classroom door had locked behind me. I woke up soaked in sweat each time, and when I told my younger brother about the dreams, he said, "Just tell Mom about the book." I was pretty sure he just wanted me to get in trouble, and while that may have been true, I really should have told my mom about the book. If I had, I could have been spared many nights of terrible dreams.

A little over a month after I checked out that terrifying book, the library called and left a message on our answering machine. "Mrs. Beauregard, Renee is a little late returning a book to the library. If you could return it as soon as possible, we would really appreciate it." I was busted. My mom asked me about the book, and I retrieved it from under the couch, hanging my head in shame.

I got in trouble for checking the book out of the library when I knew I wasn't supposed to. But my punishment was a five-minute lecture on the inappropriateness of some books and movies for kids. Compared to the month of nightmares I had been dealing with, the lecture didn't seem like such a bad punishment. I finally got to tell Mom what was scaring me, and talking through it with her really helped. I didn't have any more nightmares about clowns after that. Maybe they were caused by fear, and maybe they were caused by guilt. Either way, it was a huge relief to be done with the bad dreams.

~Renee Beauregard Lute

75

The Coolest Friend Ever

Courage is what it takes to stand up and speak; courage is also what it takes to sit down and listen.
~Winston Churchill

When I turned twelve, I hung out with a kid named Raymond Sproat. We became friends and classmates in the eighth grade. Raymond was willowy and dark-skinned, and had eyes the color of cinnamon toast. He was the coolest kid I had ever known. He used foul language, smoked cigarettes, and could hit a baseball farther than anyone I'd ever seen. He would do the wildest things and take the craziest chances. Raymond cheated on exams, cut classes, and picked fights with kids twice his size. He had a scar on his chin from where he dove from a bridge and hit the bottom of the river.

We hung around a lot together that year, even though we weren't very much alike. Neither of us had other friends. I think we had an unspoken respect for one another.

I admired and envied Raymond. He was fearless, confident. He never backed away from trouble. I wanted to be more like Raymond because I was tired of being picked on. I was sick of bullies hawking snot on my shirt and then howling like monkeys when I tried to wipe it off. I had had enough of being taunted with nicknames like Dork Face whenever I walked past them.

My faith in Raymond was boundless. I remember riding down the steepest streets in town on the handlebars of his rusty old bicycle.

We flew down those streets. If we had hit a rock or a pothole I would have been ground into the pavement, probably splitting open my head in the process. But I wasn't worried. He led me into danger many times, but he always led me out again.

Raymond and I did some wild things together. Sometimes we would hop aboard a lumber train headed south and ride it for several miles, with the poison heat of the diesel exhaust sweeping back into our faces. I always went along with whatever he said. I never questioned Raymond's judgment.

That is, until one day just before the start of school.

It was the first week of September. The weather was unseasonably cold and damp. A drab cloak of low clouds had swallowed the town and sunk down against the earth itself. I woke early, tugged on my jeans and T-shirt and headed for Raymond's house. I knocked and he came out.

"Let's get out of here," he whispered, letting the door close softly.

"Where are we going?" I asked, but he didn't answer. With Raymond leading we headed east, toward the edge of town. By then I knew where we were going.

Our clubhouse was located deep in a forest of second growth redwood. The woods were thick there, branches coming to within four feet of the ground in many places. There was no path leading to the place. It was well concealed, hidden away in the thicket. The clubhouse was little more than a few planks nailed together to keep out the weather, but it was ours. We walked along without speaking, pushing our way through a tangle of salal and blackberry vines.

At one point Raymond stopped and pointed to his jacket: "Check this out," he said. The metal tip of a flat bottle protruded from a side pocket.

"What is it?" I asked. Raymond laughed.

"What do you think?" He pulled out the bottle and held it up for me to see. "It's whiskey. I stole it from my old man."

"What are we gonna do with it?"

Raymond laughed again. "We're gonna drink it."

I must have made a face because Raymond looked at me and

said, "You're not chicken, are you?" I nodded. I never thought of lying to him. He cuffed me on the shoulder lightly. "Don't be scared. Booze can't hurt you."

I nodded again, satisfied. Raymond smiled and took off, climbing the hill with me in hot pursuit.

Halfway up the ridge it began to rain. Thunder whacked and cracked. Lightning flashed so close that I could smell it, and not far away there was a splintering, rending sound as a tree fell.

We reached the clubhouse and crawled in through the entrance. It was damp and dark inside, and laced with a myriad of spider webs that clung to my face. With a wave of my hand I brushed them aside, shuddering at the thought of a spider making tracks along my neck.

Raymond removed the bottle from his jacket, unscrewed the cap and took a long drink. He handed the bottle to me.

"Try it," he said. "You never tasted anything like it in your life. Tastes like fire." Bravely, feeling privileged and adult, I took the bottle and raised it to my mouth. Then I stopped.

"No, thanks," I told him. "I don't want any."

He looked shocked. "What do you mean?"

"Just what I said."

I realized that my refusal to drink with Raymond was testing the limits of our friendship. That he might not want to pal around with me any longer. But I also knew that a true friend wouldn't force you to do things you didn't want to. I had already seen what liquor did to adults, how it brought out the worst in them and made them act irresponsibly. I wanted no part of that.

Raymond sat there for a moment, just staring at me. Then he shrugged and said, "That's okay, Tim. I understand."

It was the coolest thing I'd ever heard my friend say....

~Timothy Martin

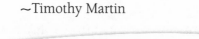

I Pledge Allegiance

I like to see a man proud of the place in which he lives. I like to see a man live so that his place will be proud of him.

~Abraham Lincoln

The first day of junior high school! Excitement crackled in the air. My mom dropped me off at the curb, and I practically skipped onto my brand new campus. Everywhere, kids were greeting each other, grinning and laughing. I waved at familiar faces and called out, "Hi!"

It was weird, but after just three months, everyone looked so different — taller, with new haircuts, new clothes.

I had P.E. for first period. I didn't mind it that much, since it meant I'd get it over and done before the heat of the afternoon. I was weirded out by the locker room though. It even smelled funny — stale and musty. We all bustled around each other, shoving our backpacks beneath the benches, trying to figure out the combinations on our new locks. I smiled at the girls next to me and they smiled back.

In a far corner of the room, a speaker squawked on. "Good morning, Woodrow Wilson Junior High School students! Welcome to the first day of a fabulous new school year. We'll begin with the Pledge of Allegiance."

I tugged my gray gym shirt over my head and my right hand immediately rested over my heart. Around me, other girls froze in place, all of us looking towards the flag draped near the speaker.

A few tears came to my eyes. Every time I did the pledge, I

thought of my grandpa. He had died almost a year before, but I still missed him every single day. Grandpa served in World War II and the flag had very special meaning for him. Even if we heard the pledge or the national anthem on TV, we stopped everything and saluted. He would get this distant look in his eyes, like he could see all the way to India and China where he loaded bombers during the war. It had made him proud and sad all at once.

The principal finished reciting the pledge. The other girls unfroze and resumed dressing. The day continued, full of reunions and excitement and groans as we confronted our first homework assignments of the year.

The next morning in the locker room, I noticed something odd. Some of the girls talked through the pledge and continued to change clothes. The morning after that, even fewer paused to place their hands over their hearts. I looked at the gym teachers' cubby and was shocked that they talked and laughed through the pledge, too.

By the second week of school, I was the only girl in the whole locker room who did the Pledge of Allegiance. I stood out. That's when the comments started.

"What do you think you're doing?" sneered one girl.

"The pledge," I said.

"What's wrong with you? We don't have to do the pledge any-more." She tossed her hair over her shoulder.

"Yeah," another girl chimed in, "there's no one to make us do it!" They shared a triumphant grin.

I had known some of these girls since second grade, but now it was like I didn't know them at all. It wasn't just their hairstyles and bodies that had changed over the summer. Something else had changed, too.

The next morning, I hid in a bathroom stall to switch clothes. When the pledge started, I faced a graffiti-covered metal door as I mouthed the words. I couldn't see the flag. My stomach clenched in a great big knot. It felt so wrong to be hiding like that.

I kept hiding for the next week, and it felt worse every single day.

The other girls left me alone, and that should have made me glad. It didn't. Instead, I felt like I was betraying the memory of my grandpa. He risked his life fighting for that flag. I rarely saw him cry, but when he'd hear the song "I'm Proud To Be An American" by Lee Greenwood, tears would fill his eyes. Now, tears were filling my eyes as I cowered in a bathroom stall. I wished that I could go to the teachers for help, but they didn't seem to care about doing the pledge, either.

I cared. I cared a lot.

I spent a weekend gathering up my nerve and practicing what I would say. By the time Monday came, I was nervous, but also calmer than I had been in a long time because I knew I was doing the right thing.

I changed into my gray gym clothes right away and was standing by my locker when the principal began morning announcements. The pledge started and I put my hand over my heart.

A girl nearby slammed her locker shut and looked over at me. "Why are you doing that?" she asked. She didn't sound mean about it, more like she was confused.

"My grandpa fought in World War II and he died last year," I said. "I'm doing it for him."

She blinked. Embarrassment flickered over her face and she looked away. "Oh," she said.

Over the next few weeks, more girls confronted me, thinking they could bully me about the pledge. I gave them all that same answer. Eventually, they stopped asking.

I came to realize something. These kids thought they were rebelling against something they were forced to do in school. The fact was, every single girl in that locker room probably had a family member in the military at some point. With a Navy base nearby, some of them even had enlisted dads.

I never inspired other girls to do the pledge along with me. That was okay. They made a choice; I made mine. It was enough that I stood there, in the open, to say those words. I was doing it for Grandpa, but more than that, I was doing it for myself.

Grandpa raised me to be proud to be an American, and that pride didn't stop because I was in seventh grade.

~Beth Cato

Party Invitation

A man has to live with himself, and he should see to it that he always has
good company.
~Charles Evans Hughes

I was excited. I had been invited to go to my friend's birthday party. Tori was not my best friend, but she was in my class and we did stuff together. And I liked to go to parties. I asked my mom and she said I could go, so I told Tori that I'd be there.

And then, two days later, my very, very best friend called. She and her family were going to Disneyland for the whole day. She invited me to go with them. Disneyland! I loved Disneyland so much. I really wanted to go... more than anything. I ran to ask my mom if it was okay. That's when my mom reminded me that Tori's party was on the same day. She said I couldn't change my mind just because something better came along.

I was mad. So mad. Disneyland was my most favorite place in the whole world and I loved to go there... and I especially liked going with my best friend. My excitement about going to the birthday party was gone. Tori's party would be okay but not as fun as a whole day at Disneyland and besides that, Tori wasn't even my best friend. I begged my mom. She said no. I cried. I sulked. I pouted. My mom still said no. What I wanted to do wasn't nice. It wasn't right.

I couldn't get her to change her mind. I tried every excuse I could think of. My mom explained to me again—once you accept an invitation to something, you can't change your mind and go to something else just because you want to do the other thing more. That isn't nice. She asked me to think about how I would feel if someone did that to me. If someone had said they'd come to my party and then, because something better came along, they changed their minds and didn't come, how would I feel? I thought about it. Although I didn't want to admit it, my mom was right. It would hurt my feelings if someone did that to me. Although I didn't want to, I told my best friend that I wouldn't be able to go to Disneyland with her.

So my friend and her family went to Disneyland and my mom dropped me off at Tori's party. I did not want to be there. But something interesting happened after I got there. In spite of the fact that I had not wanted to go, I had a great time! We did stuff that was fun and different. We watched a movie that hadn't come out in theaters yet; we were the first people to see it and that was pretty amazing. There was a make-your-own pizza contest. We each got a piece of dough and then there were all of these toppings to choose from. We all got covered in pizza dough, cheese and toppings. You're supposed to take a present to the birthday person and we all did. But Tori's mom and dad had a special present to give to each of us too! That was so cool.

When my mom came to pick me up I didn't want to leave. After we got home I told my mom all about the fun things we had done. She was so glad that I'd had a good time and she told me that she was proud of me for understanding why you can't just dump someone because something better comes along. Not only did I love the party and have a great time, but I learned an important lesson. My mom was right... as usual.

~Barbara LoMonaco

Truth or Dare

Precaution is better than cure.
~Edward Coke

n fifth grade, I really wanted to be Allison's friend. She seemed to know a lot of things I didn't. Allison had an older brother and a big house, and a really sarcastic sense of humor that you didn't want directed at you. What else did Allison have? A giant slumber party for her birthday in her finished basement, complete with snacks and foosball and what promised to be a pretty exciting round of Truth or Dare. I seriously wanted to be on Allison's good side.

I was a hopeless romantic, even from kindergarten. I never had a lot of luck with diaries, but every few months I would start a new one when the agony of love was just too much to bear. "Today, Kevin came in with a haircut, and it was AMAZING," I would write. Or, "James said he would play tag with me at recess and then he DIDN'T! I am so mad at him!" In that regard, Allison had something else to offer me—she was friends with most of the boys in our grade, and she really liked to talk about it. Staying up late listening to music and discussing which boys we liked was my all-time favorite activity. For this, I would follow Allison to the ends of the earth.

One day, Allison came over to my desk to talk about the sleepover we were having that night. She said she had something awesome planned, something she had done before. "We're going to talk to guys... online," she said. "We chat with them, and we flirt with them."

"Are these boys from our class?" I asked, always looking for an opportunity to "accidentally" let slip my latest crush. I mean, if they didn't know I liked them, how would they know to like me, right?

"No, I don't even know them," Allison answered. "They're just random guys. We go online and find them and then talk about kissing them and stuff."

Something didn't feel right. It was one thing to want Jeff to know I thought he was cute. It was another to talk to some random guy online. I may have been a fifth grader, but I was still a straight-A student. How did we know these guys were our age? How did we know it was safe?

But still—I wanted to be Allison's friend. I wasn't going to be Allison's friend if I always chose "Truth" in Truth or Dare, and I wasn't going to be Allison's friend if I didn't do this thing with her. It was that kind of situation. "Okay," I said. "Sounds awesome."

That night, I was packing up my things to go over to Allison's house. I knew my mom had a strong distrust of Allison's parents and thought they were totally weird. I usually tried not to add fuel to the fire, but something just didn't feel right.

"I think we're going to make friendship bracelets," I said to my mom, "so I need to bring my string with me."

"Mmmhmm," my mom answered, otherwise occupied with making dinner.

"And then we're going to go online and chat with some boys. It's not that big a deal, just like, flirting and stuff."

"What was that?" My mom put down her knife. "Do you know these boys?"

"Well, no, they're just random guys, but it's fine. Allison said she's done it before."

My mom didn't think it was fine, not even a little bit. And I kind of knew it wasn't fine... that was why I told her. When my mom dropped me at Allison's house that night, she went in to talk to Allison's mom while I ran upstairs to get settled. My stomach was in knots. Allison would definitely know that I told on her and she would never want to be my friend now. I was pretty sure our friendship was over. I was pathetic, and she would laugh at me.

"Hey," I said to Allison. "So... my mom found out we were going to chat with boys online tonight. She says we can't do it."

I waited for her response, my stomach doing flips.

"Whatever," Allison said. "Do you want to watch a movie?"

I was stunned. She didn't care at all.

That night, we didn't touch the computer. We made popcorn, watched a movie, and listened to music. In the morning, my mom picked me up. Allison never mentioned it again. I know now that what I did was right—no friendship is worth doing something unsafe and wrong.

And you know what? I was invited to her big slumber party after all. It was awesome.

~Madeline Clapps

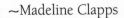

Chicken Soup
for the Soul

The Shirt Off My Back

If you haven't any charity in your heart,
you have the worst kind of heart trouble.
~Bob Hope

t was as if a supernatural force had overtaken me. My heart fluttered and my legs had a mind of their own.

"Look, Mom!" I exclaimed, pointing to a giant sign across the mall.

"What is it?" she asked.

"Everything is ninety percent off!" My voice reached an octave higher than normal.

"Let's take a look," Mom said.

"Wow! Good find, Andrea," said my sister Juliana.

We marched straight to our favorite store. Once inside, we found ourselves amidst the bustling frenzy of shoppers. We strolled through the cloud of perfume, past the cosmetic counters, directly to the racks of clothes.

"These T-shirts are only two dollars!" Juliana exclaimed.

We snaked through the crowd. I started grabbing as many shirts as I could. There were five different shades of purple and since I couldn't decide, I took all of them.

"This sale is awesome!" I said as I flipped through the sea of blues.

"Try them on," Mom said. "They are so cheap."

I snatched them all off the hangers. Before I went into the

changing room, Mom whipped out her calculator, punched in numbers and calculated our savings.

"These jeans are only seven dollars," Juliana said, leaning over Mom's shoulder.

Even though I didn't need them, I carried the jeans into the fitting room. The shopping ritual was something I experienced each year during the holidays and before school. I had taken whatever was in reach and the miniscule changing room was overflowing with clothes. As I stood knee-deep in a colorful mountain of T-shirts, I realized I did not have enough room to store them all. Did I really need these?

I started thinking about all the children who never got new clothes. I lived the first year of my life in an orphanage in Buzau, Romania where the children had nothing. My sister and I were both adopted from there, and my mother made sure to ship boxes of clothes to the orphans in Romania every year. Each summer, my parents, sister and I dedicated a day to sifting through our closets and choosing some clothing to share.

Sometimes my mother convinced me to give away clothing that I still liked a lot, but other times it wasn't as hard as I often had brand new clothing that I had been given for Christmas or birthdays that I didn't even use.

As I stood among the piles of clothes in the cramped dressing room, I turned to Mom as she neatly folded the shirts I set aside to purchase. "I have enough," I said.

Mom stared blankly.

"I'm not going to buy these."

"Which ones did you decide not to buy?"

"I want all of them, but I don't need anything." I licked my lips and sighed deeply. "I'm not going to buy any of these." My eyes glistened with tears as I pictured dozens of kids running around, playing happily in my hand-me-down clothes. I certainly didn't need any new clothing, when I already has so much. A smile tugged at the corners of my mouth. "I need to go home and clean out my closet." I don't know any of the Romanian orphans, but I know I would give them the shirt off my back.

~Andrea Canale

80

Alice and Snowball

No act of kindness, no matter how small, is ever wasted.

~Aesop

On my twelfth birthday my mother handed me a square box. "Jamie," she said, "this is something you've wanted for a long time."

My heart beat fast as I opened the box. Out popped a fluffy, white Poodle puppy! I let out a whoop. "Thank you, Mom! I'm going to name her 'Snowball.'"

My mother smiled. "That's a good name," she said. "Now a few things: pets come with responsibility and since this is your dog, you will have to feed her, walk her, and clean up after her. Is that understood?"

"Yes, Mom," I replied.

I set to training Snowball right away, having her walk by my side on a leash. She didn't do it perfectly but I knew she would in time. I decided to take her for a short walk down a nearby, quiet lane.

As we turned into the lane, we saw an old woman sitting in her yard. When we passed by, she called out, "Is that a new dog? I know all the dogs in the neighborhood but I've never seen this one before. My name is Alice," she said, as she came toward us on the sidewalk, dragging an aluminum canister on wheels behind her. She collapsed onto a chair near her gate, gesturing for us to come in. "It's not easy for me to breathe," she wheezed. "That's what this machine is for." I tried not to stare.

"What is this little one's name?" she asked.

I picked up my puppy and placed her on Alice's lap. "Her name is Snowball and mine is Jamie," I replied. "I just got her for my birth-day today!"

"It's very nice to meet you Jamie and Snowball, and a very Happy Birthday to you," Alice said. Soon Alice had lost herself in snuggling Snowball. With Alice's eyes closed, I felt it was okay to study her breathing machine. It reminded me of something out of a science fiction book. When I looked back at Alice, I saw her clutching and patting the calm dog and softly humming to her. As I watched, I saw tears roll slowly down Alice's cheeks.

"What's the matter?" I asked.

She said, "I used to have a Poodle years ago. Holding your dog brought it all back."

"Why don't you get one of your own?" I asked.

"I'm too old for a dog," she replied.

I just sat quietly because I could not think of anything to say.

"Well," she said, smiling, "I guess it's time to give you back your dog. I do so love a little dog to snuggle with. You two will visit me again now, won't you?"

"Of course," I said, as Snowball and I walked away from her down the lane. But I was thinking I would never go back there. I didn't want to see her again with her old lady smell and her scary breathing machine.

I lay awake for a long while that night. I felt torn because even though I didn't want to visit the old woman, I knew that it would be the right thing to do. She was sick, alone, and old—older even than my own grandmother, who was pretty old! And Snowball seemed to comfort Alice so much.

The next morning I hooked Snowball to her leash and we set out for her morning walk. I found myself taking a turn into the lane where Alice lived. Maybe we would find her out in her yard.

~B.J. Lee

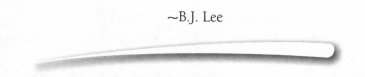

81

Not Such a Good Idea

You will do foolish things, but do them with enthusiasm.
~Colette

never did like the term "tomboy" but that's what I was, a twelve-year-old girl who'd rather hang out with boys than girls. Even though some of the boys were bullies, I preferred them over girls who were drooling over the Beatles and David Cassidy or talking about clothes, shoes and make-up.

Stupid girls they were. On this beautiful summer day, they were sitting in front of the TV rather than enjoying the sun and cloudless blue sky. I sighed with contentment as I gazed over the green fields, dotted with buttercups and daisies, not knowing that I was about to do something stupid too.

In the distance some Jersey cows were grazing. I could see their pink tongues curling around the long grass, ripping it from the earth. I was familiar with the various cows. I had even petted a couple of them on my way to school. They were gentle animals, with sad brown eyes and huge wet noses.

Upon hearing footsteps, I turned around and saw Danny and his gang approaching. Danny was considered the leader of the boys in the neighborhood and whoever wanted to join the soccer, bicycle, running, or badminton team had to have Danny's approval.

"Hi," he said with a grin. "Your brother tells me that you want to join us for next week's soccer game."

"Yeah." I felt confident. Even though not an official member of the team, I had been a goal replacement on several occasions and prided myself on my blocking abilities.

"I wouldn't mind having you on the team," Danny said. "Everybody knows you're not a girl like the other girls, but you still have to prove your worth. Show that you have courage."

I shrugged. "Just tell me what you want me to do."

Danny nodded. "Okay. I want you to walk up to those cows in the field and pull the tail of that black one."

Mistaking my confusion for doubt, Danny crossed his arms over his chest. "I dare you; I double dare you."

"That's what you want me to do?" I asked incredulously. "Pull the tail of a cow?"

"Not just any cow," Danny reminded me. "That black one over there."

Wondering about this odd test, I climbed through the fence and confidently walked up to the black animal. Some courage test this was. Pull the tail of a cow… ridiculous.

I was only a few meters away from the beast when it snorted and kicked the soil under its front paw.

That's when I saw it. This wasn't a cow; this was a bull! And he seemed upset.

I had seen the running of the bulls in Seville and knew those beasts were not only fast, but trampled anything in their way.

To heck with the dare. Quick as I could I did an about face and raced across the field, occasionally glancing over my shoulder to see if the bull was following me.

He was, and I ran even faster. My heart was hammering and my muscles were screaming. I'd lost my shoes somewhere along the way, but I didn't care—escaping was all I could think about. Stupid Danny. When he selected the black beast he must have known it was a bull and not a cow.

Up ahead two of the boys held the horizontal wires of the fence open and without thinking I launched myself through them, the way a swimmer would dive into the water.

I lay there, breathing heavily, feeling silly. How could I not have noticed the difference between a cow and a bull? When I looked up, I saw Danny grinning down on me.

As I scrambled to my feet I didn't know what I wanted more... accusing Danny of setting me up, or running home, hoping they would forget this whole thing ever happened.

"I guess this means I can't join the club, huh?"

"Are you kidding me?" Danny said. "See you tomorrow for the 100 meter sprint. Welcome to the club."

Now that I think about it that was a pretty dumb thing to do! But... live and learn.

~Conny Manero

Chapter
9

Think Positive
for Kids

Being Responsible

A Little Effort Goes a Long Way

Whether you think you can or you think you can't, you're right.
~Henry Ford

Growing up in Michigan, delivering newspapers was a great way to make a few extra bucks. For the most part, it was a pleasant, uneventful job—unless it was winter. Winter was a different story. Winter was brutal.

One particular January weekend was a doozy when I was twelve. On Friday, a freezing rain coated the roads with a half-inch of ice. On Saturday, a swirling blizzard dumped eight inches of snow on top of that. Bear in mind, our neighborhood wasn't a flat grid with regular street maintenance; this was a maze of winding, narrow, sometimes hilly dirt roads. We were on our own.

Miraculously, the newspaper distributor managed to get the papers to the top of a steep hill at the edge of the neighborhood, but Mom's trusty station wagon was no match for incline, ice and slush. How the heck was I going to get all those newspapers where they needed to be? The task ahead seemed impossible. But the idea of *not* delivering the papers loomed even larger. After all, the newspaper boy takes his cue from the mailman and the UPS driver—come rain or shine, you have to deliver.

I put two and two together and figured out a plan. I played hockey on a league at that time and was pretty good at skating. The

ice on the roads would provide a familiar surface. We loved to toboggan and had a full-sized wooden beauty in our garage. The solution:
lace up my skates, load the newspapers on the back of the toboggan,
strap them down and tow the whole rig. It was slow going for sure,
but I have never witnessed more sheer gratitude than that day. Every
customer, even the surly ones, greeted me with a smile and a hand-
shake for getting the job done. Personally, this was a great example
of how a seemingly insurmountable challenge was overcome *and*
yielded unexpectedly positive results!

I had another winter experience during my childhood that had
a big impact on the adult that I became. In junior high, I was on the
worst hockey team in the league. One day we were scheduled to play
the best team in the league. It seemed like a hopeless exercise, since
we all knew—even the coach—that we were going to get destroyed.
But the coach gave us great advice. He told us that just because we
were going up against a scary opponent, it didn't mean that we gave
up. On the contrary, we had to try even harder.

Our ragged team took his words to heart and played the game
of our life. We were sliding into slapshots, checking their star players
into the boards and giving them the surprise of their lives. Did we
win? Heck no! We got our butts handed to us, but the other team
went out of their way to congratulate us for the way we played, with
heart and effort.

After the game, our coach was almost in tears—but not because
he was sad or angry. He was overjoyed that we tried so hard to win.
To him, it was our best game and we should remember the great feeling of giving it our very best—win or lose. For the rest of the season,
we all skated a little taller.

In a twist of fate, a year later I wound up on the best team in the
Little League. That part was great. The bad part was that I was the
worst guy on the team. It was very frustrating to watch home runs
and great defensive plays being made all around me, but I wasn't a
part of them. I struck out at the plate so many times I'm sure I was
approaching a season record.

These are the moments when you have a choice. Do you fold

and bemoan your miserable status as "team loser," or do you try and do something about it? I hated the idea of not contributing to the team, so I decided to just plain "get better" at baseball. If I didn't have the natural gifts the sport demanded, I would practice until I figured out some way to hit and catch and throw that ball.

Slowly, almost imperceptibly, I got better—and as I improved, so did my attitude. I figured if I could improve a little bit, maybe I could improve *more* than a little bit. This thinking served me well when our team, the "White Sox," got into the Little League World Series against the "Pirates." The teams were evenly matched. The Pirates won the first game and the White Sox took the second. Game three was important because it could give a mental edge to our team and create momentum. We needed to win.

With building confidence, I decided to put my fears aside and play the best that I could. During my first at bat I took a fastball in the thigh from their best pitcher, simply because I refused to back away. That was a bad idea—it left a gnarly, circular bruise for weeks. Still, the incident dampened any remaining hesitation and I hit four-for-five that day. During my last at bat, I whacked a grand slam home run that won the game. There was no more glorious feeling than to help the team win—even if it was *really late* in the season. (Full disclosure, the other team won the championship, but it was a great series).

At the Baseball Awards banquet, I was humbled to get Most Improved Player. Of course, that meant it was official that I was awful at the beginning of the season, but they were acknowledging my efforts and I was no longer awful. The icing on the cake was taking home the Best Sportsman trophy as well. The sweet message behind that award meant that I didn't let being a poor player get me down, or negatively impact my team.

These incidents as a kid helped me to accomplish more as a young adult. When I was twenty-one, I came up with the crazy idea to make a movie, executive produce it, star in it, and sell it around the world. The idea still seems crazy to me all these years later, but I had seen how tackling problems usually ended up with a positive outcome, so I was not to be deterred. Our scary little movie, *Evil*

Dead, became a great success and it paved my way into the film business where I've stayed ever since.

If there is a moral to this story, it would be this: don't be fooled into thinking that childhood adversities and triumphs have no bearing on your adult life. To the contrary, they *define* your adult life. The events decades ago proved to me that just because something *seems* impossible, it doesn't mean that it *is*.

~Bruce Campbell

I Can't Believe I Did That

Only surround yourself with people who will lift you higher.
~Oprah Winfrey

was dangling my legs in the pool when Linda swam up and blocked me. Something about Linda always made me a little uncomfortable. I wanted her to like me, mostly because none of my classmates lived close enough to hang out after school. Linda lived only two houses down from mine. But this warm spring afternoon, her words made me shiver.

"You've got to do what I say," she commanded, her voice low. "Otherwise, I'll tell your mom you did it anyway."

"She won't believe you," I protested.

Linda glanced a few feet away at our moms in their pool chairs. We could hear them laughing and chatting. They weren't listening to us. Linda tossed her wet ponytail over her shoulder. "Oh, I don't know... maybe she will. And even if she doesn't, my mom wouldn't talk to yours anymore either."

Uh-oh. Linda's ideas weren't always fun. And sometimes they were downright mean. "What do you want me to do?" I squeaked.

"You know those new people in the house on the corner?"

"Yeah," I answered.

"We-ell... they're such pains," Linda declared. "All I have to do is put a toe on their precious lawn and they come running out to make sure I didn't run over their flowers with my skates. I have an idea that will show them."

Linda pulled me down into the shallow water beside her and whispered her hideous plan.

"Soooo.... you just bring me a bag of your grossest garbage tonight," she said. "Then, when it's dark enough, we can pull our stuff down there in my wagon...." Her voice sounded mysterious, like a kid detective. Only she wasn't solving crimes. She was planning one.

"But..." I tried again. "I don't like this. What if they see us?"

"Don't be a baby," she said flatly. "They won't."

Maybe I could do it after dinner when I was supposed to be taking the trash out anyway. But I was feeling sicker by the minute. Why was I doing this? So what, if Linda dumped me. I knew it was wrong. I didn't even know those people. But it was like Linda had some sort of hold on me that I couldn't explain.

As Mom and I left, Linda wrapped her dripping arm around my shoulders and laughed loudly like we were best buds. "See you later!" she said.

"Feeling okay, hon?" Mom asked when I could barely eat my dinner.

"I'm just... not... too hungry, I guess," I said. Now I was lying too! How did I get in this mess?

I pulled the kitchen trash bag to the door. "Be back in a bit," I called.

Outside, I nearly abandoned the whole idea. But there was Linda, waiting at the end of our driveway. She must've known I'd chicken out and she wasn't going to let me.

"C'mon!" she urged, tugging our cargo down past her house to the corner. The home was dark. "Perfect!" she said in her director's voice. "Now!"

And suddenly, there we were, tossing all that yucky grossness onto the clean driveway. Lettuce leaves and greasy foil wrappers and wads of smelly tissue landed at my feet. I could hear cans dinging and rolling behind the bushes.

My heart was pounding, and my feet felt glued to the pavement in horror at what we'd just done. Somewhere a light went on in the back of the house. "Run!" Linda cried, yanking the rattling wagon and pulling me down the street. I never ran so fast in my life.

The next morning I truly did feel sick. But somehow I made it through the door, into the car with Dad, and on to school. "Have a great day!" Dad called. I hugged my books to my chest and clunked the door behind me. I didn't think I'd have a great day ever again.

I flubbed the easiest math problem when Mrs. F. called on me. I couldn't concentrate on my favorite reading book. I could barely swallow my peanut butter and jelly sandwich at lunch. And by the time I got home, my insides felt as wobbly as Jell-O Jigglers.

"Is something bothering you?" Mom wondered when I turned down Toll House cookies. Her voice was quiet, but I could hear a firmness in it. I knew she wouldn't let this one slide.

Suddenly, I couldn't hold it in any longer. "I think I did something... terrible!" I blurted on a sob. "And I'm... not sure... how... to fix it."

Mom just listened, pushing my bangs away from my eyes as I choked out the whole disgusting story. I was sure she was going to be so disappointed in me. More than I was in myself... and that was huge.

But she only looked into space for a moment. "I saw the husband out trying to scrape his driveway this morning," Mom told me then. "His wife is recovering from a fall she had last month and he told me how glad he was she didn't trip over any of that slop today."

I looked into her eyes, miserable. She reached over and tucked her finger under my chin. "I think you know what it feels like to be the new kid in school. And how they feel being new on our block...."

"Yes," I admitted softly. Then, after a moment, it was like I suddenly woke up from a nightmare. Yes! I did know. And I also knew how much I wanted people to like me and to fit in. So much that I let someone talk me into doing something so unlike me that it left me heartbroken. I had hurt someone for no reason. And like Mom always said, "hurting someone else hurts God, too."

Suddenly I was angrier than I was afraid. Mostly at myself—for letting Linda talk me into such a plot. I wanted to march two houses down and tell her my own plan. And if she didn't care to join me, that was her problem.

Linda did go with me, hanging behind as I rang the bell. I stuttered our apology to the woman in her wheelchair. At first, her black eyes flashed, reminding me of dark skies on a stormy day. I could tell she wasn't sure if we were really sorry, or if someone was making us confess. But after we finished hosing down her driveway she asked us in for lemonade. She told us about her grandchildren, who were our age and lived in another state. I confided how I loved to read and that Linda was a great swimmer. By the time we left, I had a new friend, and dinner sounded good again.

Even Linda seemed relieved. It was almost like she had needed me to stand up to her. Maybe all her crazy ideas were because she tried too hard to feel... important. Because she wanted me to like her, too. I hadn't thought of that before.

"Hey! Race you to your house!" I dared.

I was through doing whatever old thing Linda said. But after today, maybe, we could be real friends....

~Pam Depoyan

84

Chicken Soup
for the Soul

Take the Bull
by the Horns

I quit being afraid when my first venture failed and the sky didn't fall down.
~Allen H. Neuharth

The summer after fourth grade I went to a sleep-away camp in Maine for the first time. It was an old, rustic place on a lake called Moose Pond. Campers slept in log cabins or platform tents. Traditional activities like hiking, canoeing, campcraft and archery were emphasized.

Multi-day hiking trips that involved camping in the mountains quickly became my favorite activity. There were usually about ten campers and a couple of counselors on each trip. We'd head off into the Appalachians or the White Mountains for a few days at a time, each of us carrying a pack loaded according to our size and strength.

Each day we hiked ten, fifteen or even twenty miles. When we arrived at a campsite in the evening, the counselors would assign everyone—including themselves—a task. Some would string up tarps between trees. Others would bring jugs and filters to a river to purify water. A few were placed on firewood duty, gathering twigs and splitting small logs. The rest would begin preparing dinner.

The tasks were important. Each one needed to be completed in order for the group to be fed and rested by the next morning. But the tasks were also simple. Most of my friends went about them with little guidance. If they made a mistake, a counselor could usually remedy it.

For some reason, to me, the prospect of making a mistake was particularly concerning. As my friends began their work, I sat thinking about what to do. I didn't want to take the first step without being sure I was doing it just right. If I was supposed to tie up a tarp, I'd ask what kind of knot to use. Then I'd have a counselor double check to make sure I'd done it right. If I was on water duty, I'd ask what part of the river to go to. When I got back I'd confirm that I'd been in the correct place. If I was making dinner, I'd double check about cooking times. I wouldn't split a piece of wood without consulting a counselor on the proper size. Packing, I'd ask if I was folding tarps and clothes properly. The questions were constant. If a counselor assigned me a task, he knew he'd be hearing from me without pause until I was done.

Eventually I could tell the counselors had gotten frustrated with me.

There's nothing wrong with asking for help when you need it—the counselors knew that. But the fact was that I didn't need any help. Generally, I was asked to carry out tasks I had completed before. Even if I hadn't, I should have been able to figure it out for myself. If I knew enough about knots to ask which one to use, couldn't I just have picked the one I thought would work best? The counselors thought so.

One evening at the campsite I approached a counselor with my most recent question—it had to do with how to wash the dishes properly. He turned to me and said little more than, "Mike, take the bull by the horns." It was clear he'd said this out of frustration. But the message behind it—or at least the message I took from it—was clear. I could do these things on my own; I could make decisions for myself. However I decided to complete the task would probably work, even if it wasn't exactly what the counselor had in mind.

It was a minor comment, but it changed the way I approached campsite setups. The next day, before I asked a counselor a question, I asked myself first. I found that I was smart enough to always come up with the answer. In fact, as I worked through problems on my own, I realized that there was no reason to assume that a counselor could always come up with a better answer than I could. I could decide what knot was best for tying up a tarp. I could find the place on the river that had the cleanest water. I knew how to build a fire, so I could figure out what kind of wood was needed.

Solving these little problems had a big impact on my confidence. Even after camp ended that summer I thought about what the counselor had told me: "Take the bull by the horns."

I found that in other parts of my life, I was capable of getting things done on my own. In school, I could work out a math problem without asking a teacher to walk me through it step by step. In sports, when I made a mistake I knew I could try again without having a coach intervene. At home, I went about my chores more independently. Perhaps my parents noticed I was growing up.

Many years later, I haven't stopped thinking about that one counselor's comment. It reminds me that I can manage on my own. I can do it.

~Michael Damiano

85

The Case of the Busted Lunchbox

There are always three sides to every story:
your side, the other side, and the truth.
~Author Unknown

received the following note from the mother of one of my students: "I need to inform you that two boys in Timmy's class smashed his new lunchbox in the school cafeteria. I think they should pay for a new one."

As the teacher, I had to solve this mystery before the school day ended or else Timmy's mom would not be happy with me. It's tough being a detective while you're supposed to be actively involved in teaching almost thirty students, but I promised myself that I would give it my best shot.

During reading class, I talked to Timmy in the back corner of the classroom and he told me the names of the two so-called villains, George and Mike. I approached George and Mike separately, and I asked each of them independently what had happened to Timmy's lunchbox. George and Mike both told me the same story, which was surprising because usually when kids are guilty they don't keep their stories straight. How interesting! They didn't even have time to rehearse it, and their versions were identical. And what they said was probably true. They admitted to smashing the lunchbox, but said, "Timmy wanted us to wreck it."

When I heard that, I tried not to fall out of my chair laughing in disbelief. I interviewed Timmy again, but all he did was show me the dented unusable lunchbox.

I told Timmy that I was going to solve this mystery, and I slid him a piece of paper with these words: "Did you in any way encourage George and Mike to dent in your lunchbox?" After what seemed like a very long wait he wrote: "Sort of."

Aha! Now I was getting closer to the truth. Timmy finally admitted what happened. He hated his Campbell's® soup lunchbox. Kids had made fun of it. He wanted a "cooler" one. There was only one way in Timmy's mind that his mom would buy him a new one. The new lunchbox had to be wrecked beyond repair. And it was, thanks to his two pals, George and Mike.

I asked George and Mike, "Would you leap off Niagara Falls because your friend Timmy asked you to do so?

Right after school, as the buses left the building, I called up Timmy's mom, and I explained what happened. She wasn't exactly happy with Timmy.

So what happened to Timmy? Did he get a new lunchbox? No way! He had to brown bag it the rest of the year. Things worked out perfectly.

And I think Timmy learned four important things:

1. Don't try to fool your mom.
2. Don't try to fool your teacher.
3. The truth works better than lies.
4. Don't make your friend part of your lies.

~Joe Sottile

Love, Loss, and a Goldfish

If you want children to keep their feet on the ground, put some responsibility on their shoulders.

~Abigail Van Buren

was seven years old when I got my first pet. My family always had some sort of animal around, but none of them were truly mine. But then I won George. At the time, my father was a janitor in a neighboring school district. When fall came around and the leaves began to change colors, his school held its fall carnival. I was about as excited as any seven-year-old could possibly get without wetting herself. When we pulled into the parking lot, I didn't even wait for my daddy to shut off the old Ford before my feet hit the gravel. Like a bullet I was off! Three of the biggest buildings I'd ever seen and every one of them filled with carnival splendor.

I closed my eyes, spun around seven times, and stopped with my finger pointing at the old elementary building. I ran as fast as my legs could carry me towards the bright red double doors. I had ten dollars in my pocket, and I knew I couldn't spend it all in one place. I walked up and down the hall, carefully inspecting every room and trying to decide what was worth my precious allowance. I didn't need to gamble a whole dollar on the cake walk when I could buy a cupcake next door for a quarter. The duck pond wasn't necessary either, as the prizes always got lost or broken. Then I saw it. The perfect reason to spend my precious money. There were about fifteen fish bowls and a basket full of ping pong balls. I didn't see anyone else playing as I shyly entered the room. There was a high school girl working the game. She was tall, blond, and pretty. I nervously walked up to her and whispered, "How do you play this game?"

She smiled sweetly and said, "Oh. It's easy and super fun. All you have to do is bounce a ping pong ball off of one of those buckets and into one of the fish bowls."

"Oh. That sounds easy enough." I smiled at the thought of victory. "What do I get if I win?"

I was expecting some plastic bracelets or a pencil topper. None of those prizes compared to what she said next.

"If you win you get whatever goldfish is in the bowl you hit."

My jaw nearly hit the ground. A fish? All I had to do was get the ping pong ball in a fish bowl and I got to take home a real, live, breathing, swimming goldfish?

"Okay. I can do it. How much does it cost?"

"Its ten cents per try or fifteen tries for a dollar."

A dollar? A whole dollar? Well… it was worth it. It was only a dollar, and I had ten of them. I handed the pretty girl a dollar and she gave me a basket of fifteen ping pong balls. I held the first one in my hand until it was warm. Then I took aim and bounced it off of the bucket directly in the middle of the line. It hit the rim of the closest fish bowl and bounced onto the floor. I was disappointed, but I had fourteen more tries.

Again and again I aimed and bounced but to no avail. I was down to my last ping pong ball and my spirit was low. I held the ping pong ball for nearly a full minute before I took aim, closed my eyes, and tossed the ball. I stopped breathing and opened my eyes. For a second I thought I had finally done it. Then I saw the white sphere bouncing across the tile floor. I reminded myself that it was just a fish and tried to stifle the tears that were threatening to spill onto my red cheeks. The pretty teenager took one look at me and said, "Oh, honey, please don't cry. Here, I'll give you an extra shot, just because you tried so hard."

She handed me one more ping pong ball. This time, the ball was orange. The difference in color may not have meant much to anyone else, but to my seven-year-old self, it was a sign. A sign that this ball was the one I would win my fish with. Instead of aiming to the buckets this time, I aimed to the fish. All of the fish were golden except for one. He was sitting in the back, and tiny compared to all the others. I decided that he would be my fish. I took aim and didn't think about it. I just threw the ping pong ball. Time seemed to slow down as the ball soared in a perfect arc and landed with a plunk in his bowl. For a split second, I didn't realize that I had done it. Then, beaming, I turned to the girl as she handed me the bag with my white and black goldfish swimming serenely around in it. I hugged her and ran out into the hallway. I ran around the school grounds until I found my parents. With my fish hidden behind my back I put on my best sad face and walked up to them.

"Oh, no. What's with the face?" My mom cooed.

"Oh, nothing. Except that I won...." My face lit up as I prepared to show off my prize, "...THIS!" I swung my arm out from behind my back to show my parents my new fish.

"Oh, sweetie, that's great! Dan, look, she won a fish! How much did you spend, dear?" asked my mother.

"A dollar. The girl running the game was really nice and she gave me an extra try. That's how I got my fish." I couldn't stop smiling as I recalled how the pretty teenager had helped me.

"Well, cupcake," Dad said. "What're you going to spend the rest of your money on?"

"Him. My fish needs a bowl and some rocks and some food and I want to get him a little castle so he can pretend to be a king."

My father chuckled. "Well, okie dokie, then. I guess we need to make a trip to Walmart."

Mom bought us all candied apples and we headed back to the truck. I couldn't stop staring at my prize. He looked so serene and at ease. I kept thinking about the castle he was going to have, and how good a king he would make. Suddenly I had the perfect name for him.

"George!" I exclaimed.

"What?" My mother looked startled.

"My fish's name is George. Like King George, you know? Because he's going to have a castle and rule the land. I mean rule the water." I felt so clever as I explained my choice.

"Sounds like a good name to me," my dad agreed.

We all piled into the truck and headed the fifteen miles to Walmart. We pulled into the parking lot and once again filed out of the truck. I practically dragged both of my parents to the pet section and then carefully examined every fish bowl. I immediately realized that some of the nicer ones were way out of my budget.

"Look at this one," my mother called to me. "It's clean and simple. And it's on sale for five dollars."

I skipped down to where my mother was standing and followed her finger to the bowl. It was perfect. Tire shaped, with a flat bottom and a curved rim. It was crystal clear, so I could watch what George was doing any time I wanted to. I carefully pulled it down and hugged it close.

"Now, I need gravel."

"Well, what color did you feel like getting? It looks like they have blue, purple, black, rainbow, and just plain white."

I thought for a moment before saying, "Just plain white I think. It'll look brighter, and I want George to have a bright kingdom."

"Good choice. I agree," said Mom as she grabbed a bag of white gravel and continued down the aisle to the fish food. She handed me a bottle simply labeled "Goldfish Food."

"Okay, now, one last thing." I turned and walked back to the gravel section to look at tank decorations. I looked past the novelty signs and the skyscrapers until I found the perfect tiny castle. It was brown stone, with one tower and a hole for a door.

"I found the castle, Mom. Let's go find Dad and go home."

We went to the entertainment center to find my father and then headed to the cash register. I was worried that I didn't have enough money for all of George's things. I cringed every time the cashier rang up an item.

"Your total is $11.75." She sounded cavalier as she delivered the bad news.

"I guess take off the castle," I muttered.

"Now hold on just a minute, cupcake," my dad piped up, "I think I can spare the extra three dollars for that castle. You can't be a king without a castle."

I beamed as my dad handed the lady the extra three dollars. I scooped up the bag full of goodies and skipped out to the truck.

It took about thirty minutes to get home. I devoted the entire trip to imagining what my life with George would be like. His bowl would be cleaned every Friday, and I would have to feed him every day when I woke up and when I got home from school. He would live on top of my nightstand, right next to my bed. I couldn't wait until we got home so I could see how he would look swimming around next to my pillow.

As we pulled into the driveway I once again descended from the truck. I ran as fast as my little legs would carry me into the house and down the hall to my room. Gently placing George's bag on my bed, I went to the bathroom and first dumped the white gravel into the bottom of his fishbowl. Then, after settling the castle firmly in the middle, I filled the bowl with lukewarm water. As carefully as I could, I carried the full bowl into my room and set it on the night-stand. I asked for my dad's assistance in transferring George from his bag to his bowl. Without realizing it, I held my breath as my dad scooped up George and dropped him with a satisfying plunk into his brand new home. George did a couple of victory laps around his bowl, before settling into his castle. I grinned as I took a seat on my bed to stare at my new best friend.

Two years passed and George remained on my nightstand. Every Friday I would clean out his bowl as promised. I found myself turning down invitations to go somewhere immediately after school, because I would have to feed my fish first. George never did any tricks or anything out of the ordinary, but to me he was golden. Every day he would remind me that I was needed, that I had someone depending on me.

One day, I came home from school and headed to my room to feed George. When the door to my room swung open, a terrible sight met my eyes. George was floating, upside down, at the top of the water. I dropped my book bag and ran over to his bowl. I watched my best friend floating around lifeless and I couldn't do anything but stare. Finally, my mom walked into the room.

"Hey, sweetie, what do you want for din…" my mom started to say.

I turned around as tears started to well in my eyes. "Mommy, I think George d…d…died." With that last word I started bawling uncontrollably. My mother came to my side as I crawled onto my bed and hid my face in my pillows. George was gone. My best friend, keeper of secrets, was now floating around the top of the bowl. I cried and cried. Finally, I ran out of tears and I just lay there and thought about my fish. Suddenly, a realization hit me.

George hadn't just left me. Maybe it was true that he was just an ordinary fish, but he had taught me something. My goldfish had taught me what responsibility meant. I learned through feeding him and cleaning his bowl and making sure that the water was perfect that life was a complex thing. I had taken care of him, and that made me feel good. I had accepted the responsibility for another living thing and I had excelled at it. To my nine-year-old self, this was a giant achievement. Slowly, a smile crossed my face. Maybe George was gone, but the lessons he taught me would forever be carved into my memory. As Dr. Seuss said, "Don't cry because it's over. Smile because it happened."

~L. A. E. Howard

Cell Phone Madness

Everything in moderation... including moderation.
~Julia Child

"Surprise!" was the first thing I heard as soon as I opened the door. My family and friends were all gathered together. There were colorful balloons all over the house, a big poster that said "HAPPY BIRTHDAY," and of course a cake with a number 12 candle. It was a wonderful feeling knowing that I had finally turned twelve and I might possibly get the thing I wanted most.

I saw my mom and dad coming towards me with a small package wrapped up with really nice pink paper with flowers on it. When I ripped the paper and opened the box, I couldn't believe my eyes. I had really gotten a cell phone! I ran to give my mom and dad the biggest hug ever. "Thank you! I love you guys!"

"You're welcome. We knew this was going to make you happy but we didn't only get you this because you turned twelve, but also because you are doing well in school. We expect you to keep getting good grades."

"Of course I will!" I said confidently.

As soon as I got to school the next morning I was showing off my phone and asking everyone for their number. It was cool how I got so many contacts on the first day.

It felt like I didn't even exist in that class anymore. I wouldn't pay much attention to the teachers because I was too busy on my phone. Luckily, I didn't get caught using it.

I'm pretty sure that the teacher did notice that I stopped paying attention to her because a week later we took a test and I failed. To make matters worse, my mom had to sign the test.

It was hard to show my mom the test. She was used to seeing A's and B's on my tests. Well eventually I showed her and she couldn't believe it. She was angry but most of all, she was disappointed. Seeing her like that made me feel bad.

Weeks passed and my dad started to dislike the fact that I had a phone. We would argue every day about why phones are bad for us. He would say, "Anahy, can you please stop texting?"

"I'm not doing anything wrong, I'm just texting my friends. I don't think there is a reason for you to get mad."

"I don't mind if you text your friends, but don't do it when someone is talking to you, when you are eating, doing homework, or when we have guests. It's rude."

My mom also joined the conversation "Anahy, I have also noticed that you never pay attention to us, your brother or sister. It's like you have your own little world now and we don't communicate as much with your phone between us."

I acted like they were wrong but then I started to wonder if it was true that I was being impolite.

A week later I tried going a whole day without a cell phone and it didn't go that badly. My relatives came over and it was the first time that I wasn't using my phone. Everyone noticed because they were asking me about it. It got really annoying because everyone exclaimed "Wow!" Finally you are not using your phone." That day I had so much fun because I was actually spending time with my family and paying attention to them. From that day, I had a different point of view towards cell phones.

Phones really take you away from the rest of the world. When you use your phone you move from the real world to a technological world. I'm not saying that phones are bad and not to use them, but you do have to make some time to spend with your family too and not get stuck with your phone all day. My phone took away time from my homework and from my family. It also affected my grades.

I will keep using my phone, but I have it under better control now so that it doesn't interfere with my real life.

~Zulema Anahy Carlos

The Visitor's Secret

No one keeps a secret so well as a child.
~Victor Hugo

One snowy Saturday when I was five, our cozy house smelled of rising bread. Earlier I'd helped knead the sticky dough. After it rose, Mommy let me punch it down before she divided the rubbery blob into three pieces. I smeared one pan with greasy Crisco and shaped my own loaf while she formed two others. Grandma Donna's kitchen rule said helpers were tasters, but Mommy wouldn't let me nibble. "Raw dough can give you a tummy ache," she warned. "You can taste it when it's cooked."

While the bread baked we snuggled on the couch reading storybooks, until the doorbell rang unexpectedly. Mommy opened the door, and I shivered at the freezing air as a bundled woman stepped inside.

"Teresa," Mommy said, "please go play in your room for now." It was not a request. I inhaled deeply, filling my nose with the yeasty scent as I left, hoping the visitor wouldn't stay long.

Soon I served imaginary homemade bread to the stuffed animals and dolls attending my bedroom tea party.

Mommy's loud kitchen timer dinged that the real bread was ready. I sprang from my room but hesitated when I saw the lady—now red-nosed and puffy-eyed—on our couch. She dabbed at her eyes and dropped a limp Kleenex into the open purse beside her. Reaching for another tissue, she noticed me staring. Her mouth turned up like a smile, but I knew it wasn't real.

I followed Mommy, who'd already opened the oven door. "Mommy, I'm hungry. Can I have some now?"

The oven rack screeched as she slid it toward her, but her voice was gentle. "May I have some now, please?" she corrected, lifting the first shiny pan onto the countertop. "I'm sorry, but not yet, sweetie."

She tipped each fragrant loaf upside-down from its pan onto the thick oven mitt covering her left hand and flicked the bottom crust with a fingertip, nodding at the hollow thumps. "These need to cool before we cut them." She placed all three golden-brown loaves on raised wire cooling racks and rubbed the crusts with pale butter.

It smelled wonderful. "When, Mommy?"

"After my friend goes home we'll have a snack. Please go back to your room until then. Understand?"

"I'm starving," I whined. "Can't you make her leave now?"

"Teresa Lynn..."

Uh-oh, not my full name! "I'm sorry, I'm going." I spun around and fled to my bedroom, throwing the woman my fiercest "go away" look and stomping my annoyance at her presence.

I wanted that lady to leave. My tummy growled over the bread's aroma. It wasn't fair to wait in my room! I yearned for the crunchy end slices I liked, covered with melting butter and gooey honey. My mouth watered, and I could almost hear milk splashing into my pink cup.

I didn't close my door. I needed to listen. What if the lady left and Mommy forgot? I broke up the tea party. I was too hungry to play with pretend food and fancy manners.

My Barbies and I played house for a little while, but that fresh bread smell was as tantalizing in my room as in the kitchen. When Barbie wouldn't give her children any bread, either, we switched our game to a fashion show.

I listened to see if the lady had left yet. I didn't hear voices or crying anymore, so I crept out of my room until halfway down the hall I heard the visitor again. Mommy's "feel-better" voice said, "There, there. You'll be okay."

They spoke softly. From my room I couldn't tell when the lady left. I decided to let Barbie and Ken model their outfits down a runway like the ones on television. I helped my plastic friends strut farther down the hallway with every pass. Soon their stage was just inside the doorway where we could all hear.

I thought my stomach would bore a hole right through me before I finally heard the woman's first encouraging words. "Betsy, thank you for listening. I didn't have anyone else to talk to, and I know you won't breathe a word."

"Of course not," Mommy soothed. "Wait one second."

No, I thought, don't wait — leave! But it got worse. To my dismay, before the woman said goodbye she gasped, "Why, thank you for the bread. It smells delicious. We'll have these with supper tonight."

I peeked around the corner. When Mommy turned from locking the door, she spotted me and smiled. "You were such a good girl to wait so patiently." She crossed the room and scooped me into a big hug, but her eyes widened at my fashion show dolls and stuffed animal audience strewn throughout the hallway. A troubled look crossed her face. "Teresa, were you playing out here instead of inside your room?"

She looked disappointed. I lowered my head and confessed the truth. "Yes, Mommy. I'm sorry."

"Sweetie, could you hear Mommy and her friend talking?"

"Yes, ma'am."

Mommy sighed. She set me down and took my hand. "Come into the kitchen, sweetheart. We'll talk while we have our snack."

A lone, lumpy loaf remained on the countertop. Mommy sliced it and placed several thick pieces on a plate she set aside. "These are for Daddy when he gets home from work tonight." She centered ours on plates and took the honey from the cabinet. "These are for us."

For a few minutes, I concentrated on eating my bread and drinking my milk. Then Mommy spoke. She was smiling, but her voice was serious. "Did you hear what my friend and I talked about today?"

"Some." I hadn't paid attention—I was doing more interesting things while waiting—and they'd used many words I hadn't known. But I'd grasped others. "The mommy and daddy are fighting and they have money trouble." Mommy's forehead creased, and I didn't like the unfamiliar frown pushing her mouth down at the corners. "Can—may I have seconds, please?"

As I chewed she said, "Teresa, I need to tell you something very important that I want you to always remember."

"Okay, Mommy." She didn't even remind me not to talk with my mouth full.

"If my friend brought money in her purse when she visited us, would that money become ours or would it still be hers?"

"Hers."

"What if she left her purse open on the couch while she went to the restroom and we could see the money inside? Would it be ours to use?"

"No."

"What if she left her purse, if it were still here? Would that money be ours now? Could we give it to someone else?"

"No, Mommy. It's still your friend's money."

"That's right, sweetie, and her words belong to her just like her money does. The things she said inside our house are still her words, not ours to take or to share with anyone else."

"I understand." Although she didn't use the word "confidential," I learned the value of keeping secrets that winter day in Mommy's kitchen. I still feel her warm approval with every confidence I keep.

~Teresa Bruce

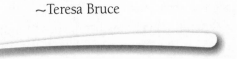

What I Learned in Gym Class

Correction does much, but encouragement does more.
~Johann Wolfgang von Goethe

'Did you forget your homework?" my sixth grade math teacher asked. I nodded my head with a feeble "yes." I could see the neatly completed math assignment in my mind's eye, problems lined up in straight rows on my notebook paper, lying on the kitchen counter at home.

"You will have to take a zero then," my teacher said.

I was stunned. I'd never received a zero. But those were the rules, and the teacher had to be consistent in enforcing them. That was also part of the problem—I was a rules follower. I always tried to do what I was supposed to do. However, I was also a daydreamer—a wonderful quality for years later when I would become a writer, but in elementary school, not so much.

I immediately fretted about my final math average—would I get a C? Would I be in trouble with my parents? And what about that 'permanent record" I'd heard so much about? Would my zero follow me around for the rest of my life?

My next class was gym, and as I walked single file with my peers down the hall, all those feelings came spilling out in the form of hot tears. I wiped them away as best I could, but when we entered the gym and sat down in our assigned spots on the floor, it was obvious to everyone around me that I'd been crying.

Gym was not my favorite class, mainly because I wasn't very good at it. My teacher, Ms. Brown, was nice enough, but I still felt like I didn't fit in. I assumed Ms. Brown saw me the same way I saw myself, as a klutz.

Ms. Brown was not, by any standard, a klutz. She was tall, trim, fit, and tan. Everybody talked about how pretty she was. Her class was a good mix of calisthenics and athletic games that gave us all a good workout.

Ms. Brown and I got along. I showed up for her class. She told us the rules, and I followed them. She gave directions and I listened. Even with my imaginative ways, I paid attention in her class. She got to the point—she didn't drone on forever like some adults. She could be firm with kids who were disrespectful or didn't try their best, but she overlooked the fact that I couldn't complete every physical task in gym. At the time, I thought it was because, like me, she had given up on my abilities. I didn't understand it was because she was compassionate.

Ms. Brown was prompt and started class on time. However, the morning I got the zero, she did something different. She walked over to where I was sitting and sat down next to me.

"Are you okay?" she asked.

I was afraid if I answered I'd start sobbing, and I really didn't want to humiliate myself anymore. One of my friends told her what happened.

Ms. Brown thought for a moment and then spoke in a reassuring tone.

"We all make mistakes. A few days ago, I was driving down the road with my head in the clouds and I crashed into the back of a truck. No one is perfect."

I was shocked. I thought Ms. Brown was perfect. I could never see her making a mistake like crashing her car. Was it possible she was a daydreamer too? It put my zero in perspective. And she had gone out on a limb admitting a mistake to make me feel better.

Ms. Brown sat with me a little longer, and then said, "Do you want to talk about this anymore?"

I shook my head "no" and wiped away a stray tear.

"Okay, I'll go away now and leave you alone," she said, patting me on the arm.

But I didn't want her to go away then. I felt better after she talked to me, and I saw her in a different light. She understood much more than I had thought she did.

The world didn't end because I got a zero in math class. I worked hard the rest of the grading period, and in the end, my average was a B. The zero didn't show up on any records, my parents understood, and the course of history didn't change. For that matter, neither did my life. It seemed so important at the time, but today I don't even remember what that math lesson was about. It wasn't the last time I forgot my homework during my scholastic career, and today, even as a responsible adult, I forget things. No matter how many sticky notes I leave myself, no matter how many lists I make, or timers I set, I will always be somewhat absentminded. That's just me.

However, from that day on I was a new kid in gym class. No, I still couldn't climb the rope to the top, or kick the ball to the fence, or run the fastest. But I took gym more seriously because Ms. Brown was teaching us and I had a new admiration for her. She taught me that two people who seem different are still the same, we all make mistakes, and we all deserve understanding and compassion.

That lesson stayed with me forever.

~Janeen Lewis

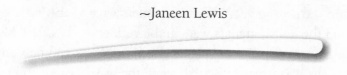

90

Better Safe than Sorry

Stand up and face your fears, or they will defeat you.
~LL Cool J

positively begged my mother to let me go to camp. I'd made fast friends with my neighbor Ellen and she went to Camp St. Mary's every summer. She wanted me to go with her in June.

"Please, Mom, please let me go. Ellen says there's swimming every day, and they'll even give me lessons!"

My mom wasn't impressed with daily swimming or the lessons. Mostly, she was concerned with me just getting through the day. I'd never spent even one night away from home. And now here I was, begging to go off to a camp for two whole weeks!

"You won't know anyone but Ellen," she said. "And she'll be in a different cabin."

My mother made a good point. Ellen was two grades ahead of me. In the fall, I'd be going into fourth grade and Ellen would be going into the sixth grade. The sixth graders were in the older girls' cabin, and the fourth graders were in the younger girls' cabin. Mom appreciated my enthusiasm, but she also knew I was naturally shy. I could tell she was worried that I'd get all the way to camp and then beg to come home.

In the end, Ellen and her mother came to my rescue. They some how convinced the camp director to allow me to stay with Ellen. So when I got to camp, I unpacked my bags in the older girls' cabin.

Boy, did I feel cool! I was only going into fourth grade, but there

I was, hanging out with Ellen and the older girls! I didn't have time to be shy. I was too busy being super cool!

All too soon, it was our last evening. The whole camp buzzed with the special Saturday activities. The cookout would be followed by roasting marshmallows and then, campfire songs and ghost stories!

Of course, all the younger kids would leave before the ghost stories started. But the older campers were allowed to stay up extra late and hear the counselors' spooky tales. And because I bunked with the older girls, I had the privilege of staying up and enjoying the thrills and chills with Ellen and my bunkmates. I could hardly wait!

I can still remember how exciting it was to sit around in that big circle, the fire crackling, the nervous laughter, shoulder to shoulder with friends, waiting for the stories to begin. I can even remember the very first story: Leapin' Lena.

I can't recall too many of the details, though. All I remember is shivering in my shoes, knees practically knocking, and my mouth dry as toast. I was sure that any minute Leapin' Lena would spring across the river and make me her next victim!

I sat there trembling because I'd suddenly realized why the younger kids weren't allowed to stick around for the ghost stories—they were too scary! And I desperately wished to be back in my little bunk bed, safe and sound. But how could I leave? I was in the cabin with the older girls. I was way too cool to admit I was scared.

Wasn't I?

I sat in agony around that campfire. I didn't want to have anything more to do with ghost stories. I knew that if I stayed, I'd just get even more frightened. But if I left, I'd have to stand up in front of all the cooler-than-me campers and find my counselor. I was very nearly close to tears. Afraid to stay and afraid to leave.

It wasn't easy. But I screwed up my courage, figuring I'd rather be safe than sorry. I found my counselor and explained the situation. She was happy to take me back to the cabin—and she stayed with me, assuring me that plenty of campers didn't like the ghost stories.

I ended up having a great time on my last night at camp—back in my cozy cabin. And when the older girls returned, they reassured me as well. They all agreed that if Leapin' Lena had scared me, I would never have lasted through... well. That's a scary story for another campfire night!

~Cathy C. Hall

Think Positive for Kids

for Kids

Being Grateful

91

Reach Out for Perspective

I have always thought it would be a blessing if each person could be blind and deaf for a few days during his early adult life. Darkness would make him appreciate sight; silence would teach him the joys of sound.
~Helen Keller

was fifteen years old. It was early August and summer was winding down. Around the corner, school, and my entrance into the tenth grade, was looming. I was going to be a sophomore in high school and I could hardly contain my excitement—not that I was overly excited for school to start. Nope, that was not the reason for my eagerness. The reason was high school football! You see, football was my favorite sport and I just couldn't wait to get out on that field and play the game I loved.

I had been playing organized football since I was nine years old. And I had not only been playing it all those years, but studying all the college and pro games on TV. My weekends were spent watching the games and scrutinizing the two positions I loved most: wide receiver and linebacker. I was a pretty good player and could play both those positions on the field. In fact, I almost never came off the field during a game, except to let special teams, punt teams and kickoff teams do their thing. Other than that, I was out there the whole game and I loved it!

As was the normal procedure for any organized sport, before

they'd let you play, they needed the doctor to sign off on your physical. A physician checked you over to make sure you were fit to play the game. I remember it was a hot August afternoon as I rode my bike up to the Mound Medical Clinic for my appointment with our doctor. I sat in the waiting room, appropriately named since they make you wait so long before going into the examination room. There were two other teammates there for their physicals and we talked about the upcoming football season and what kind of season we would have. We had achieved a 9-1 record as freshmen the year before and knew we had a great chance to have another fantastic season!

Eventually… the nurse called my name and I followed her into my room after she weighed me. I waited some more, leafing through magazines, not really paying attention to what I was reading, but rather killing time. I just wanted to get this over with, get my "okay to play" and get home for dinner. I was getting hungry.

Finally, Dr. Olson came smiling through the doorway. I knew him well. He was our family doctor; we lived a block apart in our small community, and his daughter was a good friend my whole life. Susie and I hung out all the time together at their house on the lake where we would swim and fish. I was also a paperboy and had been delivering their newspaper for the past six years. Yep, right out of a Norman Rockwell painting. (If you don't know anything about Norman Rockwell, your parents will.)

After some small banter about the pending school year and how my summer had been he got into the basic questions about my health and how I was feeling and so on. Then the hands-on part began. He took out his instruments to peer into my nose, ears, and throat. With cool, practiced hands, he felt around my neck, my stomach, and checked my shoulders, elbows, and knee joints. The little reflex hammer inevitably made my leg jump, and he seemed satisfied. I always struggled a little with the necessity of getting physicals, because I knew how I felt—healthy as a horse! But rules are rules, and I guess they are they for a purpose, as I soon discovered.

After that part of the physical was over, in a matter of a few minutes, then came the part I always hated. The drop-your-pants and cough part, to check for a hernia, which can be caused by a muscular injury. I turned my head and coughed. He asked me to cough again. And again. He sat back and scowled. He said he would be right back and left the room.

At this point I had no idea what was going on and I did not like it. I didn't know much about hernias, but the doctor wasn't smiling anymore, and that scared me. Dr. Olson came back in with another doctor who I knew from my church and whose daughter was in my class as well. Now it was his turn to have me cough three or four more times. He looked at the other doctor and confirmed that I did have a hernia. They gently explained to me what it was and said surgery would be necessary. Translation: I would have to sit out the entire fall football season! Their consolation was that I should be good to go by the time basketball season was upon us. I just sat there in a daze, trying desperately to maintain total denial about the information they had just given me.

The bike ride home was slow and long. I breathed hard while I struggled to grasp what not playing football would be like, but I was just coming up with a big pit in my stomach. I felt like someone had just sucker-punched me in my solar plexus: devastated. I was going to have surgery. I felt like my life was over.

I rode my bike up our driveway, laid it down, and walked into our small three-bedroom house. My mom, dad and little brother were getting ready for dinner in the kitchen. I stopped in the front hallway and just stood there, looking at them in their happiness and ignorance, while my world crumbled around me. I could feel the blood drain from my face. Mom saw me standing there and asked what was wrong. I broke down. I spat out the news about the doctor, the hernia, the surgery, and finally, the lost football season. She tried to comfort me, but I was too caught up in my own misery, feeling sorry for myself. Mom was a nurse. She carefully explained how simple the procedure was and that I would be better than new, but I didn't want to hear that. I was thinking only of football. And myself.

Within a few days my parents checked me into the hospital for my surgery. All I could think was woe is me. Poor me. Why did this have to happen to me? So unfair! As I lay in my hospital bed, another patient was wheeled in to be my roommate. He was a seven-year-old kid. Could my day get any worse? I didn't need some little punk kid sharing a room with me. He was with his parents, who introduced themselves to me along with their son, named Jack. They were very friendly so I forced myself to be nice, but they surely realized I was a surly teen who could barely be bothered.

Surgery was scheduled for the next morning, bright and early. Though Mom tried to prepare me, I was scared and uncertain as to what to expect. After the scrub-down they put a needle in my arm and told me to count backwards from 100. I made it to 94 and then lost consciousness. The next thing I knew, I woke up in the recovery room feeling queasy, like my head and mouth were filled with cotton. I was so groggy from the drugs they used to knock me out, and my abdomen... I remember comedian Bill Cosby talking about his hernia operation from a record one of my older brothers had. Bill talked about waking up and how it felt like they had sewed his leg to his stomach. I now understood that joke!

Once they wheeled me back to my room I slept most of the rest of the day with my parents checking on me. It was late that night when I woke up to see Jack, my seven-year-old roommate, looking at me. He asked me how I was feeling and I told him about the surgery, or at least what it felt like afterward. He seemed kind and interested. My football season was lost, and I was starting to accept that fact. Life would go on. Jack seemed nice enough to talk to, and he was a good distraction from my cares, too.

After we chatted for a while about my surgery, and life in general, I finally asked him why he was in the hospital. "I have cancer," he said without missing a beat. I froze. I looked at this little kid and couldn't believe what he had just told me. For him, it was like he was talking about what he ate for breakfast, simple. I noticed how sickly he looked, pale and drawn. We talked about it for a while and I was even more surprised at his candor and acceptance of his situation.

Here I was, twice Jack's age, and all I had was a hernia. Nothing life-threatening. Nothing I wouldn't get over. I had been grumpy and pouty for a week, feeling so sorry for myself—how my life had been derailed (temporarily) and how unfair everything was—when in front of me was a little boy whose short life was going to be cut even shorter by cancer. This was an example of true struggles, and yet Jack acted so much wiser and older than me. I was ashamed. I felt like the biggest fool. When he finally went to sleep, I remember just staring at him. I prayed for him and asked God to forgive my selfishness. Then I cried for him.

Life is short. Life is precious. We spend so much of our time worrying about the little things and blowing them out of proportion because, after all, they are happening to *us*! We get all caught up in our own problems, making them so much bigger than they really are, assigning them too much importance. We lose sight of the real problems that are out there.

Think back on the last crisis you faced, the last thing you were worried about, and I'll bet you realize now how unimportant it is/ was. I learned that from my lost football season. After my operation, I recovered and had a very successful basketball season. Football the following year was just as fantastic as I had dreamed it would be in tenth grade. I had lost one season of play, but I learned an important lesson: problems are as big as you make them, because no matter how insurmountable you may think your troubles are, there is always someone out there who has a bigger mountain to climb. Maybe the solution to your cares is as simple as opening your eyes and reaching out a helping hand to another person, to put your own problems in perspective.

~Kevin Sorbo

92

The Gift

If you want to turn your life around, try thankfulness.
It will change your life mightily.
~Gerald Good

The day was bright and sunny, clear, crisp and beautiful, exactly the opposite of my attitude, which was rotten and sad, ungrateful and sour.

The day I am referring to was no different from any other day except for the fact that I was skiing in the beautiful Eastern Sierras in California. It is a place that many find uplifting and spectacular, but I found hard to see because most of my days back then involved a bad attitude.

I was fifteen and a year past the death of my mother. I was mad at the world and I wasn't afraid to show it. Gratitude was a foreign word to me. Fun was fleeting except for brief moments of snowball fights and checker games at night.

We hit the slopes early that day. My skis dangled from the chairlift as I rose high through the trees towards the top of the mountain. Halfway up my attitude went from bad to worse. I had dropped one of my ski poles! This, of course, was before the days of snowboards that don't require any ski poles. I needed two ski poles! Down it fell until it stuck far below like a toothpick in the bright white snow below the chairlift, inaccessible from the slopes.

That's when the moaning and complaining started. Not just your normal run-of-the-mill complaining, but relentless and continuous complaining. "How can I ski with one pole?" I yelled. I felt off balance and awkward. Or was it my attitude that was off balance? Either way, I wasn't a happy camper… or skier.

And so the story went throughout the day with only one pole. Then, something happened… something that I still remember to this day.

In the afternoon, when even I was tired of hearing my complaints, I decided to make one last run. Up the hill I went. Only this time I decided to go all the way up to the advanced run. I slid from the chair, looked briefly at the landscape far below and took off down the hill.

As I was swerving this way and that, I heard from behind me several "Oohs!" and "Aahs!" "Look at that guy go!" I heard people say as they watched a skier fly down the hill.

I turned around to see a kid, about my age, yelling "Woo Hoo!" as he jumped from one mogul to the next, spinning and flying through the air. He was having fun and looking good doing it. I thought, "Wow, I wish I could ski like that!" I was in awe of his skill and technique. He flew by me as though he wasn't even touching the snow.

Then I noticed… he was smiling and laughing and he didn't have any arms! Here he was, obviously a great skier, with a great attitude. Yet he didn't have any ski poles because he had no arms. I had been complaining all day long because I had lost just one of my ski poles. This kid was having the time of his life with much less. That was a defining moment for me.

Many times since that day when I have felt a bad attitude coming on, I think of the gift God gave me on that ski slope… the gift of gratitude and the perspective to see it. Many things may happen to you in your life, both good and bad, but it is how you view them that makes a difference. When you focus on what you have instead of what you don't have, you will be much happier and joyful and you will be a shining light to those around you!

~Stan Holden

93

A Piece of the Puzzle

Happiness is an attitude. We either make ourselves miserable,
or happy and strong. The amount of work is the same.
~Francesca Reigler

S ummer heat seeped into every corner of the small attic bedroom. Hot, humid air snaked across my chest and made my already labored breathing more difficult. At nearly ten years old, I thought I was too old to have the croup. The wheezing and barking cough told a different story.

Earlier that morning, fever and congestion had been my greatest enemies. Now I added anger and disappointment to the mix.

As the excited voices of my sister and two cousins wafted upstairs, I scrunched deeper into the soft bed. The slam of the front door, followed by the rumbling of my uncle's old car, plunged me further into frustration. They were off on an afternoon adventure, while I was stuck in bed. Again.

I spat out all the bad words I knew, which only served to fuel my anger and provoke a coughing spasm that left me struggling for breath. Worn out by wheezing and the heat, I fell asleep. When I awoke, my grandmother was sitting in a chair next to my bed, rhythmically shelling peas into a big pot.

She looked at me and smiled. "Good. You're awake." She reached over and pressed her hand against my forehead. "Better. In a few days, you'll be up and running around."

"Not soon enough," I muttered.

Her hands stilled for a moment, a fat pea pod held in her stocky fingers. "Ah, the trip."

I pounded my hand on the bed. "They could have waited. I'm stuck here and they're off having a good time. It's not fair." Tears welled up in my eyes as I spoke.

My grandmother remained silent. Her hands again moved smoothly, continuing to shell peas as if they had a life of their own. When she finally spoke, her voice had an edge to it. "So, who told you life was fair?"

I straightened up, surprised at her words. "What do you mean?"

"I mean that life isn't fair." She put the pot on the floor by her chair and turned to me with her this-is-important-so-listen-up look. "It's a tough lesson to learn at ten or at any age, and some people never learn it. They spend all their time being angry and waste what they do have by wanting what they don't or can't have, not appreciating what they do have."

I opened my mouth to respond, but a series of deep coughs seized my body. When I could breathe again, I protested, "But the only thing I have is the stupid croup. Who would want that?"

"Harriet, you are one smart cookie, so listen carefully. In a few days, you will be better. Some people who are sick don't get better." She leaned over me a second time and planted a kiss on my forehead. "Enough about trips. Let's play cards. This time I won't be so easy to beat."

I still felt I had gotten a raw deal, but I knew enough not to argue with my grandmother. I tucked this conversation away in the back of my mind where I could take it out later, examine it and try to fit the different pieces together. Talks with my grandmother often followed this pattern.

But right now I was more interested in playing cards than unraveling my grandmother's lessons.

For the next hour, we played gin rummy. At first, I won every game and crowed with delight between bouts of coughing. My grandmother said nothing, just played in her slow, careful way.

Toward the end of the hour, my luck deserted me and I lost one game, a second, and soon a third. With each loss, a knot of anger grew in my stomach at the cards, at my family, and at the unfairness of life. All the enjoyment of the game was gone but I played on, determined to succeed.

After winning five games in a row, my grandmother totaled the score. She had beaten me by a landslide, but instead of gloating the way I would have, she simply gathered up the cards and the pot with the shelled peas. "Enough for one day. You feel good enough to come downstairs?"

For an answer, I got out of bed and padded after her into the kitchen. I plunked down at the large, wooden table while she opened the freezer and pulled out a carton of ice cream. "You're in luck. It's chocolate. Your favorite."

She spooned two oversized scoops of chocolate in one bowl and a smaller scoop in a second one. A moment later, the bigger bowl sat in front of me. The cold velvet slipped down my throat, soothing the raw tissue.

We had just finished eating when a car door slammed outside. My sister and cousins raced into the kitchen, all talking at once. My uncle walked in behind them and held out a paper bag. "We got these for you."

I opened the bag and pulled out a package of pink cream-filled wafers. "Strawberry," I said in a small voice. Anger tightened my chest and I opened my mouth to complain—to tell them they should know I hate strawberry.

Before I could speak, the clink of a spoon against a bowl caught my attention. I turned toward the sound. As I did, a look passed between my grandmother and me. My jaw snapped shut.

The anger, the card game, and the expectant faces crowded around me all came together. A piece of my grandmother's puzzle clicked into place. I had made one bad choice that day by being angry at what I didn't have, rather than being happy with what I did have. Now I had another chance.

"Thank you," I said. "We can have these for dessert tonight."

~Harriet Cooper

94

Is That All?

Gratitude is the best attitude.
~Author Unknown

Christmas was always an amazing time in my home when I was growing up. My parents didn't have a lot of money but they were always incredibly generous when it came to giving us presents. In fact, they didn't just give presents to us children. Every year they held a Christmas Eve party and gave all the kids in the neighborhood presents as well.

One year, when I was eight years old, I was hoping against hope that I would get a bike for Christmas. I made it clear in every way I knew how to my parents. I left hints all over the place.

On Christmas morning, we had our normal over-abundance of presents. All of us kids received present after present, with the last present being the "big" one. When we got to the apparent end of the presents I was very upset. My last present had not been the "big" one I had hoped for. There was no bike for me. I blurted out, "Is that all?" The moment I said it I knew I had made a big mistake. That comment would have been inappropriate in any situation but after all those presents it was completely wrong-headed.

My parents looked unhappy, as my disappointment was obvious. I was so upset I didn't even realize how ungrateful I sounded. My entire family felt extremely uncomfortable and was on edge. For a few moments there was nothing but silence around the tree. I started to realize what an idiotic thing I had said. After my parents worked so hard, how could I complain that I did not receive a bike when I had received so many other things?

My parents continued to look very upset, and then something happened that made me feel even worse. My father got up and went outside the living room to the hallway. He came back wheeling the bicycle that they had been planning to give me after all the other presents were distributed.

Now I felt even worse than before—I had gotten the bike but had demonstrated for my parents and my siblings what an ungrateful person I actually was. How could I ever enjoy it after that? I did learn to enjoy my new bike, but it was never as good as it would have been if I hadn't said that stupid thing.

My parents were very wise people and they knew how to handle this. They told me to think about how I felt at the moment I saw that I had actually received the bike. They told me to remember that feeling so that I would never repeat that mistake and feel that way again.

For years after that, at the end of all the present giving, my father would ask me what I had to say to everyone. It had become a family joke. I would always say, "Is that all?" But what I really meant was "Thanks so much." And everyone knew that.

~Bill Rouhana

95

The Boy Who Had Everything

Gratitude is an art of painting an adversity into a lovely picture.
~Kak Sri

When I was a baby, my parents gave me anything I wanted. We would walk into a store, and anything that I wanted was mine; all that I had to do was to ask. I would play with a toy for a while, get bored, and ask my parents for a new toy. Then my dad died when I was two and a half, and I got even more stuff as my mom, friends and family gave me more and more stuff to try to make me feel better. My mom continued to treat me to whatever I wanted until I was seven and my world changed.

That was when the real estate market crashed. My mom had thought that buying houses was a good idea as a way to invest her money to take care of us. After the crash, I went from the kid who got an iPod when his tooth fell out and who had the coolest house to hang out in, to literally having nowhere to stay. My mom's best friend, my Auntie Loren, took us in until my mom could figure out what to do.

After the real estate crash, when I would ask for a new toy, or bike, or even to see a movie my mom would say "maybe for your birthday" or "I'm sorry honey, but we can't really afford that right now." I didn't know it then, but my mom had grown up in a family where money was never a problem, so this change was as big for her as it was for me. My constant requests for toys and video games were not helping my mom, who was already a widow, deal with her feelings about our new crisis—our financial situation. But I wasn't used to hearing "no" so for a year or two I kept asking.

Then something happened that would change my way of thinking forever. My mom had been working really hard all year, just to pay for the necessities, like our water and power bills. When she asked me what I wanted for my birthday I said that I wanted a new video gaming system. I didn't know that it was expensive. All I knew was that my friends had them and that I wanted one too.

On my birthday, I started opening my presents, believing that I would get what I asked for. As I opened the last gift, I found two or three T-shirts and a pair of jeans. When my mom asked me what I thought, I said that I loved them, but she could tell how disappointed I was and she started crying. I hugged her harder than I had ever hugged anyone before. I realized how hard she was working and that she couldn't afford to give me anything I didn't need and that most of the money that my mom made went to paying for rent and food.

From then on I didn't expect to get everything that I asked for. When I did, I was so excited and grateful. I think I learned the difference between what I wanted and what I needed. I learned to appreciate the toys or games I did have and to take good care of them. When I wanted a new iPod, I had to work to buy it. I got a job folding clothes at our local laundromat, and after working there for just over a month every day after school, I had enough saved up to buy that iPod.

The feeling of having truly earned something is one of the best feelings in the world. I also am lucky to have wonderful people in my life. They have made me appreciate that it doesn't matter what I have or don't have. What matters more is who I am and who I get to spend time with.

It may have been hard going through that experience, but I was able to learn some really important lessons. Now I am grateful for everything I have and I understand the feeling you get from working to earn something for yourself. People used to think I was "spoiled" because I always had everything and didn't understand how fortunate I was. Recently, my godfather Ty told my mom that he loved to give me things because I never ask for anything and am always so grateful. I guess I've really changed.

~Jackson Jarvis

96

Learning to Love My Messy Life

Call it a clan, call it a network, call it a tribe, call it a family.
Whatever you call it, whoever you are, you need one.
~Jane Howard

I slowly open my front door, praying I'll find some sort of normalcy when I enter. No such luck. Two children fly past me, my sister chasing after our brother, screaming for her doll back. There is pasta sauce splattered on our kitchen wall—artwork, my dad calls it. And my mom has set up shop smack in the middle, ironing a mountain of clothes while *Law and Order* blares from our television.

"I have five siblings," I mutter to my new neighbor, Michelle. "Sorry for the mess."

I whisk her away to my bedroom. It's really a room shared with my two sisters, but that was nothing a good bribe couldn't fix. They were "gone for the day" as Michelle and I flipped through magazines and painted our toenails. Mercifully, none of my brothers came barging in, and the smell of acetone was enough to keep my dad away. When it was time for dinner, Michelle skipped back to her house, telling me she'd call tomorrow.

She did, and I happily accepted her invitation to go to her house. Any place would be better than my house. Soon, I was standing at her front door, ringing the bell. A strange woman answered.

"Hello, Miss Suzanne," she said in broken English. "Michelle is upstairs."

That couldn't be her mother. I looked up at a gleaming white marble double staircase. Michelle appeared at the top, a huge smile on her face, motioning for me to follow her. I wanted to thank the woman who had opened the door, but she had disappeared.

To say Michelle's bedroom was huge is an understatement. It was more like a hotel suite, complete with king size bed, a sparkling chandelier and every toy imaginable. I had never seen anything so glamorous. She explained to me that the woman downstairs was her nanny, Marion. I wondered if Marion was going to hang out with us, but it quickly became clear that we had total freedom. The only interruption that day was Aura, the housekeeper, who was putting away freshly-folded laundry. A nanny and a housekeeper at her disposal? Michelle was living the life.

I went over to Michelle's almost every day that summer, playing with her insane toy collection, unknowingly becoming more and more like family to her. I loved being in her immaculately clean home, having our lunches prepared for us like we were royalty. No chores, no siblings to annoy us, no parents to constantly nag us. I never noticed that her own parents were rarely home, and her nanny and housekeeper ignored her.

On one of those days, Michelle called me over earlier than usual. Her dad had given her something amazing called an Xbox, and she was dying to play it.

I raced over, flung open the door and announced my arrival. Aura crept up from the basement, greeting me the way she and Marion always did.

"Hello, Miss Suzanne. Michelle is upstairs."

"Thanks, Aura!" My voice echoed in her empty house.

It dawned on me. As I bounded up that glorious staircase, I thought, what did Michelle do when I wasn't there?

Sure, she had an endless supply of the latest gadgets. Sure, she had dance classes to go to. Sure, she had a nanny and a housekeeper. But who did she talk to? Who did she laugh with?

We spent all afternoon playing that Xbox. Time slipped away from us, and before we knew it, my mom was calling to tell me it was time for dinner. I looked over at Michelle, rolling my eyes as I begged my mom to let me miss dinner. This was not a battle I was going to win.

"Fine, Mom, I'll be home in five minutes," I grumbled through my teeth. But before I could slam the phone down, an idea popped into my head.

"Wait, Mom!" I said. "Can Michelle have dinner with us tonight?"

We had to squeeze in an extra chair for her, but she didn't mind. Her eyes shined as she looked around at our table, talking excitedly with my sisters, shoveling food into her mouth like she hadn't eaten in days. She laughed at all the things that embarrassed me. She laughed at my dad's cluelessness. She laughed at my brothers flinging lettuce at each other. She even laughed when my sister tripped over our oven door, which had a broken latch that made it fall open every five minutes. Another thing to fix on our list of things to fix.

When our meal was finished, and all the dishes had been washed (assembly line style, the custom in our house), she turned to me and whispered, "You're so lucky you have such a big family. Can I have dinner with you all tomorrow night?"

I looked over at my sloppy siblings; my brothers were making a fort with our couch cushions, knocking over everything to make room for it, and my sisters were jumping up and down in the other room, dancing to a boombox that skipped whenever they hit the floor too hard. My parents were making espresso that bubbled over every time, adding yet another layer to the permanent coffee stain on our stove. Suddenly, my house — my crowded, messy, loud house — seemed like paradise.

~Suzanne De Vita

97

Chicken Soup for the Soul

Make Your Heart Smile

You can't live a perfect day without doing something for someone
who will never be able to repay you.
~John Wooden

My grandmother beeped the horn and I ran out the front door to meet her. She sat smiling in the driver's seat.

"Where are we going?" I asked, even though it really didn't matter. I enjoyed spending time with her whatever we did.

"You'll see," she said with a sly grin. She was barely five foot tall, but made up for it in her big personality and even bigger heart.

We drove out of my neighborhood and past the middle school I attended until we ended up in a place I'd never been. At first I thought it was apartments, but the brick buildings weren't connected and it seemed more like a small community. Wet clothes hung from front porch railings and trashcans overflowed. Men walked around shirtless, staring at us as we pulled into an empty parking space. I instinctively locked my door.

"There's nothing to be afraid of, sweetheart," my grandmother said as she squeezed my hand.

Before she turned off the ignition, I spotted two familiar faces walking our way. It was a mother and daughter from our church, and the young girl went to my school.

My grandmother quickly hugged the woman and said, "Ready to do some shopping, ladies?"

I scooted into the backseat with Deidre. We chatted until pulling into our town's local mall. Deidre and I skipped to a popular store where most girls our age shopped and in the window a big banner read "Back to School Sale!" We squealed and ran in. There were racks and racks to choose from—bright colored shoes and shirts to match. My grandmother and Deidre's mom helped us find the right sizes. But before we made it to the dressing room, Deidre stopped so suddenly I nearly bumped into her.

"Look at these!" she said as she picked up a pair of orange and yellow duck slippers. She slowly slid her hand into the soft shoe before running it across her cheek. She stripped her socks off and tried them on. "Oh, it's like walking on a cloud! Aren't they the cutest things you've ever seen?"

But before I could agree, her mother quickly grabbed the slipper out of her hand and shot her a look of disapproval.

"You don't need these, Deidre," she said with a stern glare.

Deidre shook her head and put the slippers back on the shelf. Steps away, my grandmother overheard the exchange and changed the subject with lighthearted conversation (she was good at that).

Almost an hour later, with a pile of clothes in hand, we were done.

"Well, why don't you girls keep looking and we'll take care of this stuff," my grandmother said as she and Deidre's mom made their way to the cash registers.

As my friend and I looked around, out of the corner of my eye I noticed Deidre's mother wrap her arms around my grandmother before taking the bags of clothes.

After lunch, we waved goodbye to Deidre and her mom and watched the two walk back to their home.

"Did you have fun?" my grandmother asked while putting the car in reverse.

"I did. Thank you for the clothes, Grandma."

"Well, we have one more thing left to buy and we're done."

"What's that?" I asked.

"We're going back for those slippers. It'll be our gift to Deidre," she said, even though I knew she'd already given them a gift that day.

We drove back to the store that afternoon and purchased the fuzzy duck slippers.

Weeks later, our family sat around the table enjoying a meal at my grandmother's home. She had outdone herself with roast and potatoes, corn and green beans, her famous apple pie for dessert. When we were done eating, I began helping her clean the kitchen. As I brought the dishes to the sink, she leaned down and whispered, "I have something for you in my room. Go ahead, I'll finish this," she said with her hands plunged into soapy water.

I walked into her bedroom and lying on the dresser was a gift wrapped in silver paper. My name was written just below a bright blue bow. I ripped it open to find a pair of yellow and orange duck slippers with a note slipped inside one of the shoes. It read:

Some of the best gifts are practical ones, but every little girl needs a present that makes her heart smile. Always make time for what makes your heart smile.

Though I've outgrown the shoes, I haven't outgrown the message. My grandmother was happiest when she was giving to others. And I knew she wanted me to find that unique way to encourage people too.

And she was right. It would be the best moments in life — those that make your heart smile.

~Amanda Dodson

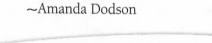

98

Like a Pendulum

Even if happiness forgets you a little bit, never completely forget about it.
~Jacques Prévert

The hallway was full of dressed-up people hiding their tears under fake smiles. It seemed like everyone wanted to break into tears. Honestly, I wanted to cry too, but I promised I wouldn't. My mom looked at me wearily, her eyes red; she tried her best to sound comforting.

"He'll be fine, Mikaela, really. He'll come back and we'll be a happy family once again," my mom whispered, her voice barely audible in the hallway. My dad, dressed in his camouflage army gear, walked up to me with a smile.

"Hey kiddo, don't worry about me, I'll be fine. Everything will be okay," he said in his loud voice. I knew he was sincere but I still couldn't help thinking that this could be the last time I would ever see him. "You promise that you won't cry for me, okay? I don't want any crying coming from you. Like I said, don't worry, I promise. Pinky promise?"

He held his pinky out to me.

I stuck my pinky out and my tongue along the way and mumbled under my breath, "Sure Dad, sure." The grin on his face grew wider.

The thoughts flooded in again, the thoughts of my dad dying. I began to imagine how devastating it would be if he were gone. I would be confused, upset. Why did my dad have to do this? Why couldn't he stay home and be there for me? Even if he were okay, I wouldn't see him for a whole year. And before I knew it, I had already broken the promise of no tears.

Soon the whole room was full of crying adults. My first reaction was to run out of there, and so I did. My chubby feet weren't that fast but I darted out of the room as fast as I could and ran to the bathroom. I shut myself in an empty stall. I stayed for what seemed like hours.

Finally, I mustered up the courage to go outside. As soon as I walked out, I could see myself in the mirror. I looked awful. My blue dress had became a crumpled, tear-stained disaster, my hair looked like a bird's nest, and most of all, my eyes were red. A girl came into the bathroom and started talking to me. "You're a first timer. Everyone starts off like this." She was a teenager, maybe fourteen or fifteen, with short curly hair and wearing casual clothes. She continued, "My name's Jessica, but you can call me Jess. My dad's a medic. How about you?"

"Mikaela. My dad's a medic too."

I started crying again. Jessica gave me a caring smile. I'm not sure why, but I told her everything.

"I know that it's so hard to know that your dad's going to be leaving you alone, but you should be proud of him. I know I am," said Jessica. "My dad's been going to war since I was six and I don't see him often. But I'm proud of him. Do you know how many lives he's saved? He's saved 100 people. That makes me happy, knowing that my dad is saving people."

I felt so selfish in that one moment. Here was a girl who had suffered much more than I had and she was happy that others were happy and grateful to her dad for serving our country. A pang of guilt ran through me.

I only knew Jessica for ten minutes but she taught me a lot. Because of my father getting deployed to Iraq, many people would have a second chance at life; many families would get their loved one back. I learned that, like a pendulum, there's always another side, a much brighter, happier side, and that I must always look on the bright side.

~Mikaela Rose

99

The Color of Gratitude

Green is the prime color of the world, and that from which
its loveliness arises.
~Pedro Calderón de la Barca

Seeing the world differently than everyone else is an experience all its own, especially when you don't even know that you are seeing things differently. I didn't know I was colorblind until I started school. I had been excited to start school and I loved everything about it — the playground, circle time, snack time, making new friends. Everything except coloring. I hated picking out crayons and staying in the lines. I never asked for a coloring book at restaurants. I just did not get what all excitement was about.

My parents didn't question it. They just assumed it was not something I enjoyed and often joked about the fact that I was very smart but was failing coloring in preschool. That is, until the day I came home full of news about my new friend, Devon, who was tall, funny and… green. My mom laughed it off at the time, assuming Devon must have been wearing a green shirt.

A few days later I attended my first flag football practice. My mom sat on the sideline watching as I learned for the first time the rules of football. I played with all my heart. At the end of the practice my new coach came up to my mom and me and told me what a good job I had done. When my dad called from work later that day to hear about my first football experience, I told him how the green coach had praised me.

The following day my mom accompanied me into the classroom to meet my "Martian" of a friend. When I pointed him out my mom began to chuckle. She told me that he was brown, not green. Within a few days I was sitting in a doctor's office taking a colorblindness exam and sure enough I tested positive. I was officially brown/green colorblind.

Since then I have learned how to deal with colorblindness by reading the names on the crayons or colored pencils. My mom has had to draw charts and label them if I need to see shades for a school assignment. But most importantly I have learned that color doesn't matter as long as I wake up each day and experience the wonders of brown grass and green tree trunks.

~Bailey Corona

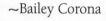

The Kind Police Officer

Service to others is the rent you pay for your room here on earth.
~Muhammad Ali

"Wake up, Heather." My mom shook me awake. "Your daddy's having a stroke. I need you to wake up."

I had heard of strokes before, but I didn't know anyone who had ever had one. I remembered an older gentleman from church had recently passed away; people said he suffered a massive stroke.

I grabbed my glasses off my bedside table and followed my mom into my parents' bedroom. My dad was moving in a jerky fashion across the bed.

"The ambulance is on the way," my mom said. "Please hold his hand while I get dressed."

I crawled beside my daddy, drool coming from his mouth and his eyes frantically moving all over the room. "I'll be okay," he slurred as if he were still half asleep.

"Yes, Daddy," I said, my voice shaking with fear, "You will be okay." Then I changed those words to a request. "Please be okay?"

"Okay, okay. I'll be okay," my dad repeated, still slurring his speech.

My mom had finished dressing, and I heard her waking my younger sister up and helping her get dressed. I heard her tell my sister in a calm, reassuring voice, "The ambulance is going to come and take Daddy to the hospital."

As I heard the sirens getting closer, my mom came back to the room and took my daddy's jittery hands from me. "You need to go get dressed now."

Scared and not wanting to leave my daddy or my mom, I went to my room and threw on some sweat pants and a sweatshirt. My sister stood at my side and waited until I was dressed before grabbing my hand with hers. It was mid-December, five days before Christmas. I pulled on some shoes and, with my sister at my side, we went to the front door to let the paramedics in.

As is standard practice, a police officer accompanied them. After he checked out my dad's situation in the bedroom, he returned to my sister and me; we were standing together in the dining room, our arms around each other.

"Does your mom have an address book?" he asked.

We nodded.

"Good. If you know where it is, go ahead and grab it. Your mom will want that to call family members once your dad is settled at the hospital. Where's her purse?"

My sister lifted my mom's purse from the back door handle where it was always draped.

"Great. She'll want to have that as well," he continued talking as he grabbed a paper grocery sack that we had in the kitchen, filling it with snacks and crayons and bottles of soda. "Do you attend a church?"

We told him our church and our pastor's name. He asked if he could use the phone and call our pastor. We heard him apologize to the pastor for calling at this very late hour and then explain that my dad would be taken to the hospital.

At about this time, my dad had been stabilized enough to transport him in the ambulance. The paramedics wheeled the gurney down our hall and out the front door.

The police officer then huddled my sister and me together. "I'm going to drive right behind the ambulance. You tell your mom to drive right behind me, okay? And tell her she has my permission to speed." He grinned and winked.

With my dad being loaded into the ambulance, my mom grabbed her keys from the hook beside the back door. The officer escorted us from our home, shutting the door behind us all. Calmly, he told my mom to follow him.

When we got to the hospital, the officer walked us inside. My mom was taken back with my dad, and my sister and I sat in the waiting room, still holding hands. After speaking with the nurse at the front desk, the officer sat down with us, handing us the paper bag he had packed from our home.

"I have to go back out on duty, but I've packed you some things from your home. You shouldn't need anything. But if you do, that nice nurse right over there," he said pointing to the front desk, "will get you anything you want. And if she doesn't, you call for me." At that time, our pastor arrived and sat with my sister and me.

The officer stood to leave and then said, "I bet your dad will be just fine. He's got two beautiful daughters to live for."

The officer was right. My dad was just fine. He spent almost two weeks recovering from the stroke, but he had very little permanent damage.

I don't remember the officer's name. I don't recall ever encountering him again, but I will always be grateful for his being there. When my mom couldn't reassure us, and we were faced with a very unclear and scary future with our dad, the officer took the extra time and effort to help two scared sisters in the middle of the night.

It's because of his encouragement that my sister and I were able to stay strong for our family that night. I'll never forget his kindness, and I try to replicate it whenever I can.

~Heather Davis

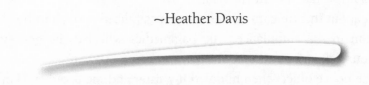

My Final Foster Home

Keep away from people who try to belittle your ambitions.
Small people always do that, but the really great make you feel that you,
too, can become great.
~Mark Twain

Moving into a foster home is quite a scary experience for a child or young teen. I moved in with my foster parents, whom I now call mom and dad, at the beginning of the second semester of my freshman year in high school. I was fifteen years old. My social worker Tonya said, "They have three children of their own, one boy and two girls, all younger than you. They also attend church regularly."

My reply was, "Okay," as I was too nervous to think of anything else to say. She continued to inform me that they were good people and had been foster parents for a long time, and that they were well known and respected in the community.

As we pulled into the driveway, my heart began to pound hard in my chest. Before Tonya could shut the engine off, a lady and two children came outside to greet us. The lady, Linda, began talking to Tonya as we began to exit the car. The children came to my side and started talking to me, all at once. They could have spoken a foreign language and I wouldn't have understood them any better. Tonya informed Linda that I hadn't said much and that I was pretty nervous, from what I caught of their conversation. As we started to remove my luggage, the children yelled that they wanted to help. They each grabbed a bag, and I grabbed my largest suitcase and another bag. We went into the house while Linda and Tonya continued to talk.

We took my luggage into Sonya's bedroom. She was the youngest and she had bunk beds, so this was to be my bedroom as well. As we laid my luggage on the floor, Sharon, the middle child, sat on the bed asking so many questions that I couldn't answer them all. Sonya remained standing beside me asking questions as well. All the questions and their excitement just added to my nervousness.

When I began to open and unpack my luggage, Sonya and Sharon showed me which drawers to put my clothes in and which drawer I could use as a junk drawer. As I emptied each bag they wanted to see what I had. Linda came to the bedroom and told the girls that they needed to quit bugging me, but I told her it was okay. They were just curious.

After I finished putting everything away, Linda went to another room and Sharon and Sonya took me on a tour of the house. Then they took me outside to show me their horses and barn. Sonya wanted to show me her swing set and asked me if I would push her on a swing for a few minutes. It was Wednesday, church night, so we went back into the house to start preparing for church.

Linda was ironing her clothes as Sharon and Sonya dressed for church. Linda and I talked about my past foster homes and about her husband Ray and Junior, the oldest child. She told me that Junior was at his cousin's house and Ray was at work. Before I could ask what time they would be home so I could meet them, the door flew open and four people came in talking and laughing loudly. They started talking to me all at once. Linda laughed and told them to leave me alone because they were probably scaring me to death, but I thought it was funny.

I was ready for bedtime that day as I was tired from all the activity. But Sonya continued to ask questions and talk to me until Linda threatened to go and get her father.

Days turned into weeks, weeks into months, and months into years. As every day went by, my foster parents treated me just as if I were their child. I lived with them for several years and even when I was acting like a typical smart-mouthed teenager, they never called Tonya to come remove me and place me somewhere else.

After living with them and seeing how life could be, I was inspired. I saw how working hard and staying away from drugs and alcohol could lead to a good life. My life before foster care always involved moving from place to place and I saw lots of drug and alcohol abuse. I am so grateful to my foster family for showing me a different and better way of life.

~Amanda Plaxico

Meet Our Contributors

Debbie Acklin has been featured in over two dozen newspapers and TV news shows for her work as a contributor to the *Chicken Soup for the Soul* series. She lives in Alabama with her husband, two grown children, and Duchess the cat. E-mail her at d_acklin@hotmail.com or visit her on Facebook at debbieacklinauthor or follow her on Twitter @debbieacklin.

Monica A. Andermann lives on Long Island where she shares a home with her husband Bill and their cat Marlo. Her writing has been included in such publications as *Angels on Earth*, *Woman's World* and many editions of both the *Cup of Comfort* and *Chicken Soup for the Soul* anthologies.

Jennifer Azantian is a published author of short stories in both fiction and nonfiction. After graduating from UC San Diego, she joined the Sandra Dijkstra Literary Agency where she brings a passion for literature born of a writer's heart to the discovery and nurturing of new talent. Follow her on Twitter at @jenazantian.

Felice Keller Becker graduated from the University of Arizona with a BA degree in Creative Writing and Phi Beta Kappa honors, and earned an MBA degree from the University of Washington. An award-winning songwriter, Felice lives with her husband and daughter in Los Angeles, where she is working on her first book.

Valerie D. Benko is a Communications Specialist from western

Pennsylvania. When she's not writing corporate material she frees her mind through creative nonfiction writing. Valerie has more than twenty stories published in anthologies in the U.S. and Canada. Visit her online at valeriebenko.weebly.com.

Emma Blandford has recently finished her master's degree in Education and is working full-time at a state university as a Residence Hall Director. She is passionate about health and physical education, water safety and directs an aquatics program during the summer months.

Jeanne Blandford is a writer/editor who, along with her husband Jack, is currently producing documentaries and creating children's books. When not in their Airstream looking for new material, they can be found running SafePet, a partnership between Outreach for Pets in Need (OPIN) and Domestic Violence Crisis Center (DVCC).

Tucker Blandford found his direction in life after completing three documentaries while still in high school. A recent graduate from UConn with a BA degree in Fine Arts for Theatre Production and Design, he is currently honing his skills creating puppets and the worlds they live in.

Christy Box is a student at the University of Central Florida. She was the Editor-in-Chief of the Florida Virtual School newspaper and was published in *EC* magazine. She enjoys writing, traveling, and reading. Christy is a screenwriter and intends to pursue this as a career. E-mail her at box.christy@gmail.com.

Michaela Brawn is a recent graduate of LaGuardia Arts high school. She currently attends Brown University, class of 2017. Last summer was spent traveling throughout Europe with her friend Griffin. She enjoys singing and horseback riding.

Richard Brookton is a retired schoolteacher from Australia. He and his wife Natalie have two married children and four grandchildren. His teaching career started in one-teacher schools in the Australian bush, and he later taught high school and science college classes. Barbershop singing (baritone) is now one of his passions.

Caitlin Brown enjoys reading, cooking, playing paintball, and filmmaking. She was homeschooled through her senior year of high school, and is now a college student majoring in cinematography. Her Christian faith is important to her, and her goal is to produce family-friendly films. E-mail her at ShoeboxGirl@comcast.net.

Teresa Bruce writes and edits for authors and publications, including the *College Park Community Paper*. Her chemical-free garden yields more harvest for critters than for friends, but her homemade bread is almost as good as her mom's was. Please read her blog, "What to Say When Someone..." at TealAshes.com.

Jill Burns lives in the mountains of West Virginia with her family. She's a retired piano teacher and performer. She enjoys writing, music, gardening and nature.

Bruce Campbell is a New York Times best-selling author several times over with his books, *If Chins Could Kill: Confessions of a B Movie Actor* and *Make Love the Bruce Campbell Way*. His day job is being an actor.

Andrea Canale is currently in her last year of college, studying Cultural Anthropology. She hopes to continue her hobby of helping others by joining the Peace Corps. Andrea enjoys drumming, reading, and cooking. She was first published in three *Chicken Soup for the Soul* books in 2008.

Zulema Anahy Carlos is a high school senior. She is an outgoing and outspoken girl who enjoys helping people, working with children, dancing and singing. Zulema also enjoys writing nonfiction because she's able to express her feelings, thoughts and talk about the real world.

Beth Cato is an active member of the Science Fiction & Fantasy Writers of America, and a frequent contributor to the *Chicken Soup for the Soul* series. She's originally from Hanford, CA, but now resides in Buckeye, AZ with her husband and son. Connect with her through www.bethcato.com.

Madeline Clapps lives in Brooklyn with her boyfriend and her cat Vanilla Bean. She went to New York University and is a singer, writer, and editor, with many stories published in *Chicken Soup for the Soul* books.

Courtney Conover is a wife, mother, and yoga instructor who writes to take the edge off. She resides in suburban Detroit with her husband Scott and their toddler son. Her blog on motherhood, "I Signed Up for This?" can be found at courtneyconover.blogspot.com.

Harriet Cooper is a freelance writer and has published personal essays, humor and creative nonfiction in newspapers, newsletters, anthologies and magazines, and is a frequent contributor to the *Chicken Soup for the Soul* series. She writes about family, relationships, health, food, cats, writing and daily life. E-mail her at shewrites@ live.ca.

Bailey Corona is a high school junior. He plays on the varsity soccer team at his high school and loves to ride his mountain bike, dirt bike and go off-roading in his Jeep.

D'ette Corona is the Assistant Publisher of Chicken Soup for the Soul Publishing, LLC. She received her Bachelor of Science degree in business management. D'ette has been happily married for twenty-one years and has a sixteen-year-old son whom she adores.

Maddy Curtis dreams of becoming a professional singer by attending Catholic University of America for her Bachelor of Music degree in Vocal Performance. She is the ninth child in her huge family of twelve and hopes to become an opera singer and use her talents to benefit children with special needs. E-mail her at maddycurtis93@gmail.com.

Emily Sheera Cutler is a sophomore at the University of Pennsylvania where she is studying Theatre Arts with a minor in Creative Writing. Emily's stories have also been published in *Chicken Soup for the Soul: Teens Talk Middle School*, *Polyphony H.S.*, and *Able Muse Review*. In 2012, Emily was selected as a YoungArts Finalist in Writing.

Michael Damiano is a nonfiction writer. He writes in English and Spanish. His first book, *Porque la vida no basta: Encuentros con Miquel Barceló*, was published in Spanish by Editorial Anagrama (and by Editorial Empúries in Catalan) in 2012.

Heather Davis is a momma, an author and a humorist. *TMI Mom: Oversharing My Life* is a collection of humorous essays that Davis has penned. She and her family live in Oklahoma where she chronicles her life at www.minivan-momma.com. And yes, she really does drive a minivan. E-mail her at Minivan.Momma.2@gmail.com.

Pam Depoyan holds a BA degree in English from Loyola Marymount University. Her writing has appeared in *Highlights*, *Pray*, *Chicken Soup for the Soul: Angels Among Us* and *Chicken Soup for the Soul: It's Christmas!* She loves crafting "word-photo stories" that draw readers into their own moments of God's wonder. Read more at wordglow.wordpress.com.

Suzanne De Vita received her B.A. degree in communications from Quinnipiac University. A lifelong writer with a passion for working with children, she plans to pursue a career in public relations with an emphasis on youth programming. E-mail her at suzdev27@gmail.com.

Amanda Dodson and her husband of seventeen years live in Walnut Cove, NC. They have three children, ages fourteen, twelve and four. Amanda is a freelance writer and author of *Revitalized Church*. She chronicles letters to her children at amandaTDodson.com.

Shawnelle Eliasen and her husband Lonny raise their brood of boys in Illinois. Her stories have been published in *Guideposts*, *MomSense* magazine, *Marriage Partnership*, *Thriving Family*, *Cup of Comfort* books, numerous *Chicken Soup for the Soul* books, and more. Visit her blog, "Family Grace with My Five Sons," at Shawnellewrites.blogspot.com.

Victoria Fedden received her MFA degree in Creative Writing from Florida Atlantic University in 2009. She lives in Fort Lauderdale, FL. She has had several stories published in the *Chicken Soup for the Soul* series as well as many other publications, and is the author of *Amateur Night at the Bubblegum Kittikat*, a memoir for adults.

Jess Forte is a sophomore in college studying creative writing and journalism. When she isn't writing or doing homework, she enjoys spending time with friends. Follow her on Twitter @authorjessforte.

Marius Forté was born in Vienna and traveled and worked extensively throughout Europe and most of North Africa and the Arabian Peninsula, exploring in depth those areas' diverse religions, cultures and political systems. He hosts the radio show *Flashpoint Live* each weekend and his book, *The Answer: Proof of God in Heaven*, is due out fall of 2013. He lives in New York with his wife, Marti, and two children.

Jody Fuller was born and raised in Opelika, AL. He is a comedian, speaker, writer, and soldier with three tours of duty in Iraq. He currently holds the rank of Captain in the Alabama National Guard. Jody is also a lifetime stutterer. E-mail him at jody@jodyfuller.com.

Gary Graham, is an American actor best known for *Alien Nation*, *Star Trek: Enterprise*, *Robot Jox* and *The Hollywood Knights*. An avid sportsman, he served sixteen years as a Ski Patroller. Also a musician, he fronts The Gary Graham Band, and he wrote the acclaimed book, *Acting & Other Flying Lessons*. E-mail him at sikesrules@yahoo.com.

Cathy C. Hall is a writer from the sunny South. Her essays, short stories, poetry, and articles have been published in markets for both children and adults. She also blogs about all things writerly. Come read what she's been up to at c-c-hall.com.

Maryanne Higley Hamilton received her BSEd-Art degree from Florida International University, and her Masters of Art Therapy degree from Vermont College. A published author, she is an art therapist at Leepa-Rattner Museum of Art. She enjoys traveling, creating art, writing children's books, and playing her clarinet in a large marching band.

Carol Harrison, B.Ed., is a distinguished Toastmaster, motivational speaker and author of the book *Amee's Story*. She also has stories in six other *Chicken Soup for the Soul* books. She enjoys time with family and friends, reading and scrapbooking. E-mail her at carol@carolscorner.ca or visit her website at www.carolscorner.ca.

Mason Carter Harvey, a student in Guthrie, OK, has been a member of FCCLA and National Junior Honor Society and the recipient of the 2013 Prudential Spirit of Community Award. He's appeared in magazines, newspapers and media including a news documentary. He enjoys football, music, public speaking and inspiring others.

Drienie Hattingh was born and raised in South Africa. She and her husband live in Ogden, UT. Her articles appeared in magazines and newspapers in South Africa and America, and her essays in *Christmas Miracles* and *Spirit of Christmas*. She published three anthologies in the *Tales from H.E.L.* series. E-mail her at DrienieM@aol.com.

Freelance writer and piano teacher **Wendy Hobday Haugh** can't wait to share these stories with her grandchildren: Marissa, Charlie, Lilli and Max. She hopes this book will help kids everywhere by offering them encouragement, fresh insights, and smiles galore. E-mail her at whhaugh@nycap.rr.com.

Stan Holden has been a professional creative director, graphic designer and cartoonist for many years. Having transitioned out of the commercial industry he now fulfills his creative pursuits through writing and illustration for fun. He lives in Southern California with his wife Renée, daughter Sara, son William and his two dogs Jack and Bella.

Neesha Hosein is a writer and editor in Houston, TX. She has written for newspapers, magazines, websites, and runs a writing business—www.RavenTreeComm.com. She self-published her first book, *I of the Storm* (Amazon, Kindle), in 2012 and is working on a nonfiction book about autism. She blogs at www.novellarella.blogspot.com.

L. A. E. Howard is a student at Missouri State University, working towards her Bachelor of Arts degree in Secondary English Education. Lisa is the happiest when writing, singing, or spending time with her dog, Todd. She plans to be a professor of English. E-mail her at erhartl@otc.edu.

David Hull lives in upstate New York. He was a teacher for twenty-five years and is now semi-retired. He has had other stories published in the *Chicken Soup for the Soul* series. David enjoys reading, gardening and spoiling his nieces and nephews. E-mail him at Davidhull59.aol.com.

Zehra Hussain is currently a high school senior from Irving, TX. Zehra has lived in Kansas, Virginia, and even Saudi Arabia. She enjoys writing stories as well as meeting new people. She plans on pursuing a career in the medical field to make a positive impact on the world.

Ben Jaeger currently attends the University of North Florida and is pursuing a BBA degree in Economics with a minor in Community Leadership, and hopes to attend law school upon graduation. Ben enjoys traveling, listening to musicals, and playing with his dog, Winn Dixie. E-mail Ben at benreallife@hotmail.com.

Tanya Janke has worked in three schools, two shopping malls, a theatre, a market research company, and a berry patch. Now she spends her days writing. Her first play, an adaptation of *The Little Prince*, was produced in Toronto in 2010.

Amy January received her BA degree in Classics and Creative Writing from Bard College in 2004. This year, she completed her post-baccalaureate certificate in Writing for Children and Young Adults at McDaniel College. She enjoys writing, working with children, traveling, and belly dancing. She misses summer camp a lot.

Jackson Jarvis is fourteen years old, into surfing and classic rock (he thinks he should've been born in the 1960s). An aspiring music producer, he's also written three yet-to-be published books including *The Book of Bad Ideas* and *The Weird Stuff I Do*. He lives in New York State with his mom, Joelle, and his dad Eric is his guardian angel.

Dani Johnson was raised on welfare, pregnant at seventeen, homeless at twenty-one, millionaire by twenty-three. Now a best-selling author, international speaker, TV/radio host and has appeared on hundreds of shows like *Oprah* and ABC's *Secret Millionaire*. She and her husband Hans have five kids, five companies, and feed thousands of orphans monthly.

Rosalie Kramer dreamed of being an art teacher but when her sons, Marc and Danny, were born with muscular dystrophy she turned to writing as solace. After their deaths, three days apart as teenagers, she wrote to help her heal. Since retirement, her poetry and prose has been published frequently.

R.K. Krochmal lives in a small town in rural North Carolina, surrounded by family and a multitude of pets.

Cathi LaMarche has contributed to over twenty anthologies. As a composition teacher, novelist, and writing coach, she spends most days immersed in the written word. Her recent story "Bountiful Harvest" was chosen for publication in Gloria Gaynor's upcoming book titled *We Will Survive*.

Carina Lamendola is a radio broadcaster, and talk show host at WYBG in Massena, NY. She studied Drama at the American Musical and Dramatic Academy in New York City, and SUNY Potsdam in Potsdam, NY. Carina is a live organ donor to her precious mother Gloria. Learn more at www.Newstales.net.

Mary Elizabeth Laufer has a degree in English Education from SUNY Albany. When she's not writing, she works as a substitute teacher for the Osceola County school district in Florida. Her stories and poems have appeared in magazines, newspapers and several anthologies.

Kathryn Lay is a full-time writer for children and adults in books, magazines, and anthologies. She enjoys speaking to schools and writer's groups. She and her husband own Days Gone By Antiques/Vintage. The site can be found on Facebook and at Etsy at LaysDaysGoneBy. E-mail her at rlay15@aol.com.

Arlene Ledbetter holds a Bachelor of Arts degree from Dalton College. She has written adult Sunday School curriculum, numerous magazine articles, and is an active member of the Chattanooga Writers' Guild.

She lives with her husband, Phil, in Georgia. Sample her stories at www.arleneledbetter.com.

B.J. Lee lives in Florida with her poet husband, Malcolm Deeley, and poodles, JoJo and Clementine. She has fifty poems published in magazines such as *Highlights for Children*; and anthologies such as *And the Crowd Goes Wild!* and *The Rhysling Anthology*. You can read more of her poems at www.childrensauthorbjlee.com.

Neal Levin is a freelance children's writer whose work has been published in a variety of magazines ranging from *Highlights for Children* to *The Saturday Evening Post*, as well as several poetry collections.

Janeen Lewis is a writer living in Smyrna, GA, and holds degrees in journalism and elementary education from Eastern Kentucky University. Lewis has experience teaching and writing, and her stories have appeared in several *Chicken Soup for the Soul* anthologies. E-mail her at jlewis0402@netzero.net.

Barbara LoMonaco has worked for Chicken Soup for the Soul as an editor since 1998. She has co-authored two *Chicken Soup for the Soul* book titles and has had stories published in numerous other titles. Barbara is a graduate of the University of Southern California and has a teaching credential.

Crescent LoMonaco is a part-time hair stylist and full-time mom. She used her experience as a former salon owner and her love of writing to write the "Ask a Sylist" column for the *Santa Barbara Independent*. She lives on the California coast with her husband and son.

Renee Beauregard Lute's work has appeared in a number of magazines and in *Chicken Soup for the Soul: From Lemons to Lemonade*. She has an MFA degree from Hamline University, and lives in Issaquah, WA with her husband, daughter, and eagerly anticipated second baby, due in January. E-mail her at renee.b.lute@gmail.com.

Amanda Yardley Luzzader is an aspiring novelist and an active member of the League of Utah Writers. She also enjoys photography and spending time with her husband and two sons.

Emily Madill lives on Vancouver Island, BC with her husband and two sons. She has a BA degree in business and psychology. Emily believes in the importance of teaching children accountability and empowerment from a young age. She has published several esteem building books for children. Learn more at www.emilymadill.com.

Kathryn Malnight is fourteen years old. She loves to read and write and work with special needs children. She hopes to one day help other brothers and sisters of special needs kids with issues that face them because of their siblings. Much love to Alex!

A former newspaper reporter, **Dawn Malone** now writes for children. Her work has appeared in *Highlights for Children*, *Pockets*, and other children's magazines. She is a member of the Society of Children's Book Writers and Illustrators. She lives in central Illinois. Visit her blog "Here's the Story" at dawnmalone.blogspot.com.

Conny Manero is the author of two novels, *Waiting for Silverbird* and *Voice of an Angel*, and two children's books, *Kitten Diaries* and *Debbie*. In her spare time, Conny is an active fund-raiser for the Toronto Cat Rescue and plays ten-pin bowling at a competitive level.

Timothy Martin is the author of numerous young adult novels and screenplays. His work has appeared in over a dozen *Chicken Soup for the Soul* books and numerous literary journals. E-mail Tim at tmartin@northcoast.com.

Jenny Mason is an award-winning author. She received a master's degree from Trinity College Dublin and an M.F.A. degree from Vermont College of Fine Arts. She dwells in the side of a gingerbread mountain in Colorado, but previously lived on the breadcrumb shores of Sandycove, Ireland. E-mail her at jen.michelle.mason@gmail.com.

Ruthy Mavashev was born in 1999. Although she is the second child in the family, she is the first American citizen. Ruthy's parents emigrated from the former USSR to the U.S. in 1996. Ruthy is an honor student and professional piano player. She enjoys spending time with her older sister Erika, playing with her cat, and helping out around the house.

Marya Morin is a freelance writer whose stories and poems have appeared in publications such as *Woman's World* and Hallmark. Marya also penned a weekly humorous column for an online newsletter, and writes custom poetry on request. She lives in the country with her husband. E-mail her at akushla514@hotmail.com.

Lava Mueller teaches creative writing at Community College of Vermont. Lava still loves to go to the beach. While the waves wash over her feet she remembers her father and silently sends him a prayer of gratitude for teaching her about the healing power and love of nature.

Scott Neumyer is a freelance journalist whose work has appeared in print and online publications like *Parenting* magazine, *New Jersey Family*, *ESPN*, *Esquire*, *Wired*, *Details*, *Babble*, and many more. He lives in central New Jersey with his wife and daughter. He also loves bacon far too much. E-mail him at scott@scottneumyer.com.

Shirley Oakes is a wife, mother, grandmother and great-grandmother who enjoys her family. She and her daughter are co-owners of the Family Affair Day Care/Pre-School. She enjoys doing family history work, sewing, painting and gardening. She has also written a children's book.

Pamela Millwood Pettyjohn, contributor to *Chicken Soup for the Soul: Angels Among Us* and *Blue Ridge Parkway—Celebration*, writes inspirational stories, poetry, and children's literature. She is a Chattanooga Writers' Guild member and former elementary schoolteacher. Pamela, husband Charles, and dog Cole enjoy hiking and photography.

Gloria Yaxiri Plancarte is a seventeen years old high school senior. She plays both volleyball and soccer for her school. Gloria loves hanging out with friends and coaching kids to better understand how fun sports and working out can be. E-mail her at gloria.plancarte@ yahoo.com.

Amanda Plaxico is currently enrolled in nursing at college. Married since 1998, she has three kids that are her world. Amanda enjoys spending time with her children, family, and friends and enjoys doing pretty much anything outdoors. She feels that God has a purpose for us all and looks to Him for guidance.

Denise Reich is an Italian-born, USA-raised freelance writer. She has been happy to contribute several stories to the *Chicken Soup for the Soul* series. Denise currently writes for the Canadian magazine *Shameless* and is shopping a novel. She recently played a dancing judge in a TV commercial and took up indoor skydiving.

Stacey Ritz is an award-winning freelance writer, author and philanthropist. Ritz is the co-founder of Advocates 4 Animals, Inc. working to create No Kill Communities. She is also the founder of Youth WRITE Now, Inc., a national writing initiative-providing Writing Mentor and Coaching programs for individuals of all ages.

Deb Roberts previously worked in the dependent care industry encouraging young children and older adults to reach their potential. Currently, she is a freelance writer working on historical fiction for young adults.

Amanda Romaniello is a Syracuse University graduate. This is her fourth story published in the *Chicken Soup for the Soul* series. When not writing, Amanda is training for long distance road races, reading, taking photos and spending time with her Dalmatian, Louie. E-mail her at amanda.romaniello@gmail.com.

Mikaela Rose is earning her middle school education with honors and plans to keep up the good grades. Writing is her favorite subject, and is also one she excels in and enjoys. Her greatest inspirations are her wonderful family, her crazy friends, and all the books she has read.

Sioux Roslawski is a third grade teacher in the Ferguson-Florissant School District. Her children — Virginia and Ian, her son-in-law Jason and her granddaughter Riley — make the world a better place with their gentleness, their kindness and their artistry. Sioux's a member of the WWWP writing critique group.

Bill Rouhana is the CEO of Chicken Soup for the Soul and is grateful to his parents for giving him the bike in his story, teaching him important lessons about living and for many other things.

Tracie Skarbo's stories have appeared in several of the *Chicken Soup for the Soul* books in the past, her book *Harmonious Flight* was released in 2011 and a second titled *Pulp Tattoos* will be released later this year. She lives on Vancouver Island with her family and enjoys running, climbing and photography.

Sam Sorbo is an international fashion model, real estate developer, actress, wife, mother of three, writer, philosopher, photographer, hospital volunteer, and founder of TrueFeminist.com. She attended Duke University to study biomedical engineering, speaks five languages fluently and advocates home schooling. Her book, *The Answer: Proof of God in Heaven*, is due out in 2013.

Joe Sottile is a children's poet, performer, and author. He is a former teacher. Joe loves to share poetry in schools and libraries from *Waiting to See the Principal and Other Poems*. His motto is "Poetry Promotes Literacy and Laughter." E-mail Joe at jsottile@frontiernet.net for a fun-filled interactive performance.

Diane Stark is a wife, mother, and freelance writer. She is a frequent contributor to the *Chicken Soup for the Soul* series, as well as many other magazines. E-mail Diane at DianeStark19@yahoo.com or visit her blog at www.DianeStark.blogspot.com.

L.A. Strucke is a writer, songwriter and producer. A lifelong advocate of the arts, she seeks to inspire others through words and music. She graduated Rowan University in 2005, and thanks her children, who have encouraged her to make a difference in the world. E-mail her at lastrucke@gmail.com or learn more at www.lastrucke.com.

Susan Sundwall is a freelance writer whose first mystery, *The Red Shoelace Killer*, was published in 2012. She lives with her husband in upstate New York. Visit her blog at susansundwall.blogspot.com.

Kristen N. Velasquez is a teacher, poet, and writer. Her story, "Backseat Driver," was published in *Chicken Soup for the Soul: Angels Among Us*. Kristen is a cancer survivor and advocates for childhood cancer patients and children with special needs. View her current projects at www.operation-gold.com and redfeathermarket.com.

Dallas Woodburn is a 2013-14 Steinbeck Fellow in Creative Writing at San Jose State University. This year she is doing a random act of kindness every week and chronicling her experiences on her blog, daybydaymasterpiece.com. Contact her and learn more about her nonprofit youth literacy organization Write On! at www.writeonbooks.org.

Meet Our Authors

Kevin Sorbo was born in Mound, Minnesota. His mother worked as a nurse and his father taught junior high school. By the time he was in college, Kevin was covering tuition costs with modeling work, which swiftly translated into a career in television.

Kevin is well known for playing Hercules, first in a series of TV films, and then later in the immensely popular series, *Hercules: The Legendary Journeys*, which became the number one show in the world. Just as the *Hercules* series came to an end, Kevin received a call from the wife of Star Trek creator Gene Roddenberry, personally requesting him to play the lead role in Roddenberry's second sci-fi series, *Andromeda*.

In 1997 Kevin accepted his first leading film role in the fantasy action feature *Kull the Conqueror*, and followed that with many more films, including *What if...* and *Soul Surfer*. He has also played characters in video games such as *Mortal Kombat 4*, *God of War* and *The Conduit*.

In addition to his work onscreen, Kevin now also produces films, and is both executive producing and starring in several films that are coming out in the 2013-14 timeframe.

Kevin recently authored the widely praised book *True Strength* that recounts the painful recovery from a series of strokes that changed his life during his Hercules years. He also wrote one of the stories for *Chicken Soup for the Soul: Billy Graham & Me*.

He and his wife Sam met during her guest appearance on *Hercules* in 1998 and they have three children together: Braeden, Shane and Octavia.

Aside from a successful career in entertainment, Kevin has always devoted a hearty portion of his time to causes he believes in. Since 1997 Kevin has donated his time as the spokesperson for the nonprofit organization, *A World Fit for Kids!*, a gold medal winner for after school programs, and in 2005 he was named successor to Arnold Schwarzenegger as the national spokesperson for The Afterschool Alliance, a nonprofit working to ensure that all children have access to quality after-school programs. All of Kevin's royalties from this book are going to *A World Fit for Kids!* to fund its programs for children.

To read more about his work please visit www.kevinsorbo.net.

Amy Newmark has been Chicken Soup for the Soul's publisher, coauthor, and editor-in-chief for the last five years, after a 30-year career as a writer, speaker, financial analyst, and business executive in the worlds of finance and telecommunications. Amy is a *magna cum laude* graduate of Harvard College, where she majored in Portuguese, minored in French, and traveled extensively. She and her husband have four grown children.

After a long career writing books on telecommunications, voluminous financial reports, business plans, and corporate press releases, Chicken Soup for the Soul is a breath of fresh air for Amy. She has fallen in love with Chicken Soup for the Soul and its life-changing books, and really enjoys putting these books together for Chicken Soup for the Soul's wonderful readers. She has coauthored more than six dozen *Chicken Soup for the Soul* books and has edited another three dozen.

You can reach Amy with any questions or comments through webmaster@chickensoupforthesoul.com and you can follow her on Twitter @amynewmark or @chickensoupsoul.

Thank You

We owe huge thanks to all of our contributors. We know that you poured your hearts and souls into the stories that you shared with us, and ultimately with each other. As we read and edited these stories, we were truly amazed by how you unselfishly shared personal memories of your childhoods, which were sometimes a bit painful or embarrassing for you. We know your stories will help other kids going through the same experiences. We appreciate your willingness to share these inspiring and encouraging stories with our readers. We could only publish a small percentage of the stories that were submitted, but we read every single one and even the ones that do not appear in the book had an influence on us and on the final manuscript.

There were several thousand stories submitted for this book and our editors Barbara LoMonaco and Jeanne Blandford read every single one. Jeanne narrowed down the list to a few hundred finalists and put together the initial manuscript for us to make the final selections.

Assistant publisher D'ette Corona did her normal masterful job of proofreading and working with the contributors to approve our edits and answer any questions they had and then our editor Kristiana Pastir proofread the book one more time and oversaw production. We also want to thank our creative director and book producer, Brian Taylor at Pneuma Books, who designed the beautiful cover and interior for this book. Once we saw that cover image, we had to make this book!

About
A World Fit for Kids!

Chicken Soup for the Soul is proud to work with Kevin and Sam Sorbo to support the efforts of the organization they chair, *A World Fit for Kids!* — a leading provider of healthy behaviors and personal empowerment programming and training that result in a triple bottom line for young people, resulting in:

- Obesity reduction
- Increased graduation rates
- Work readiness / jobs

Since 1993, *A World Fit for Kids!* has positively impacted the lives of over 200,000 youth through its healthy behaviors and youth development programs in communities with some of the highest obesity rates and lowest high school graduation rates in Los Angeles. They work to ensure that young people develop the physical, mental and emotional fitness they need to succeed. *A World Fit for Kids!* has a distinctive mentoring model that helps young people push beyond self-imposed limitations, refine existing skills and develop new ones. High school participants work with positive adult role models, discover their own strengths in leadership, and in turn, become active advocates, empowered leaders and healthy behaviors ambassadors who positively influence their peers, families, schools and communities. Students learn about healthy behaviors and quality physical activities, and teens are equipped to graduate from high school ready for higher education, the workforce, and a healthy, prosperous future.

A key example of the *A World Fit for Kids!* successful model is the Teen Mentors in Motion Program, which provides healthy behaviors and youth development training, job shadowing, and internship opportunities to teens. The program helps to increase self-awareness, build confidence, and strengthen interpersonal skills, equipping teens with important knowledge and tools that build their capacity to succeed in school, work and life. *A World Fit for Kids!* teens receive mentoring, academic assistance, and enrichment activities to support them in discovering their own capacity for success. To prepare them for a skilled workforce, participants engage in work-readiness training, job-shadowing, and have the opportunity to apply for a six-month internship as an Assistant Coach-Mentor at one of the *A World Fit for Kids!* school sites or with another youth-serving organization in a profession of their choice.

Evaluation results have shown that the Mentors in Motion Program works. In fact, 94% of students who completed the Mentors in Motion training and six-month internship program since 2003 have graduated from high school, primarily from a high school with a 49.5% graduation rate!

While the *A World Fit for Kids!* afterschool programming is only available in the Greater Los Angeles area, they maximize their impact, reach and sustainability by sharing their success strategies and expertise according to a replicable model that can reach young people all over the world by partnering with a network of service providers. Through their training, *A World Fit for Kids!* is creating a sustainable, accessible way for others to achieve the same breakthrough results.

All of Kevin Sorbo's royalties from this book, along with a share of Chicken Soup for the Soul's proceeds, will benefit *A World Fit for Kids!* To learn more please visit www.worldfitforkids.org.

Improving Your Life Every Day

Real people sharing real stories—for twenty years. Now, Chicken Soup for the Soul has gone beyond the bookstore to become a world leader in life improvement. Through books, movies, DVDs, online resources and other partnerships, we bring hope, courage, inspiration and love to hundreds of millions of people around the world. Chicken Soup for the Soul's writers and readers belong to a one-of-a-kind global community, sharing advice, support, guidance, comfort, and knowledge.

Chicken Soup for the Soul stories have been translated into more than forty languages and can be found in more than one hundred countries. Every day, millions of people experience a Chicken Soup for the Soul story in a book, magazine, newspaper or online. As we share our life experiences through these stories, we offer hope, comfort and inspiration to one another. The stories travel from person to person, and from country to country, helping to improve lives everywhere.

Share with Us

We all have had Chicken Soup for the Soul moments in our lives. If you would like to share your story or poem with millions of people around the world, go to chickensoup.com and click on "Submit Your Story." You may be able to help another reader, and become a published author at the same time. Some of our past contributors have launched writing and speaking careers from the publication of their stories in our books!

Our submission volume has been increasing steadily—the quality and quantity of your submissions has been fabulous. We only accept story submissions via our website. They are no longer accepted via mail or fax.

To contact us regarding other matters, please send us an e-mail through webmaster@chickensoupforthesoul.com, or fax or write us at:

Chicken Soup for the Soul
P.O. Box 700
Cos Cob, CT 06807-0700
Fax: 203-861-7194

One more note from your friends at Chicken Soup for the Soul: Occasionally, we receive an unsolicited book manuscript from one of our readers, and we would like to respectfully inform you that we do not accept unsolicited manuscripts and we must discard the ones that appear.